Examining Business Process Re-engineering

Current Perspectives and Research Directions

Edited by

Gerard Burke and Joe Peppard

KOGAN
PAGE

YOURS TO HAVE AND TO HOLD

BUT NOT TO COPY

The publication you are reading is protected by copyright law. This means that the publisher could take you and your employer to court and claim heavy legal damages if you make unauthorised photocopies from these pages. Photocopying copyright material without permission is no different from stealing a magazine from a newsagent, only it doesn't seem like theft.

The Copyright Licensing Agency (CLA) is an organisation which issues licences to bring photocopying within the law. It has designed licensing services to cover all kinds of special needs in business, education and government.

If you take photocopies from books, magazines and periodicals at work your employer should be licensed with CLA. Make sure you are protected by a photocopying license.

The copyright Licensing Agency Limited, 90 Tottenham Court Road, London, W1P 0LP. Tel: 0171 436 5931. Fax: 0171 436 3986.

First published in 1995

Kogan Page Limited
120 Pentonville Road
London N1 9JN

British Library Cataloguing in Publication Data

A CIP record for this book is available from the British Library.

ISBN 0 7494 1637 8

Typeset by Kogan Page
Printed in England by Clays Ltd, St Ives plc

CONTENTS

Part Five — Flat Organizations - Opportunity or Threat?

ACKNOWLEDGEMENTS

Clearly, the most important contributors to a book of collected papers like this one are the individual authors of those papers. We would like to express our most heartfelt thanks to them all. Their willingness to participate and their flexibility and speed in making suggested changes to their papers ensured that the sometimes daunting task of editing such a volume was, in fact, a pleasure.

We would also like to express our appreciation to Alex Britnell for her invaluable help and support during the production of the manuscript, to Jenny Gubbay of Kogan Page for ensuring that this manuscript in fact became a book and to Philip Mudd of Kogan Page for his encouragement and commitment to the project.

Gerard Burke and Joe Peppard
Cranfield
March 1995

LIST OF FIGURES

LIST OF TABLES

THE CRANFIELD MANAGEMENT SERIES

The Cranfield Management Series represents an exciting joint initiative between the Cranfield School of Management and Kogan Page.

As one of Europe's leading post-graduate business schools, Cranfield is renowned for its applied research activities, which cover a wide range of issues relating to the practice of management.

Each title in the Series is based on current research and authored by Cranfield faculty or their associates. Many of the research projects have been undertaken with the sponsorship and active assistance of organizations from the industrial, commercial or public sectors. The aim of the Series is to make the findings of direct relevance to managers through texts which are academically sound, accessible and practical.

For managers and academics alike, the Cranfield Management Series will provide access to up-to-date management thinking from some of the world's leading academics and practitioners. The series represents both Cranfield's and Kogan Page's commitment to furthering the improvement of management practice in all types of organizations.

THE SERIES EDITORS

Frank Fishwick
Reader in Managerial Economics
Director of Admissions at Cranfield School of Management

Dr Fishwick joined Cranfield from Aston University in 1966, having previously worked in textiles, electronics and local government (town and country planning). Recent research and consultancy interests have been focused on business concentration, competition policy and the book publishing industry. He has been directing a series of research studies for the Commission of the European Communities, working in collaboration with business economists in France and Germany. He is permanent economic adviser to the Publishers Association in the UK and is a regular consultant to other public and private sector organisations in the UK, continental Europe and the US.

Gerry Johnson
Professor of Strategic Management
Director of the Centre for Strategic Management and Organisational Change
Director of Research at Cranfield School of Management

After graduating from University College London, Professor Johnson worked for several years in management positions in Unilever and Reed International before becoming a management consultant. Since 1976, he has taught at Aston University Management Centre, Manchester Business School, and from 1988 at Cranfield School of Management. His research work is primarily concerned with processes of strategic decision making and strategic change in organisations. He also works as a consultant on issues of strategy formulation and strategic change at a senior level with a number of UK and international firms.

Shaun Tyson
Professor of Human Resource Management
Director of the Human Resource Research Centre
Dean of the Faculty of Management and Administration at Cranfield School of Management

Professor Tyson studied at London University and spent eleven years in senior positions in industry within engineering and electronic companies.

For four years he was lecturer in personnel management at the Civil Service College, and joined Cranfield in 1979. He has acted as a consultant and researched widely into human resource strategies, policies and the evaluation of the function. He has published 14 books.

THE CONTRIBUTORS

Colin Armistead is the Professor of Operations Management in the Dorset Business School at Bournemouth University where he also holds the Royal Mail Chair of Business Performance Improvement. Previously Colin was Senior Lecturer and Head of the Operations Management Group at the Cranfield School of Management. Colin has contributed to the Operations Management and Service Operations Management fields through his work on customer service, operations strategy, the design and control of service processes and capacity, quality and productivity management in service. He has written extensively on services operations in books and journal articles. Colin is a past Chairman of the Operations Management Association and is a member of the board of the Institute of Business Process Re-engineering.

Gerard Burke is a lecturer in Information Systems (IS) at Cranfield School of Management. Having obtained a degree in Maths at St Johns College, Oxford, Gerard worked as a management consultant with Price Waterhouse for 10 years and then moved to an internal corporate consulting role with the WH Smith group. He is particularly interested in managerial learning with regard to IS/IT and how to overcome the barriers and blocks to this learning, the organizational and cultural issues surrounding IS/IT in organizations and in the impact of IT on individuals, work, careers and society as a whole. Gerard continues to consult with organizations ranging from large multi-nationals to small local businesses.

Wan Wan Chew received her BSc degree with First Class Honours from the Department of Information Systems & Computer Science, National University of Singapore in 1994. She is currently on a Singapore Airlines scholarship to pursue an MS degree in Operations Research at Stanford University. Her research interest includes crew and flight scheduling, application of BPR techniques on macroscopic and microscopic levels, and Information Systems Planning.

Rainer Eisele, PhD, is Senior Lecturer for information management and Project Manager at the Institute for Information Management at the University of St Gallen, Switzerland. His main areas of research are business process re-engineering, management information systems and computer integrated manufacturing. He received a master degree in engineering (Dipl-Wirt-Ing) from the University of Karlsruhe and a PhD from the University of Nurnberg-Erlangen.

Bob Galliers is Chairman and Professor of Information Management at Warwick University Business School. Prior to his appointment as Chairman he headed Warwick's Doctoral Programme in Information Systems and its Information Systems Research Unit. He was previously Foundation Professor and Head of the School of Information Systems at Curtin University, Perth, Western Australia, where he developed Australia's first Master's Programme to emphasize the management issues associated with the introduction and utilization of IT in organizations. Prior to that he was a consultant with ISCOL Ltd, the management systems consultancy company of the Department of Systems and Information Management of Lancaster University, having previously pursued a career in public administration.

He has written many papers and articles and is editor-in-chief of the *Journal of Strategic Information Systems*. He is author or joint author of a number of books in the area of information systems management and is currently engaged in writing a volume provisionally entitled *Building Bridges: Strategies for Information Systems, Innovation and Change*.

Keith Grint is a lecturer in Management Studies at the University of Oxford and a fellow in Organizational Behaviour at Templeton College. His *Sociology of Work* (1991), *Management: A Sociological Introduction* (1995) and *Deus ex Machina* (with Steve Woolgar, 1995) are all published by Polity Press. An edited collection, *The Gender-Technology Relation* (with Ros Gill, 1995) is published by Taylor and Francis. He has published articles in diverse areas (Gender, Technology, Social Theory, Japanization, Outdoor Management Development, Labour History and Appraisal Systems) and is currently editing a collection on Leadership for Oxford University Press.

Alan Harrison is currently lecturer in Operations Management at Warwick Business School, where he has been for the last nine years. His research interests have centred on the transfer of Japanese management methods, and he is author of *Just-in-Time Manufacturing in Perspective* (Prentice Hall, 1992). Currently, he is focusing on the enablers and inhibitors to the flow of materials in different operations environments, a research programme in which he is sponsored by Exel Logistics. His interest in BPR developed from his work on just-in-time, initially in comparing continuous and breakthrough approaches to improvement and subsequently in understanding processes.

Amir Hartman is a doctoral candidate at The Katz Graduate School of Business of the University of Pittsburgh. His dissertation investigates and attempts to unveil the myth of the 'postindustrial' or 'information age'. His research interests include the critical studies of information technology, sociology of scientific inquiry, and telecommunications policy. Amir's background includes degrees in computer science, and the rhetoric of science, as well as professional experience in information systems consulting. His vices often involve, but are not limited to, 'surfing the web' and playing and coaching soccer.

Christof Hauser is research assistant and PhD student at the Institute for Information Management at the University of St Gallen, Switzerland. He studied business administration at the Universities of Luneburg and Mannheim in Germany and received a masters degree in business administration (Dipl-Kfm). Since 1992 he has been working in research projects focusing on business process re-engineering. His main research interests are market impact evaluation and cost analysis of business processes.

Frederick Hewitt is Head of Aston Business School. He holds BA and PhD degrees from Bristol University and is also professionally qualified in Education (PGCE) and Computing (MBCS). Prior to assuming his present position in 1993, he was Vice-President of Logistics for Xerox Corporation. His research interests and publications cover the areas of TQM, Benchmarking and Business Process Management, as well as Logistics and Supply Chain Management.

James Hoopes is Professor of History at Babson College in Wellesley, Massachusetts where he teaches courses in the history of ideas and in comparative business history to business students in both the undergraduate and graduate programmes. His most recent book length publication is *Peirce on Signs: Writings on Semiotic by Charles Sanders Peirce* (Chapel Hill: University of North Carolina Press). As his chapter in this book suggests, he is interested in the ways in which recent advances in philosophy of mind, especially in semiotics, might contribute to organizational science.

Matthew Jones is a lecturer in Information Management in the Management Studies Group, Department of Engineering and Judge Institute of Management Studies at the University of Cambridge. He previously held postdoctoral research positions at the Universities of Cambridge and Reading where he was involved in the development of computer-based models for use in public policy decision-making. His current research interests are concerned with the social and organizational aspects of the design and use of information systems and the relationship between technology and social organizational change. He has published widely on these issues.

Mark Keen is a researcher and visiting lecturer at Sheffield Business School and a practising organization consultant. Having gained an MSc in Organization Development, he has embarked upon a PhD investigating the implementation of BPR programmes and in particular the role of senior managers. His current research is oriented around the possible contribution of postmodern concepts, such as discourse, genealogy and 'simulacra', to the understanding and effective implementation of the BPR phenomenon. As a keen sportsman he is hoping that the worldwide growth in interest and application of BPR will continue, perhaps leading to possible research opportunities in Southern Africa in the near future.

Chris Morgan is Senior Lecturer in the Faculty of Management at Nene College in Northampton. He lectures in Operations Management and Operations Strategy to undergraduate and postgraduate students, and supervises postgraduate research activities associated with MA, MSc and MBA programmes. His current research programmes are concerned with the impact of technology and information systems on operational strategies.

Chris qualified as an electronic engineer before undertaking postgraduate studies in management and industrial relations. He is a member of the Institute of Management and of the British Computer Society. In 1981 he was awarded a Whitworth Exhibition.

Before entering academe Chris worked in telecommunications, robot engineering, computer software design, manufacturing systems design and in consulting. He has had extensive experience at all levels of management and as a consultant has been responsible for several company reconstructions.

Enid Mumford is an Emeritus Professor of Manchester University and an organizational design consultant. Prior to her retirement from academic life she was Professor of Organizational Behaviour at the Manchester Business School. She has had a long connection with the Tavistock Institute of Human Relations, serving for many years on the International Quality of Working Life Committee which had as its aim the diffusion of socio-technical concepts around the world. She is at present a member of the Tavistock Council.

She has been involved in organizational design involving new technology for many years and has tried to develop methods and tools which will assist the future users of new systems to play a major role in their design. One of these is ETHICS. She has an intimate knowledge of the long wall method of coal mining as, in the 1960s, her research group at Liverpool University was asked to carry out a study of industrial relations problems in coal mining. This led to her spending 12 months working underground in the Maypole Colliery near Wigan.

Professor Raghu Nath is on the graduate faculty of The Katz Graduate School of Business of the University of Pittsburgh where he has been coordinator of The International Faculty Group and Director of Management Training Laboratory. He is the President of INSOHP and INTEGRATED SYSTEMS which specialize in the development of effective organizational systems by deploying an integrated multistage strategic process model. The model is based on a socio-technical approach to organizational learning and improvement.

Dr Nath has consulted widely with international organizations, governmental departments, and multinational corporations in the United States and abroad. He has authored over 50 publications, presented papers at several international conferences and given many invited addresses in the United States and abroad. Dr Nath was Chairman of The International Division of The Academy of Management and is a fellow of The International Assocation of Educators for World Peace.

Joe Peppard is EU Management Fellow at Cranfield School of Management and on the faculty of Trinity College, Dublin. An honours Business Studies Graduate at Trinity College, he previously spent five years lecturing at his *alma mater*, joining Cranfield in 1992. During 1993, he was a visiting scholar at Groningen University in Holland and is currently external examiner at a number of universities. He has considerable expertise in the areas of information systems strategy, business re-engineering, electronic data interchange, executive information systems and the impact of IT on organizations and society, consulting with a number of European and Scandinavian organizations in these areas.

Joe was involved in establishing the Information Systems Research Centre at Cranfield and is involved in a number of the centre's research activities, including projects examining future IS/IT skills, managing IT infrastructure and business re-engineering. His publications include *IT Strategy for Business* (Pitman Publishing, 1993) and (co-authored with Philip Rowland) *The Essence of Business Process Re-engineering* (Prentice-Hall International, 1995) as well as articles in both academic and general business journals.

Hean Lee Poh received his Diplom-Ingenieur in Electrical Engineering from the University of Paderborn, Germany, in 1982, his MS degree in Computer Science from the California Institute of Technology in 1987, and his MS and PhD in Engineering-Economic Systems from Stanford University in 1991. He is currently a lecturer at the Department of Information Systems & Computer Science, National University of Singapore. He has published journal and conference papers in the areas of neural networks, marketing and financial modelling as well as decision support systems.

Ian Preece is an internal consultant working for Mercury Communications specialising in process oriented change programmes. Prior to this he worked in the IT and oil industries. He is currently researching into BPR at Cranfield University and, together with Joe Peppard, was the co-leader of a business sponsored BPR research project at Cranfield.

Lance Revenaugh is serving as a lecturer in Information Systems at City University of Hong Kong. He holds a PhD from Arizona State University and an MBA from Baylor University. In the past, he has been a member of the faculty at the University of Idaho, Biola University (Los Angeles) and California State University Fullerton. He has served as a consultant to several organizations including Motorola and US West. His research activities are focused on information systems architecture, IS strategy and its implementation, BPR and its implementation, and assessing the impact of information technology. He currently lives in Kowloon, Hong Kong with his wife Heidi and three young children.

Jeremy Rose read English at Cambridge University and subsequently worked as a professional musician and music administrator until injury prompted a change of career. After completing an MSc in Information Management at Lancaster University, he joined Manchester Metropolitan University as a Senior Lecturer in Business Information Technology. He is currently working on a major project evaluating Information Systems in the National Health Service.

Philip Rowland now works for a leading management consultancy following two years as a teaching fellow in operations management at the Cranfield School of Management. During this time his main research area was business process re-engineering and he co-authored *The Essence of Business Process Re-engineering* with Joe Peppard. Philip completed his MBA at Cranfield following six years with Ford Motor Company in the Systems Department working on a variety of projects from manufacturing to finance and product development.

Ranjit Tinaikar is a doctoral candidate at the Katz Graduate School of Business of the University of Pittsburgh. He is majoring in the area of Management Information Systems. His dissertation investigates the phenomenon of IT-driven organizational transformation by developing and testing a network theory of organizational learning. His research interests include the philosophy of Information Technology (IT), sociology of organizational change, and strategic planning and control of IT. Ranjit's background includes degrees in computer engineering and management, as well as professional experience in information systems consulting. His personal passions include his wife Dee, dramatics and cricket.

Richard Vidgen worked for a software vendor on leaving university, where he was involved in developing and supporting financial applications. For a number of years he worked as a freelance consultant, designing and implementing IT solutions for the banking and insurance industries. More recently he was employed as a system development manager for a UK bank. In 1992 he joined the University of Salford as a Lecturer in Information Systems, where his research interests include Information System development methodologies, Information System quality, business process re-engineering, and data and object modelling.

Hugh Willmott is Reader in the Manchester School of Management, having previously worked at Aston Business School and Copenhagen Business School. His work has appeared in a wide range of leading management, accounting, finance and social science journals. With David Knights, he co-founded the International Labour Process Conference which he organized for a number of years. He is currently working on a number of conceptual and empirical projects whose common theme is the critical examination of the changing organization and management of work in modern society. His most recent books are *Labour Process Theory* (Macmillan, 1990 co-edited with David Knights), *Critical Management Studies* (Sage, 1992, co-edited with Mats Alvesson), *Skill and Consent* (Routledge, 1992, co-edited with Andrew Sturdy and David Knights) and *Making Quality Critical* (Routledge, 1995, co-edited with Adrian Wilkinson). *Making Sense of Management: A Critical Introduction* (Sage, co-authored with Mats Alvesson) is to be published later this year.

James R G Wood is currently Senior Lecturer in Computer Science at the University of Salford and, together with Professor Wood-Harper, is Joint Director of the Doctoral Programme in Information Systems. After graduating in operational research he worked in the engineering industry as a systems analyst before undertaking research and joining Brunel University as a lecturer. He holds a Masters degree in business systems analysis and is presently completing his PhD on the methodological basis of information systems development. He is currently leading a group of researchers looking at the potential use of advanced information technologies, including multimedia, within health care, and at the likely impact on the pharmaceutical industry of the structural and managerial changes currently taking place within the National Health Service.

Trevor Wood-Harper is currently Professor of Computer Science and Information Systems at the University of Salford where he leads a research group in information systems methodology, evaluation and quality. His degree is in computer science and he holds a Masters in systems engineering (with Peter Checkland) and a PhD in information systems. Prior to his academic career he was a senior systems analyst with Granada Television and British Airways. He is perhaps best known for his work on the Multiview methodology, and presently holds visiting positions in Denmark and the United States. He has published widely, with more than fifty research articles and five books to his credit.

INTRODUCTION

Every so often, a new phenomenon is discovered in the constellation of management thinking. Some of these come and go quickly like visiting comets which we can only observe for a few fleeting moments. Others burst into life like bright stars seeming to shine a brilliant new light on our previous and current experience of organizations and management. Suddenly, we can see with startling clarity where in the past we have been stumbling in the dark. Some of these stars establish a permanent position in the constellation providing extra light to illuminate old problems in new ways and perhaps opening our eyes to problems which previously we could not see.

Researchers and academics are usually the first to observe the new phenomenon using their powerful scientific equipment. Their discoveries are then publicized and managers in the wider world are made aware. However, practising managers are usually obliged to observe the new discovery with the naked eye. This can be difficult since detail will not be visible and it is easy to be dazzled by the hullabaloo. The casual observer may also find it difficult to identify and differentiate the new phenomenon in a sky which is already dotted with shining stars.

Sometimes, and even more confusingly for the untrained observer, these seemingly new discoveries have actually been there all the time but have not previously been observed and labelled.

One such recent discovery is Business Process Re-engineering (BPR). The first glimmerings of this phenomenon were being observed in the 1980s but it wasn't until the early 1990s that it burst into dazzling light. With tub-thumping certainty, the management astronomers assured the watching world that here at last they had discovered the centre of the management universe. With messianic fervour, they assured us that all organizational black spots could be enlightened by the blinding rays of BPR. Some practising managers, like the Three Wise Men of the Christian nativity story, have followed the star religiously. Others, more sceptical, have sought to examine the BPR phenomenon in more detail and have asked questions like

'Where in the sky should I look for it?'

'Is it visible through the clouds?'

'How will I know that I've seen it and that I haven't mistaken it for a reflection of another star like TQM?'

'Is it a new star or something which has been around for many years under other names?'

'Which way does this particular star lead?'

'How do we follow the star?'

'Is it really a star or is it a visiting comet which will soon disappear from the management constellation?'

In order to observe the new phenomenon more closely and address these questions thoroughly, one requires a powerful 'telescope' which will have features such as: access to and experience of many different organizations, objectivity, appropriate research methods, availability of a wide body of work from which to draw and, perhaps, most importantly of all, time. Inevitably, such a 'telescope' is more commonly available to researchers and academics than to practising managers.

We are very fortunate to have such a 'telescope' and through it we have been observing BPR for the past five years. In this time, we have built up a rich picture of this new phenomenon. This has included an industry-funded research project, three symposia of practising managers, and experience from our own consultancy work.

In 1993, we felt that clear observation and deep appreciation of the new phenomenon was being obscured by clouds of evangelical preaching, natural scepticism and misinterpretation. Therefore, we instigated the first European academic conference on BPR, entitled *BPR: Academic Directions*, with the aim of blowing away the clouds by taking a considered academic view and, hence, moving towards a consensus.

However, at that time, very few European-based researchers were actively training their 'telescopes' on BPR. Therefore, we invited a number of leading thinkers to present their views and provide a variety of different perspectives on the new phenomenon. The insights and discussion provoked us to pen our proposed 'Research Agenda' for BPR which was published in the first edition of *The Journal of Business Change and Re-engineering* in the summer of 1993.

Since that time, many other researchers have begun to focus on BPR and there was an overwhelming feeling that we should coordinate a second conference to take place in 1994. This time, however, we decided to issue a general call for papers. The response was overwhelming with submissions from researchers all around the world. The task of selection was arduous. However, after much deliberation, the editorial board chose

36 papers to be presented at the conference.

At the same time, our colleagues in the Information Systems (IS) Group at Cranfield School of Management were organizing the first *Management Challenges in IS* conference. One of the tracks of this event was also looking at BPR but specifically from an IS perspective.

Through these activities, we believe that we have one of the most finely tuned and specifically focused 'telescopes' currently trained on BPR. Our objective with this book is to invite you to look through this 'telescope' at the rich picture of BPR which it provides. In order to sharpen the focus for you, we have selected the most illuminating and insightful papers from the *BPR: Academic Directions* and the *Management Challenges of IS* conferences. We have also included a particularly clear-sighted and probing paper, written by Enid Mumford, which we received while we were preparing this book.

Before we take our first look through the 'telescope', in **Part 1,** we first describe a brief history of the new phenomenon of BPR and pose a series of questions which form the basic guide for our subsequent exploration.

As we progress through the book, we move the 'telescope' across the surface of the new phenomenon to delve below to discover its composition, origins, messages, life expectancy and applicability. Our journey of discovery focuses on selected areas of particular interest. Within each of these areas, the authors of the individual chapters are our expert guides providing commentaries on the emerging landscape. The selected areas form the sections of the book as follows

- **Part 2 – Definitions and models of BPR re-examined**
  In this initial view, we take a critical look at the plethora of explanations and definitions of the new phenomenon. We highlight the inconsistencies and apparent contradictions between each of these explanations and between the various definitions and the oft-quoted examples of manifestations of BPR. Bringing together the slightly different perspectives of each of our guides provides rich added insight.
- **Part 3 – Learning from earlier improvement philosophies**
  As we adjust our focus, the new phenomenon of BPR is compared with more established approaches to performance improvement such as Total Quality Management (TQM), Just-in-Time (JIT) and Socio-Technical Design. These comparisons lead to some important lessons with regard to both the types of techniques which may be useful in pursuing BPR initiatives and the critical issues which influence success or failure.
- **Part 4 – Implementing BPR-related change**
  Here, our expert guides share some of their hard-won experience of implementing changes brought about by BPR. Based on this experience

and their knowledge of other management phenomena, they enlighten us with regard to the key issues to be managed and put forward some new frameworks to help us deal with them.

- **Part 5 – Flat organizations – opportunity or threat?**
  In this final view, we look at the likely impact of BPR-related changes in terms of the way in which organizations are structured and the people within those organizations. Our first guide takes the view that so-called flat organizations are more conducive to the human condition and should, therefore, be welcomed, while our second guide offers the perspective that the very people who must be most involved in a BPR exercise are also the ones who are most affected by it. He asks: 'Will the turkeys vote for Christmas?'

By focusing on these specific areas and by providing the added insight from our expert guides, we believe that we have provided a uniquely comprehensive and considered view of the new phenomenon of BPR. We are delighted to invite you to look through our 'telescope' and we trust that you enjoy your journey of discovery with us. Come on, let's take a look!

Part One

A RESEARCH AGENDA

1

BUSINESS PROCESS RE-ENGINEERING: RESEARCH DIRECTIONS*

Gerard Burke and Joe Peppard,
Cranfield School of Management

Few management concepts, even including 'Total Quality' and 'Excellence', have generated such enormous media and business interest so quickly as the recent phenomenon of Business Process Re-engineering (BPR) – otherwise known as Business Re-engineering, Business Process Redesign, Core Process Redesign, Business Process Transformation and any other permutation of the same half dozen or so words depending on who you talk to!

A cynic might say: 'Every consultancy is jumping on the BPR bandwagon as a new service they can sell. Every IT supplier is interested because they see BPR as a new way to identify opportunities for computerization and, hence, for them to sell more hardware. And every IT manager is clinging to BPR as the latest way to justify his/her existence! BPR is now being portrayed as the panacea to all organizational ills!'

On the other hand, many large organizations, including AT&T, Ford, Texas Instruments, Mercury, Rank Xerox, National and Provincial, Grand Metropolitan, Leeds Permanent and BT claim to be embracing BPR and achieving real and significant benefits.

Clearly, something is happening out there! (See also Edwards and Peppard (1994).)

However, a scan of the academic journals and conference papers reveals little, if any, rigorous academic research published in the UK and Europe explicitly on the subject of BPR. In this chapter, we set out to lay the foundations for such research to take place by proposing a research agenda.

---

* A version of this chapter appeared in *The Journal of Business Change and Re-engineering*, Vol 1, No 1, 1993.

SOME BACKGROUND TO BPR

The term business process redesign was first used in the Massachusetts Institute of Technology's (MIT) research programme 'Management in the 1990s' which ran from 1984 to 1989. During this project, researchers such as Davenport and Short (1990) observed that successful organizations were using IT systems in ways which were more advanced than the traditional automation of clerical and operational tasks. Venkatraman (1991) elaborated on these observations and identified BPR as the third of five levels of IT-induced organizational transformation. The term BPR was used quite precisely to describe the use of IT to transform the way in which an organization works internally rather than simply to automate the way that it already worked.

The ideas were then further popularized by Hammer in his seminal article 'Re-engineering Work: Don't Automate, Obliterate' which appeared in *Harvard Business Review* in 1990. He warned against 'paving the cow paths' with IT and suggested that organizations should rethink their business by capitalizing on the opportunities provided by the new information technologies.

FIRST EUROPEAN ACADEMIC CONFERENCE ON BPR

Most research and writings on BPR have emanated from the US, with both academics and practitioners publishing voluminously on the subject. However, on this side of the Atlantic, we appear to have been more restrained, perhaps reflecting our stronger social sciences tradition in management research.

It was against this background that Cranfield School of Management ran the first European academic conference on BPR in June 1993. The conference, entitled *Business Process Redesign: Academic Directions*, was attended by 70 delegates from over 40 UK and European academic institutions.

One of the main objectives of the conference was to move towards a consensus on an agenda for academic research in BPR.

A PROPOSED RESEARCH AGENDA

We now put forward such an agenda based on:

- The results of small group discussions at the *Business Process Redesign: Academic Directions* conference during which delegates were asked to identify areas where academic research was required
- Reviews of published material in this field which has revealed gaps in the published knowledge of BPR

- Discussions with practising managers who have been involved in projects which set out to transform the way their organizations work. These discussions sought to reveal how academic research could be of benefit to practitioners in this developing field.

While not claiming to be academically rigorous in our methodology, we have consolidated our findings from these three avenues of investigation and propose a research agenda in terms of the ten questions which appear in Table 1.1

Table 1.1   A research agenda for BPR

1.   What is BPR?
2.   Where does BPR fit with other management disciplines?
3.   What makes BPR happen?
4.   Where are we now?
5.   Where do we want to be?
6.   How do we get there?
7.   How will we know if we've got there?
8.   How will this affect me?
9.   How do we keep it going?
10.   What is really happening?

The very purpose of this chapter is to set out areas where research is required. Clearly, these questions cannot be answered until that research has been completed. However, there is a body of knowledge from a number of different disciplines which may help in discovering the answers to these questions. Therefore, where appropriate we may make reference to this body of knowledge in the discussions which follow.

What is BPR?

The clarity and precision of the MIT concept of BPR seems to have been obscured by a combination of the passage of time and the media and consultancy hype. We are now in a position where:

- We have a myriad of names for what is seemingly the same concept
- There are as many definitions as there are names. For example:

   ... a way of transforming the business, which frees it from the restrictions of the traditional approach by cutting across functional divisions. Information systems ... are the fundamental ingredient of redesigned business processes ... (Butler Cox Foundation, 1991)

A revolutionary new approach that uses IT and HRM to dramatically improve business performance. (Davenport, 1993 [apologies for the grammar which is not ours!])

The fundamental rethinking and radical redesign of business processes to achieve dramatic improvements in critical contemporary measures of performance such as cost, quality, service and speed. (Hammer and Champy, 1993)
... re-engineering [is] analysing and altering the basic work processes of the business. (Morris and Brandon, 1993)

The transformation of a company from one based on functions such as accounting, marketing and manufacturing to one based on processes such as order processing and fulfilling customer expectations. (Business Intelligence, 1993)

- No distinction is made between Venkatraman's (1991) levels 3, 4 and 5 of transformation, ie Business Process Redesign, Business Network Redesign and Business Scope Redefinition
- The emphasis on *IT-induced* transformations appears to have diminished – as one can observe from the above definitions.

Because of this loss of precision, and adding to the confusion, some people question whether BPR is anything more than a number of older techniques, such as Organization and Methods (O&M), Total Quality Management (TQM) and Just-in-Time (JIT), dusted down and repackaged.

Therefore, clearly the first and most pressing need is to develop a consistent definition and a common vocabulary which will include resolution of the following questions

- How does BPR differ from other performance improvement programmes?
- What is a process and are there different levels of granularity?
- What is the role of IS/IT?
- Why has the concept of BPR emerged now and not earlier? Were senior managers straining at the leash to undertake radical transformation as soon as the technology became available? Or has the technology been the spark that caused the revolution?

This would provide a firm foundation to move on to consider such issues as

- Ways of classifying BPR projects (for example, in terms of the scope and degree of change) which might indicate different management approaches for different classes of project (Edwards and Braganza, 1993)
- Ways of classifying processes, for example, in terms of their contribution to the organization using a mechanism similar to Ward *et al.*'s (1990) application portfolio. Such a classification might indicate dif-

ferent management approaches for projects aimed at transforming different classes of processes (Bytheway, 1992)

- Whether there might be generic processes for organizations operating in the same industry in the same way as there are generic critical success factors.

However, clearly the reader needs some form of understanding of what we mean when we use the term BPR in the remainder of this chapter. Therefore, without wishing to add to the confusion, we have drawn the most common themes from the above definitions and others which we have found, and have characterized our use of the term BPR, for the purposes of this chapter only, as

An approach to organizational improvement

- Which seeks opportunities for fundamental transformations
- By focusing on the processes by which the organization delivers products or services to its stakeholders.

We do not suggest that this is a sufficient definition of BPR although it may be the starting point for such a definition.

Where Does BPR Fit with Other Management Disciplines?

While BPR has its origins in research within the IT field, fundamental changes such as those implicit in the concept of BPR will inevitably require a more holistic view. This begs the question

- Is BPR a new management discipline in its own right?
  or
- Is it a meta-discipline which is superordinate to more traditional disciplines such as operations management, human resources, strategy and IT?
  or
- Is it a multi-disciplinary approach to organizational improvement with each individual specialty having a role to play?

Having resolved this, one might move on to consider what type of individuals or group of individuals should practise BPR.

What Makes BPR Happen?

Organizations tend to embrace the need for radical change only when there are significant external threats or pressure. Are there particular types of threat which prompt organizations to undertake BPR as opposed to any other type of improvement programme?

Even then, organizations which wait until the external threat is so great that they are forced to act may be too late. Perhaps we should be looking for ways in which to encourage organizations to change during the 'good times'. Of course, this may be overtaken by the ever increasing rate of change and turbulence in the overall business environment which may mean that organizations are in a constant state of crisis anyway!

There may also be a number of internal circumstances which need to be in place before BPR can be considered. What might these be?

How are these external threats and internal circumstances translated into objectives for a BPR programme? And is there a link between these objectives and the success or failure of the programme? (For example, is BPR more likely to be successful if the objectives relate to improved service rather than to cost-cutting?)

Where Are We Now?

Writers on learning theory suggest that learning cannot take place without first 'unlearning' (Burgelman, 1983). Many of the proposed methods for undertaking BPR also suggest that an organization must first understand its current processes before attempting to redesign them. On the other hand, it could be argued that paying too much attention to the current way of doing things may constrain the likelihood of identifying radically different approaches. Perhaps this is a question of achieving an appropriate level of understanding of current processes – but what is that level?

Having decided the level of understanding required, organizations must then address the question of how this understanding is to be elicited, represented and communicated. With regard to elicitation, perhaps cognitive mapping (Eden *et al.*, 1979) and soft systems methodology (Checkland, 1981) are approaches which might be appropriate and useful.

On the other hand, representation and communication will require some form of process modelling. In our view, the techniques which appear to have the most potential in this area are two extensions to Porter's value chain (1985), namely value process models (Macdonald, 1991) and the notion of natural and contrived value chains (O'Sullivan and Geringer, 1993).

Where Do We Want to Be?

Having achieved an appropriate level of understanding of existing processes, an organization undertaking BPR must then design the way in which it wants those processes to work in the future. If truly radical change is required, then something of a creative, or perhaps intuitive, leap will be necessary. This gives rise to the following questions

- How does an organization encourage creativity and radical new thinking in managers who are immersed in the current day-to-day operations?
- How do managers assess the opportunities provided by new information technologies when many of them are still not IT literate?
- Are there any sources or guidelines which might help the organization in identifying new ideas and alternative approaches?

One source of ideas may be the plethora of articles and books over the last few years describing the organization of the twenty-first century. Emotive terms such as the virtual organization, the hollow corporation, the learning organization, the intellectual holding company, the networked organization and the modular corporation have been used to describe these new organizational forms. While these may give us a number of possible destinations in general terms, they say little about how an organization chooses one form over another (Lambert and Peppard, 1993).

In particular, there is no clear link between organizational form and business strategy. Does the new behavioural perspective of strategy, which emphasizes core competencies (Hamel and Prahalad, 1990) and organizational capabilities (Stalk *et al.*, 1992) provide a more useful reference point for BPR than the traditional market and product focus?

How Do We Get There?

The key question on every manager's lips is: 'If BPR is such a good idea, just tell me how to do it?'

One of the first issues to be resolved is who should be involved, their level of involvement and what skills they should bring. Does this depend on a possible classification of BPR projects and/or processes as described above?

Every consultancy has their own method for doing BPR. Many authors have also proposed approaches (for example, Butler Cox, 1991; Davenport and Short, 1990; Kaplan and Murdoch, 1991). Our observations conclude that, in fact, these methods are all very similar and follow the broad steps represented in Figure 1.1.

However, as we have seen, these steps raise more questions than have yet been answered. In particular, none of the proposed methods goes into any great detail about the actual implementation of the newly designed processes. These methods prompt a whole series of further questions including

- Is it possible to implement radical changes in a step-by-step fashion or must a 'big bang' approach be adopted? In particular, is it possible to pilot a change in a subset of the organization when that change will actually involve the whole organization?
- Is IT able to deliver the applications and technical infrastructure to support the new processes quickly enough? Is a new set of IT development skills, approaches and tools required?

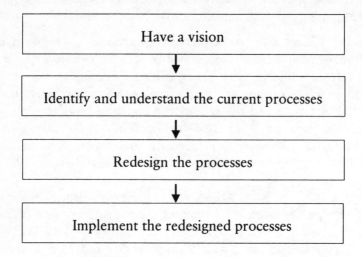

Figure 1.1   Generic steps in a BPR method

How Will We Know If We've Got There?

Having designed the new processes and implemented the changes, an organization needs to know whether they have achieved what they set out to? This will involve measurement against a set of criteria.

What are these criteria and measures? Clearly, they are likely to be linked with the objectives of the BPR programme (see above under 'What makes BPR happen?').

However, it is likely that the criteria and measures will need to be far more sophisticated than the type of performance measures currently used since they will be attempting to measure processes which cut across several functions. Indeed, measurements may need to capture an understanding of the process and its capabilities. Is there a role for benchmarking here? Perhaps activity-based costing (ABC) offers a way forward?

Whatever the solution to these issues of measurement, the resulting mechanisms must remain reasonably simple and straightforward to assess. Otherwise we may repeat the mistakes of some costing systems, where the effort involved in collecting the data outweighed the benefits and obscured the original purpose, or of some IT charging mechanisms which gave the wrong message to the users and resulted in unsound and expensive decisions (Ward and Ward, 1987).

How Will This Affect Me?

Clearly, changes of the type envisaged by BPR will have potentially significant organizational impacts.

Indeed, some of the definitions of BPR explicitly include the notion of moving from functional organization structures to ones which are based around processes. Some questions worthy of investigation in this regard are

- Does this thinking invalidate the functional organizational forms which have been put forward in the literature for many years (for example, Mintzberg, 1979)?
- Is such a radically different organization structure really necessary or can the same results be achieved within traditional functional structures or by using cross-functional teams?
- Is a process-based structure always appropriate or only for certain organizations, strategies or environmental situations?
- Is it possible or desirable to have a composite structure some of which is based on functions and some on processes?

If processes do become the focal point of organizational form, then there are implications both for structure and for the individuals who work in these organizations.

With regard to the structural implications, the following questions arise

- Functional structures are often linked with the concept of the command and control hierarchy. Will process-based organizations be flat or will hierarchies remain, possibly in a different manifestation?
- What is the appropriate level of process around which to structure the organization?
- How do the processes interact and interface with one another?
- How would the underlying principles of reporting differ from a functional organization?
- How are shared resources (eg the operation of a computer which supports several processes) positioned within the structure?
- Is team-based working a necessary part of a process organization?

Moving on to the impact of process-based organizations on individuals, we might ask

- Do processes require individuals from many disciplines and how might they be managed?

- Do board directors' roles also need to change from a functional orientation to process leadership?
- Will there be a need for a new type of manager, perhaps called a 'transform manager', who is knowledgeable in many disciplines and has the ability to look across an organization, identify opportunities for transformation and then implement these changes? Will this need breathe new life into general management development programmes such as MBAs which traditionally provide an insight in to the full range of management disciplines?
- Yet specialist functional expertise will clearly still be important. How is this expertise to be maintained and developed without the focus provided by the functional groupings?

The move towards process-based organizations will almost certainly impinge on such nebulous but potent concepts as power, authority and culture. These can present considerable barriers to the successful implementation of change initiatives. Some of these issues are

- The paradox that those with the knowledge of a process do not usually have the authority to redesign it and vice versa
- Redesigning organizations is likely to undermine the existing power base in an organization. Such a power base need not necessarily coincide with seniority but may lie with a 'dominant coalition'.
- The current organizational culture may mitigate against the new process-based organization and the change in work practices, job content, relationships, etc which it would entail
- Processes in multinational organizations may well cross national boundaries. The differences in cultures between different countries will then present further difficulties.

We would suggest that the large body of knowledge in the organizational behaviour field relating to the management of change will be relevant to dealing with these types of issues in relation to BPR.

How Do We Keep It Going?

Consider the following argument:

> Over the last thirty or so years, the business environment has been changing at an ever faster rate. This has been caused by a whole series of factors including globalization, technological development, demographic changes, ever shorter product development timescales and lifecycles, competition from developing countries, wider and wider ranges of more and more sophisticated products and services, increasingly discerning consumers demanding higher quality and better service.

And all the signs indicate that this is likely to continue!
Therefore, in order to survive organizations must be flexible, dynamic and constantly seeking to improve.

If this thinking is correct, then the inevitable, but somewhat daunting, conclusion is that a one-off dose of radical change is unlikely to be enough to ensure continuing good health.
This prompts many interesting questions including

- BPR is the latest approach to radical improvement but will there be new approaches next year and the year after that?
- How do organizations embrace the need for continuing change and instil this need in the hearts and minds of their managers?
- How does this need for continuing change relate to the concept of organizational learning?
- How often will organizations need to undertake radical change as opposed to continuous incremental improvement?

What is Really Happening?

Because of the stage of development of this field, qualitative research may well be more appropriate than quantitative analysis. Therefore, the ability of researchers to answer any of the above questions will be dependent on identifying and studying significant examples of organizations which have attempted and/or achieved real transformations. Unfortunately, many of the examples published to date have been somewhat superficial and the published material does not provide for the opportunity of in-depth analysis. Descriptive cases such as these are only valuable if the lessons learned are made explicit.

CONCLUSION

We believe that BPR is a subject worthy of much further research work. We also believe that this research is likely to be cross-disciplinary and will certainly build on published material and current work in many disciplines including strategic management, organizational design, change management, operations management, logistics, finance and information systems. We hope that our proposed research agenda provides a starting point.

REFERENCES

Burgelman, R A (1983) 'A Process Model of Internal Corporate Venturing in a Diversified Major Firm', *Administrative Science Quarterly*, 28 (2), 223–244.

Business Intelligence (1993) *Business Re-engineering: the use of process redesign and IT to transform corporate performance*, Research report.

Butler Cox Foundation (1991) 'The Role of Information Technology in Transforming the Business', *Research Report 79*, January.

Bytheway, A (1992) *Business Process Reengineering*. Paper presented at EDI 92, Birmingham, UK. Paper also available from Cranfield School of Management, Cranfield, Bedford.

Checkland, P (1981) *Systems Thinking, Systems Practice*, John Wiley & Sons, Chichester.

Davenport, T H (1993) *Process Innovation: Re-engineering Work through Information Technology*, Harvard Business School Press, Boston, Mass.

Davenport, T H and Short, J E (1990) 'The New Industrial Engineering: Information Technology and Business Process Redesign', *Sloan Management Review*, Summer, 11–27.

Eden, C, Jones, S and Sims, D (1979) *Thinking in Organizations*, Macmillan, London.

Edwards, C E and Braganza, A (1993) *The BPR Change Web*. Paper available from Cranfield School of Management, Cranfield, Bedford.

Edwards, C E and Peppard, J W (1994) 'Business Process Redesign: Hype, Hope or Hypocrisy?', *Journal of Information Technology*, pp 251–66.

Hamel, G and Prahalad, C K (1990) 'The Core Competence of the Corporation', *Harvard Business Review*.

Hammer, M (1990) 'Re-engineering Work: Don't Automate, Obliterate', *Harvard Business Review*, July/August, 104–112.

Hammer, M and Champy, J (1993) *Reengineering the Corporation: A Manifesto for Business Revolution*, Nicholas Brealey Publishing, London.

Heygate, R and Brebach, G (1991) 'Corporate Reengineering', *The McKinsey Quarterly*, Summer, 44–55.

Kaplan, R B and Murdoch, L (1991) 'Core Process Redesign', *The McKinsey Quarterly*, Summer, 27–43.

Lambert, R and Peppard, J (1993) 'IT and New Organizational Forms: Destination but No Road Map', *Journal of Strategic Information Systems*, 2 (3), 180–205.

Macdonald, K H (1991) 'The Value Process Model', Appendix D in Scott-Morton, M (ed), *The Corporation of the 1990s: Information Technology and Organizational Transformation*, Oxford University Press.

Mintzberg, H (1979) *The Structuring of Organizations*, Prentice-Hall, Englewood Cliffs, New Jersey.

Morris, D and Brandon, J (1993) *Re-engineering Your Business*, McGraw-Hill, New York.

O'Sullivan, L and Geringer, M J (1993) 'Harnessing the Power of Your Value Chain', *Long Range Planning*, 26 (2), 59–68.

Porter, M E (1985) *Competitive Advantage*, Free Press, New York.

Stalk, G, Evans, P and Shulman, L E (1992) 'Competing on Capabilities: The New Rules of Corporate Strategy', *Harvard Business Review*, March–April, 57–69.

Venkatraman, N (1991) 'IT-induced Business Reconfiguration', in Scott-Morton, M (ed), *The Corporation of the 1990s: Information Technology and Organizational Transformation*, Oxford University Press, Oxford.

Ward, J and Ward, K (1987) 'The Transfer Pricing of Information Technology', *Management Accounting*, February.

Ward, J, Griffiths, P and Whitmore, P (1990) *Strategic Planning for Information Systems*, John Wiley & Sons, Chichester.

Part Two

DEFINITIONS AND MODELS OF BPR RE-EXAMINED

Today, BPR is firmly established as part of the management vocabulary. Organizations in all sectors of the economy and in countries throughout the world are looking to BPR to achieve dramatic improvements in performance. The recent CSC Index survey *The State of Re-engineering* reported that 69 per cent of US companies and 75 per cent of European companies claim to have at least one re-engineering initiative currently underway. BPR has become big business.

Yet, despite these obvious manifestations, there remain a number of fundamental questions about the very nature of the BPR phenomenon. Perhaps most fundamental of all is the question 'What *is* BPR anyway?' This question is often manifested in a number of guises including

- 'Is it new or is it just a concoction of well-established principles in shiny new packaging?'
- 'What is a process?'
- 'Is it about radical change or about continuous performance improvement?'
- 'What is the role of IT in BPR?'
- 'If BPR is such a wonderful thing, how come 70 per cent of all BPR initiatives fail?'
- 'Isn't it just about eliminating jobs and delayering?'

The purpose of this part of the text is to explore these issues about the nature of BPR from a number of different perspectives.

In Chapter 2, Matthew Jones tells us that BPR remains surprisingly ill-defined and that the principles of BPR promulgated by its leading proponents show considerable differences. Through an examination of the literature, he highlights a number of significant contradictions, both within and between what he refers to as the various 'theories' of BPR. For example, is it an essentially 'engineering' activity, or is it a 'hearts and minds' exercise? How can the emphasis on top-down, senior executive leadership be reconciled with the concerns with employee empowerment? He concludes by addressing the question of whether these contradictions undermine the case for BPR and highlights some of the ways in which the BPR literature seeks to resolve them.

One of the key pillars of BPR is the focus on business processes. Yet the crucial question of 'what is a process?' has, surprisingly, received little attention in the literature. Drawing on his reference discipline of operations management, Alan Harrison addresses this question in Chapter 3. On examining a selection of definitions, he concludes that no clear picture emerges. He contends that this lack of clarity casts some doubt on the credentials of BPR and its ability to deliver quantum leaps in performance. He puts forward a classification of four process types together with a 'business process breakdown structure'.

Empirical studies, such as those by Hall, Rosenthal and Wade described in their *Harvard Business Review* article 'How to make re-engineering *really* work', show that while BPR can lead to dramatic improvements in time, cost and quality, the overall profit improvement for a business unit or an entire company are sometimes disappointing. Taking this as their start point, Christof Hauser and Eisele Rainer recommend that in order to avoid such deficiencies an economic evaluation of business processes should be undertaken prior to implementation. In Chapter 4, they seek to outline a concept for such an evaluation whereby the emphasis is placed on the quantification of market-related benefits. In addition, they illustrate how to select those business processes most in need of redesign and to incorporate a market orientation into BPR.

Much of the thinking about BPR appears to derive from an essentially engineering reference point. In this way, the organization is a metaphorical machine which can be pulled apart and rebuilt almost like Lego™. However, many people would argue that it is more helpful to think about organizations as cultural, social and political artefacts. It is from this cultural, social and political perspective that the next two chapters attempt to view BPR. Both draw on elements of social theory to advance their arguments.

In Chapter 5, Keith Grint develops a sociological perspective of BPR. He begins by setting out the general principles of BPR and subjects each to a brief historically based critique that disputes its novelty. He then goes on to consider why BPR might still be regarded as novel, and why the historical antecedents of BPR might be useful in accounting for its apparently limited success rate. In particular, he suggests that re-engineering is most likely to fail where it is construed as a method and a goal of change that is premised upon rational analysis, where the decision-making is incremental, where the methods of execution depend wholly upon assumptions about rational individuals, and where its legitimizing characterics are regarded as self-evident and lie in its internal and objective value. Re-engineering, Grint argues, might be better configured as a Utopia, and it embodies the same kind of possibilities and problems that Utopias throughout history have manifested. In effect, the chapter argues that for re-engineering to work as a radical and long-term change approach, the focus should be more about re-engineering the way managers think and work than about re-engineering the way processes operate. Furthermore, he contends that the methods by which re-engineering might be achieved have to be more firmly rooted in the current cultural climate of the organization.

In Chapter 6, Ranjit Tinaikar, Amir Hartman and Raghu Nath present an analysis of contempory BPR literature to justify their allegation of its narrow Tayloristic perspective and lack of a theory. They make the case for a more well-grounded, theoretical foundation to BPR. They claim that this is not a righteous call for the total rejection of BPR, but rather an attempt to encourage a more balanced approach through greater circumspection to the study and practice of BPR. They, therefore, put forward an alternative definition of BPR, which they have developed from a social constructionist perspective, and discuss its implications.

In Chapter 7, Bob Galliers questions IT's centrality in BPR and attempts to locate an appropriate role for IT in BPR. He contends that BPR as currently practised and discussed in the literature, far from being a new departure, is in fact a reversion of the classical school of strategic thinking popularized in the 1960s. He presents a case for a more holistic and even-handed stance on BPR which sees the process as a learning experience requiring ongoing assessment and review. The focus should not be on process alone, neither should it depend solely on the opportunities provided by new technology.

In the final chapter of this part, Chapter 8, Hean Lee Poh and Wan Wan Chew revisit some of the most widely referenced definitions and models of BPR which paves the way for comparisons of different frameworks and models proposed by researchers and consultants. In particular, Porter's competitive strategy framework, the Scott Morton and Rockart's *Management in the 1990s* framework and Hammer and Champy's framework 'the business system diamond' are studied, compared and unified. Based on this unification, Lee Poh and Wan Chew then propose their own framework for executing BPR. They argue that this bridges the gap between frameworks proposed by consultants and methodologies useful to practitioners. Finally, the chapter critically surveys a number of further frameworks proposed by various researchers and consultants, and tries to reduce them into a special case or an extended case of their unified framework.

THE CONTRADICTIONS OF BUSINESS PROCESS RE-ENGINEERING

Matthew R Jones, Judge Institute of Management Studies, University of Cambridge

INTRODUCTION

Business Process Re-engineering (BPR) has been described by *Business Week* as the 'hottest management concept since the quality movement' (Byrne, 1993), by *Fortune* as the 'hottest trend in management' (Stewart, 1993), and by *The Financial Times* as 'one of the key management concepts of the 1990s' (Fintech, 1992b). The same *Financial Times* article also reported forecasts of a worldwide market for BPR products growing at 46 per cent per annum to reach $2.2 billion by 1996. What is more, from an IS perspective, many of the leading proponents of BPR identify a central role for information technology. It would therefore seem clear that BPR is a major new development in management thinking which deserves the serious attention of IS researchers.

This does not mean, however, that we should treat these claims of BPR's significance uncritically. Perhaps it is simply another management fad, like any of the more than two dozen others whose waxing and waning over the past thirty years has been mapped by Pascale (1990). Or, maybe worse, it is just a fashionable label to be attached to outdated and ineffective techniques, or merely a new euphemism for sacking staff (Warren, 1993). But even if it is true, as no less an authority than Peter Drucker has argued, that BPR 'is new and it has to be done' (Hammer and Champy, 1993), then we may still usefully question what exactly this revolutionary new concept actually involves. In this chapter, therefore, we will seek to explore the nature of BPR as it is described in the literature and also as it is practised in a number of different organizations.

THE NATURE OF BPR

The origins of BPR are usually traced to an article by Michael Hammer in *Harvard Business Review* entitled 'Re-engineering Work: Don't Automate, Obliterate' (Hammer, 1990). In this he described the dramatic achievements of re-engineering in a number of companies and set out seven principles which had been 'discovered' as a result of their experience (as shown in Table 2.1).

Table 2.1 Hammer's principles of re-engineering

- Organize around outcomes, not tasks
- Have those who use the output of the process perform the process
- Subsume information processing work into the real work that produces the information
- Treat geographically dispersed resources as though they were centralized
- Link parallel activities instead of integrating tasks
- Put the decision point where the work is performed and build control into the process
- Capture information once and at the source.

At about the same time another article, on 'business process redesign' was published in the *Sloan Management Review* (Davenport and Short, 1990). This made similar claims about the transformatory potential of process-oriented approaches to organizational change, laying particular emphasis on the potential of IT in achieving this.

Since then there has been a deluge of articles on the subject (a recent on-line search identified more than 3500 in the past five years). Much of this literature, however, consists of descriptions of the BPR phenomenon for different audiences or reports of BPR 'success stories' produced by the companies involved. Only a few articles seek to develop the original concepts or to present critical analyses of BPR practice. Our discussion in this chapter will therefore use the descriptions of BPR offered by Hammer and Davenport and Short as the main starting point, supplementing this with contributions from other authors as they support or contradict their views. In addition, since, as Jones (1994) argues, the rhetoric of BPR is an important feature of the concept, extensive use will be made of the authors' own words to capture the style as well as the content of their argument.

The analysis is grouped around four key questions.

- What is it?
- Who needs it?

- How do you do it?
- What do you get from it?

What is it?

The Origins of BPR

Hammer and Champy (1993) describe re-engineering as emerging from their practical experience as consultants to a number of major US corporations, and are emphatic that it 'has little or nothing in common with [normal business improvement programmes] and differs in significant ways even from those [approaches] with which it does share some common premises'. Re-engineering, they argue, is 'a new beginning' that involves 'rejecting the conventional wisdom and received assumptions of the past ... [and] inventing new approaches to process structures that bear little or no resemblance to those of previous eras'.

Davenport and Short (1990), however, present BPR as an extension of established management approaches, in particular Industrial Engineering (IE). It therefore draws on the unrivalled power of the 'mechanizing vision' of F.W. Taylor's *Scientific Management*. Similarly, Wilkinson (1991) describes re-engineering as 'Industrial Engineering in action'. On this basis, Klein (1993) argues that the US Navy was involved in re-engineering around the turn of the century and that 'what Henry Ford did to automobile manufacturing in 1910 was also BPR'. Although they do not make such extreme claims, other authors such as Parker (1993) and Morris and Brandon (1993) identify 'time and motion' and other IE techniques as important components of BPR.

A third perspective is offered by Shillingford (1992) and Lopes (1993) who see BPR as emerging from Japanese-style quality programmes. The rationale of BPR, Shillingford (1992) argues, is that 'concepts like Japan's "best manufacturing practice", which uses just-in-time techniques, can be applied to the office as well as the factory'. Johannson *et al.* (1993) also propose that BPR, Just-In-Time (JIT) and Total Quality Management (TQM) are 'of one family'. BPR they argue, however, is 'an escalation of the efforts of JIT and TQM', which 'pushes the JIT and TQM philosophies upstream and downstream to the customer and supplier'.

The Scope of BPR

A concern with a process-oriented, as opposed to functional, perspective on organizations is perhaps the only consistent feature of the many different approaches to BPR discussed in the literature. This does not necessarily mean, however, that they share a common understanding of what a process is. Thus, even if there is no disagreement with Hammer and Champy's definition of a process as 'the collection of activities that takes one or more kinds of input and creates an output that is of value to the customer', the scope of BPR will differ significantly depending on who is taken to be the customer.

If, for example, as appears to be increasingly popular, we take customers as potentially internal to a firm, then a process could consist of an individual work task. Thus Davenport and Short (1990) discuss 'interpersonal processes' within and across small work groups which typically operate 'within a function or department', and Hall *et al.* (1993) suggest that processes 'can be as narrowly defined as a single activity in a single function'. A slightly larger-scale view of processes would consider those that combine a number of different work tasks within a department. Morris and Brandon (1993), for example, define a process as 'larger than a task ... [but] smaller than an area of business such as operations, human resources or shipping'. A third view of processes would locate them predominantly at an organizational level. Hammer and Champy (1993), for example, stress the need to 'look at an entire process ... that cut[s] across organizational boundaries'. Finally, processes may be seen as extending beyond the boundaries of any single company. Thus Venkatraman (1991) talks of 'business network redesign'.

Depending on the scale of the process seen to be involved, therefore, BPR might be used to describe a small-scale reorganization of customer complaints handling, or the complete realignment of an organization's supply chain. Michael Hammer is particularly insistent that BPR should involve nothing less than 'fundamental rethinking and radical redesign' (Hammer and Champy, 1993). 'Re-engineering', he argues, 'is an all-or-nothing proposition'; it is 'about beginning again with a clean sheet of paper'. Other writers, however, would suggest that there is a spectrum of re-engineering strategies, ranging from incremental improvement to complete transformation (Wilkinson, 1991; Davidson, 1993). Davenport (1993) seeks to argue that these are actually two distinct approaches, that he terms *process improvement* and *process innovation*. Johannson *et al.* (1993) also distinguish between the two, but argue that the first is a necessary precondition of the second.

The Role of IT

Hammer (1990) makes frequent reference to using 'the power of information technology' in re-engineering, while Hammer and Champy (1993) argue that the importance of information technology to re-engineering is 'difficult to overstate'. Similarly, Davenport and Short (1990) propose that BPR may be 'IT-driven' and that 'BPR and IT have a recursive relationship ... each is the key to thinking about the other'. A number of IT/IS consultants also appear to see BPR predominately as an approach to applying IT in organizations (see, for example, Heygate and Brebach, 1991; Aikins, 1993). The term has also come to be associated by some writers with particular types of IT system, such as workflow software and document image processing hardware (Lopes, 1993; Shillingford, 1992), to the extent that these are sometimes sold as re-engineering tools.

Perhaps in reaction to this, other writers argue that 'BPR and IT are certainly not synonymous' (Warren, 1993), rather re-engineering should be 'the common-sense practice of redesigning business processes before bringing in technology' (Fintech, 1992a). Davenport (1993) also reports the view that the approach to re-engineering should be 'first think about the process, then think about the systems', but argues that this may 'ignore valuable tools for shaping processes'. An apparent compromise, which is widely adopted is therefore to describe IT as an 'enabler' of re-engineering. For example, Hammer and Champy (1993) talk about IT as an 'essential enabler' while Davenport (1993) describes it as 'the primary enabler'.

Who Needs it?

Hammer and Champy (1993) describe re-engineering as becoming 'a competitive necessity' and argue that 'America's largest corporations – even the most successful and promising among them – must embrace and apply' its principles. They also identify three types of company that undertake re-engineering: those that are in deep trouble; those with prescient managers seeking to avoid impending crises, and finally market leaders who wish to maintain their advantage. BPR thus appears to be a universal solution, relevant to almost any company.

Stewart (1993) argues, however, that 'BPR is strong medicine, not always needed or successful'. Klein (1993) also suggests that 'there are younger companies that have invented themselves (and/or their industries) in such a way that we can think of them as "engineered" corporations'. Walmart, GM Saturn, Microsoft and Federal Express are cited as examples. Hammer and Champy also write approvingly of Walmart's practices and identify the threat of startups as a motivation for other companies to re-engineer. Does this mean therefore that some companies have re-engineered themselves without knowing it, or that it is possible to achieve its results without adopting its methods? Moreover, as Wheatley (1994) points out, what happens after re-engineering? Is further improvement possible?

How Do You Do it?

Making Re-engineering Work

No specific guidance is offered in either Hammer (1990) or Hammer and Champy (1993) on how to carry out BPR. Indeed Hammer (1990) argues that re-engineering 'cannot be planned meticulously'. Instead there is much talk of visionary leadership and boldness of the imagination. 'Commitment, consistency – maybe even a touch of fanaticism – are needed,' Hammer (1990) argues. This is not to say that he denies the 'difficult, strenuous work' re-engineering entails, but that the emphasis is very much on inspiring with the promise of great rewards, rather than the mechanics of how to achieve them. He is not alone in this, as Klein (1993) observes. 'Some writers assert that it is impossible to be prescriptive about BPR,' he argues, 'they describe it as a creative act in almost mystical terms – terms like "paradigm shift" or "breaking frame".'

Other authors, however, appear to see BPR as a much more systematic approach. For example Wilkinson (1991) describes re-engineering as a 'clear-cut procedure', while Guha *et al.* (1993) propose a 'comprehensive re-engineering methodology'. Davenport and Short (1990) describe BPR as 'a straightforward activity', which consists of five major steps involving extensive quantitative analysis. Morris and Brandon (1993) also identify a 'systematic methodology' as essential for re-engineering success.

Who Will Achieve it

'One factor that is necessary for re-engineering to succeed', according to Hammer (1990), is 'executive leadership with real vision'. This is reiterated in Hammer and Champy (1993) where it is stated that 're-engineering never, ever happens from the bottom up' because only senior management will have the necessary broad perspective to envision organization-wide change and the authority to make it happen. Thus 're-engineering is always born in the executive suite'. Davenport (1993) is also very clear that BPR requires 'strong direction from senior management'.

In parallel with this emphasis on a top-down approach to re-engineering, however, there is much talk of empowerment, teamworking, and flattening of organizational hierarchies. Workers are to take on new responsibilities, become multiskilled and customer-focused, facilitated rather than controlled by their managers. Hammer and Champy (1993) devote a whole chapter to describing this 'new world of work'.

What Do You Get from it?

The BPR literature is replete with success stories of companies which 'slashed' a seven-day turnround to four hours, reduced the number of people involved in a process by 75 per cent, halved the time from design to production and reduced tooling and manufacturing costs by 25 per cent. All that is needed, Hammer (1990) argues, is the vision to aim for such goals, then 're-engineering will provide a way'. These rewards are presented as the payoff for the pain and disruption that re-engineering will inevitably involve.

Hammer and Champy (1993) also seek to present BPR as essential if American companies are to overcome the 'crisis of competitiveness' that currently afflicts them. 'The alternative,' they argue, 'is for corporate America to close its doors and go out of business.' A similar siege mentality pervades the accounts of many other authors. This would appear to suggest that re-engineering is inevitable and that companies have no option but to pursue it if they are to survive.

Compare this, however, with the dangers of re-engineering failure. According to Hammer and Champy (1993) '50 to 70 per cent of organizations that undertake a re-engineering effort do not achieve the dramatic results they intended.' Despite this they argue that re-engineering is 'not a high-risk endeavor'. So long as you avoid a few common mistakes, which they kindly identify, 'you can't really fail'. Davenport (1993), however, is more ready to acknowledge that BPR may be risky and uses this to justify the adoption of a narrow scope for re-engineering efforts, perhaps restricting the change initiatives to a 'business unit on the periphery of the organization, in a single plant or small division', at least in their early stages.

THE CONTRADICTIONS OF BPR

From this discussion we can see that there are some widely differing perspectives on BPR. These may be seen as involving a number of significant contradictions. Some of these exist between different authors, but others lie at the heart of the concept itself. We will now consider a number of the more important of these.

New vs Established

Is re-engineering, as Hammer and Champy (1993) assert, new and different from preceding organizational change initiatives, or is Klein (1993) correct in arguing that the only thing that is new about BPR is the label? Moreover, if re-engineering is based on existing techniques, is it the analytical tradition of Industrial Engineering, or the more holistic approach of Japanese-style quality programmes that provides the inspiration?

These questions matter because they shape perceptions of the nature of the concept. Thus, while Hammer and Champy's argument for re-engineering's novelty may be seen as an attempt at product differentiation in the crowded market for management solutions, it also conveys other important messages. If re-engineering is new, then it is untainted by the problems and failures of previous approaches. If it is new, then it may be easier to believe that it is capable of the dramatic results which its proponents claim. If it is different from TQM, then it can be argued that it 'takes advantage of American talents and unleashes American ingenuity' (Hammer and Champy, 1993), rather than being dependent on alien ideas imported from Japan. The argument that BPR emerges from Hammer and Champy's consultancy experience rather than theory may also be seen as appealing to practically-minded managers.

If BPR is an extension of existing approaches, on the other hand, then there may be existing staff members, industrial engineers for example (Klein, 1993), skilled in supporting it. Similarly, it can draw on a tried and tested tradition with well-established methods and proven effectiveness. It may therefore appeal to managers as being less risky and disruptive. While this is clearly anathema to Hammer and Champy, it may make it easier to sell the concept to clients.

Radical vs Incremental

A related issue concerns the character of re-engineering. Hammer and Champy (1993) present it as an unequivocally radical approach, which involves 'reversing the industrial revolution' and 'inventing new approaches to process structure that bear little or no resemblance to those of previous eras'. Their argument that it 'can't be carried out in small or cautious steps' would thus seem to be incompatible with the quality movement approach of continuous, incremental improvement. It would also suggest that processes to be re-engineered should be organization-wide rather than restricted to a single department. This is reinforced in Hammer and Champy's discussion of the causes of re-engineering failure, the first of which is 'try to fix a process instead of changing it'. Many of the other 'common errors' they identify also stress that a half-hearted or narrowly defined approach is unlikely to meet with success.

One advantage of presenting re-engineering as a revolutionary activity is that it makes the claimed transformation of organizational performance more plausible. Without a willingness to 'obliterate' existing processes and to rethink the whole way that work is done, improvements are likely to be marginal and the 'orders of magnitude' breakthroughs that re-engineering promises will not materialize. Radical change also fits in well with Hammer and Champy's argument that American business is in terminal crisis: desperate times call for desperate measures. Internally, a willingness to fundamentally rethink an organization's activities, to challenge the rules that underlie existing practices, may also symbolize the seriousness of the endeavour and help to promote employee commitment.

As we have seen, however, some authors would include more restricted, incremental forms of process redesign within the ambit of re-engineering, while others would identify an essential commonality between TQM and BPR, seeing them as a necessary precursor or extension of each other. This may be seen to be a safer strategy which integrates different change initiatives rather than setting BPR up as the one and only solution. JIT and TQM may also promote a discipline in the treatment of organizational resources and an awareness of business processes, as well as providing specific techniques, which may make a valuable contribution to re-engineering. Moreover, as Craig and Yetton (1994) point out, incremental improvement over a number of years may achieve the same results as re-engineering without the pain and uncertainty.

IT-led vs Process-led

Through the use of terms such as 'enabler', and careful reference to the inseparability of technical and organizational change, Hammer and Champy seek to avoid the accusation made by some critics that BPR is 'just a way for IT companies to sell more IT' (Warren, 1993). An examination of their argument, however, suggests that they see IT as having a very dominant role. Thus they state that 'a company that looks for problems first and then seeks technology solutions for them cannot re-engineer', and illustrate this with a discussion of a number of information technologies, such as expert systems and interactive videodisks, identifying the way in which they 'break the rules that limit how we conduct our work'. By privileging the role of IT in this way and suggesting that organizational change stems reliably from specific technologies, the view of re-engineering as being IT-led is promoted.

Other BPR writers, in contrast, place much less emphasis on IT. Morris and Brandon (1993), for example, describe it as just one of the resources to be re-engineered. This does not mean that they dismiss its potential though. For example, although Grover *et al.* (1993) state that BPR 'does not need to be associated with IT ... it has the capability to transform the design of business processes within and between companies'. Their view of re-engineering, however, may be described as more process-led (as opposed to IT-led) than is the case with Hammer and Champy for example.

By focusing on the importance of IT in BPR, writers such as Hammer and Champy evoke a powerful explanator of change with potentially profound effects on the spatial and temporal nature of organizations.

Despite the acknowledged failure of IT to achieve its widely predicted transformatory 'impacts' on organizational performance in the past, however, a case is still made that BPR is 'the best hope we have of getting value out of our vast information technology expenditures' (Davenport, 1993). This message may be expected to be attractive to companies disappointed with the effectiveness of past IT investments and to organizational IT specialists for whom this offers renewed influence.

By downplaying the role of IT, in contrast, a distance can be maintained from past failures, and a more complex, multifactorial model of IT effectiveness advanced. It may also be argued (Johannson *et al.*, 1993) that identifying technological opportunities is a relatively small (and straightforward) part of the organizational change process, the main challenge of which is to alter organizational value systems.

Universal vs Specific

The presentation of re-engineering as a universal solution clearly widens the potential market for the concept and avoids the need to differentiate alternative types of BPR (for services or manufacturing, for example, or large or small firms). Similarly, the specific conditions under which particular approaches apply need not be identified. Many, quite disparate change initiatives may therefore be embraced by the term, enhancing the cumulative bandwagon effect.

If some companies don't need to re-engineer, however, then we will require some mechanism to enable us to identify which these are. The development of such a mechanism and of more specific re-engineering approaches for different contexts might also lead to a clearer definition of the concept, and hence provide a more reliable means of distinguishing between 'true' re-engineering and its imitators. Another useful outcome of such an exercise might be to encourage consideration of the issue of what, if anything, follows BPR.

Inspiration vs Engineering

Hammer's use of the term re-*engineering* to describe his particular approach to process-oriented change might be seen as identifying it with a particular mechanistic model of organizations as Wheatley (1994) argues. Yet the approach he advocates is much stronger on exhortation than on method, as Klein (1993) complains. This evangelistic style has been noted by Stewart (1993) who describes Hammer as 're-engineering's John the Baptist, a tub-thumping preacher'. While such an approach may be effective in selling the technique and in creating the hype surrounding the concept, as Klein (1993) observes, it is not much help as a practical guide to how to re-engineer.

A more rigorous, procedural approach, based on a specific methodology, is therefore proposed by a number of authors, especially those from an industrial or software engineering background, such as Davenport and Short (1990), Wilkinson (1991) and Guha *et al.* (1993). This is seen to be desirable as a way of promoting a more standardized approach to re-engineering which systematically addresses the critical issues. In practice, however, many of the published methodologies provide insufficient detail to be used directly by practitioners (perhaps because many of the authors have a consultancy product to sell). There is also a danger, as Wheatley (1994) warns, that methodologies may stifle initiative and creative thinking.

Top-down vs Bottom-up

The view that re-engineering requires senior executive leadership may be seen as a necessary result of the level of change it involves. Only those at the highest levels in the organization can be expected to have the company-wide vision to identify the opportunities, access to the resources to make it happen, and the power to see the changes through. By implication, therefore, those at lower levels lack these and have therefore to be led, motivated and, if necessary, forced to pursue their superiors' vision. As Stewart (1993) reports, however, this does not mean that employee involvement cannot have a vital role, at least in planning how to implement the new processes once they have been redesigned.

While such a top-down approach may be expected to appeal to senior management, it may appear less welcome to those at the lower levels of the organizational hierarchy, especially if their jobs are to be re-engineered out of existence. Indeed one Dutch consultancy recommends that only staff deemed to be capable of operating within the re-engineered organization should be involved in process redesign, if necessary by recruiting a whole new staff team to plan and operate the new processes. Senior management-driven BPR also sits uneasily with the idea of an empowered workforce, of which there is much talk in the re-engineering literature.

More generally, we may also question the concept of empowerment which suggests that power is something that managers can hand to subordinates, rather than a property of the relationship between them (cf. Clegg, 1989). The limits of this view are evident from a closer examination of the scope of empowerment described by Hammer and Champy (1993), where it is made clear that subordinate autonomy is clearly constrained by the 'boundaries of their obligation to the organization'. Even this form of empowerment, however, is seen by Hammer and Champy as requiring a broadening of recruitment criteria to include the individual's *character* (emphasis in the original). This points to a more fundamental contradiction of empowerment, and of the wider culture management literature of which it may be seen to be a part – the tension between its emancipatory image and its attempt to extend management control into the realm of individual subjectivity (Willmott, 1993).

Clement (1994) argues that this arises from the confusion of two distinct types of empowerment: 'functional' and 'democratic'. The former predominates in the BPR literature and focuses on 'improving performance in the interests of organizational goals that are assumed to be shared, unproblematically by all participants'. The other, which emphasises the 'rights and abilities of people to participate as equals in decisions about affairs that affect them' is more typical of Scandinavian work organization (see, for example, Floyd *et al.*, 1989). Much of the 'potency and appeal' of 'functional' empowerment, Clement argues, derives from its association with this more emancipatory tradition.

Rewards vs Risks

It would not seem difficult to identify the benefits to re-engineering of its promise of dramatic improvements across all aspects of a company's activities. Anybody offering an infallible method for 'quantum leaps in performance', backed by evidence from blue chip companies, would seem likely to attract more than a little interest.

It may be less clear, though, what advantages are gained from such up-front discussion of re-engineering failure, notwithstanding Hammer and Champy's assurances that this is a danger only if certain avoidable errors are committed. The vagueness of the description of these errors offered by Hammer and Champy (1993), such as 'quit too early' and 'skimp on the resources devoted to re-engineering', however, might suggest that it would be difficult for just about any company which fails at re-engineering to have avoided them all. There may also be inconsistencies between them, for example 'neglect people's values and beliefs' exists alongside 'allow existing corporate cultures and management attitudes to prevent re-engineering from getting started'. Re-engineering failures may therefore be attributed to deficiencies of the company and BPR itself exonerated from any share of the blame.

High failure rates may also be seen as increasing the plausibility of BPR – nobody would believe that such results could be guaranteed. It also raises the stakes for those investing in the concept, perhaps increasing their determination to beat the odds. In the end, though, if re-engineering is, as Hammer and Champy claim, 'a competitive necessity' then companies may have no choice. But they cannot claim that they have not been warned about the dangers ahead.

DEALING WITH CONTRADICTIONS

Given these contradictory aspects of re-engineering, three means of handling them may be identified: denial, resolution and accommodation. Only the first two of these receive much attention in the BPR literature.

The Strategy of Denial

Authors who adopt this approach either do not recognize the contradictions or seek to argue that they are due to misconceptions about re-engineering or manifestations of some form of improvement programme other than BPR. Heygate and Brebach (1991) or Parker (1993), for example, unequivocally link re-engineering with an IT-led, 'engineering' approach. Davenport (1993), however, reserves his preferred term 'process innovation' for those approaches which are radical, top-down, clean-slate, high-risk, information-technology enabled and so on. While this may lead to some differences of opinion with other writers, such as Morris and Brandon (1993) for example, who present a much narrower, more incremental, process-led approach, these can be rejected as a mislabelling of traditional process improvement.

The effectiveness of this strategy, however, would seem likely to be constrained by the absence of any agreed definition of re-engineering or of a mechanism for achieving it. Different organizations discussed by Jones (1994), for example, used the term BPR to describe: the redefinition of organizational value metrics; upstream management consultancy work to capture new information systems development work; and an adaptation of Checkland's Soft Systems Methodology to assist the planning of a major organizational restructuring exercise and associated information systems. While none of these may match Davenport's view of 'process innovation', it is not clear how anyone might be able to enforce a single, self-consistent definition. The current situation of multiple, competing forms of BPR as described by Warren (1993), though condemned as unsatisfactory by almost every writer on the subject, would therefore seem likely to continue.

The Strategy of Resolution

There are two ways in which writers on re-engineering seek to resolve the contradictions within the concept, either by demonstrating that the apparent contradictory elements are actually compatible, or by drowning them in rhetoric. The first approach is illustrated by the argument presented in Stewart (1993) that re-engineering's promotion of both top-down and bottom-up initiatives is not inconsistent, they just apply to different aspects of the process. This leads to a similar claim with respect to the relationship between BPR and TQM – they operate at different levels.

Hammer is perhaps the best exponent of rhetorical 'resolution'. While acknowledging possible contradictions in the concept of re-engineering, these are dissolved by grand statements which provide assurance of their compatibility. By focusing on the pragmatic origins of BPR, Hammer and Champy are also able to suggest that contradictions are resolved 'in practice'. Ultimately, though, Hammer argues that re-engineering depends on an act of faith. 'It's a theology', he argues, 'because it requires a belief that there is a different way of doing things' (quoted in Byrne, 1992). To doubt its coherence would therefore be an act of impiety. While such a tactic may be effective in selling the re-engineering message, it is likely to lead to confusion and cynicism as the concept is subject to more critical scrutiny.

The Strategy of Accommodation

Perhaps a better option is therefore to accept that there are contradictions in BPR. There will be tensions, for example, between providing the vision and leadership to carry through a major change initiative and engaging the energy and creativity of those who will be involved in carrying it out. This may lead to conflict and delays, but these will not be solved by imposing a rigid, formulaic approach which may achieve compliance, but not commitment. Wilful disregard of the differences of interest between organization members does not make them go away.

At a more fundamental level, it may be argued that contradiction is inherent in the nature of being. Dialectical thinking, for example, which has a long tradition in Chinese Taoism as well as in classical Greek philosophy (Heraclitus) and German Idealism (Hegel), proposes that all things contain two opposing principles which are in constant interplay. Night and day, hot and cold only make sense in terms of the relationship between them. Autonomy and control, or the technical and social aspects of information systems, are therefore not independent of each other but are inextricably linked (Han and Jones, 1993). A similar perspective on contradiction is offered by French Post-structuralism, notably the work of Derrida (Cooper, 1989). Any 'text' such as re-engineering is seen as being structured around binary attributes, one of which dominates the other, but is constantly undermined by it. The two terms thus mutually define one another in an undecidable manner. Method is therefore seen to be shadowed by inspiration, or success by failure.

This is not simply academic philosophical speculation, but points to the need to acknowledge the contradictory character of phenomena such as re-engineering, rather than seeking to ignore or eliminate it. Moreover, contradiction may be a dynamic and creative force, as is being increasingly recognized in the popular management literature. Pascale (1990), for example, discusses how organizations can harness 'contention' on various dimensions to stimulate change and adaptation. Similarly Handy (1994) characterizes the influences currently shaping organizations in terms of 'paradoxes'. Rather than seeing the contradictions of re-engineering as a deficiency of the concept, therefore, we may see them as a normal feature of organizational life, which may be managed in a positive and constructive way.

DO THESE CONTRADICTIONS MATTER?

Although articles such as Wheatley (1994) may be signs of the start of a backlash, and writers such as Davidson (1993) are already talking of new developments 'beyond re-engineering', the contradictions discussed in this chapter within and between the arguments of its proponents do not seem to have dampened interest in the topic. It may therefore be argued that they are not important. Any problems are, as Hammer and Champy (1993) suggest, resolved in practice through commitment and leadership.

In the timescale of the management fads identified by Pascale (1990), however, it may still be too early to say whether re-engineering is more than just another gimmick, especially in Europe where its growth is probably 18 months behind that in the USA. If re-engineering does endure, though, it may be because of its contradictions rather than despite them. They mean that it can be all things to all people. If you want a systematic methodology that stresses the role of IT, perhaps because you are a technically oriented consultancy, then a version of BPR can quite legitimately be developed for you based on well-supported views in the literature. On the other hand, if you want a radical organizational change programme, then this too can be accommodated. There is no authority that can enforce a single, 'correct' definition, so different audiences are able to find in it what they want. The ambiguities surrounding re-engineering that arise from the contradictions may therefore make the concept more attractive and resistant to criticism.

Finally, it is important, despite Hammer's protestations, not to treat re-engineering as an isolated phenomenon, but to recognize its links with other currently fashionable conceptualizations of organizational change. The similarities between the recommendations of Hammer and Champy (1993) and those, for example, of proponents of the 'horizontal' organization (Ostroff and Smith, 1992) may be seen not as coincidences, but as manifestations of the influence of broader social discourses. The contradictions evident in re-engineering may thus reflect general tensions inherent in modern organizations and are therefore all the more deserving of our attention.

REFERENCES

Aikins, J (1993) 'Business Process Re-engineering: Where Do Knowledge-Based Systems Fit?', *IEEE Expert*, 8 (2).

Byrne, J A (1992) 'Management's New Gurus', *Business Week*, 31 August, 42–50.

Byrne, J A (1993) 'Re-engineering: Beyond the Buzzword', *Business Week*, 24 May, 5–6.

Clegg, S (1989) *Frameworks of Power*, Sage, London.

Clement, A (1994) 'Computing at Work: Empowering Action by "Low-Level Users"', *Communications of the ACM*, 37 (1), 53–63.

Cooper, R (1989) 'Modernism, Post Modernism and Organizational Analysis 3: The Contribution of Jacques Derrida', *Organization Studies*, 20, 479–502

Craig, J F and Yetton, P W (1993) *The Dual Strategic and Change Role of IT: A Critique of Business Process Reengineering*, Working Paper 94-002, Australian Graduate School of Management, Kensington, NSW.

Davenport, T E (1993) *Process Innovation: Re-engineering Work Through Information Technology*, Harvard Business School Press, Boston, Mass.

Davenport, T E and Short, J E (1990) 'The New Industrial Engineering: Information Technology and Business Process Redesign', *Sloan Management Review*, Summer, 11–27.

Davidson, W H (1993) 'Beyond Re-engineering: The Three Phases of Business Transformation', *IBM Systems Journal*, 32, 65–79.

Dichter, S F (1991) 'The Organization of the 90s', *McKinsey Quarterly*, 145–155.

FinTech (1992a) 'Business Process Redesign: IT Suppliers Take Lessons from Users', *FinTech Electronic Office*, 9 September, p. 1.

FinTech (1992b) 'Spotlight: Business Process Redesign Brings Big Benefits', *FinTech Electronic Office*, 2 December, p. 4.

Floyd, C, Mehl, W-M, Reisin, F-M, Schmidt, G and Wolf, G (1989) 'Out of Scandinavia: Alternative Approaches to Systems Analysis and Design', *Human Computer Interaction*, 4, 253–350.

Grover, V, Teng, J T C and Fiedler, K D (1993) 'Information Technology Enabled Business Process Redesign: An Integrated Planning Framework', *Omega*, 21(4), 433–447.

Guha, S, Kettinger, W J and Teng, J T C (1993) 'Business Process Re-engineering: Building a Comprehensive Methodology', *Information Systems Management*, Summer, 13–22.

Hall, G, Rosenthal, J and Wade, J (1993) 'How to Make Re-engineering *Really* Work', *Harvard Business Review*, November–December, 119–131.

Hammer, M (1990) 'Re-engineering Work: Don't Automate, Obliterate', *Harvard Business Review*, July–August, 104–112.

Hammer, M and Champy, J (1993) *Re-engineering the Corporation: A Manifesto for Business Revolution*, Nicholas Brealey Publishing, London.

Han, P and Jones, M R (1993) *The Dialectics of Information Systems*. University of Cambridge Research Paper in Management Studies 1993–1994 No. 4, Judge Institute of Management Studies, Cambridge.

Handy, C (1994) *The Empty Raincoat: Making Sense of the Future*, Hutchinson, London.

Heygate, R and Brebach, G (1991) 'Corporate Reengineering', *McKinsey Quarterly*, Summer, 44–55.

Johannson, H J, McHugh, P, Pendlebury, A J and Wheeler, W A (1993) *Business Process Re-engineering: Breakpoint Strategies for Market Dominance*, John Wiley, Chichester.

Jones, M R (1994) 'Don't Emancipate, Exaggerate: Rhetoric, Reality and Re-engineering', in Baskerville, R L, Smithson, S, Ngwenyama, O and De-Gross, J I (eds), *Transforming Organizations with Information Technology*, North Holland, Amsterdam, pp. 357–378.

Kaplan, R B and Murdock, L (1991) 'Core Process Redesign', *McKinsey Quarterly*, Summer, 27–43.

Klein, M M (1993) 'IEs Fill Facilitator Role in Benchmarking Operations to Improve Performance', *Industrial Engineering*, September, 40–42.

Lopes, P F (1993) 'Fine-tuning Re-engineering with Workflow Automation: Blueprint and Tool', *Industrial Engineering*, August, 51–53.

Morris, D and Brandon, J (1993) *Re-engineering Your Business*, McGraw-Hill, London.

Ostroff, F and Smith, D (1992) 'The Horizontal Organization', *McKinsey Quarterly*, 148–168.

Parker, J (1993) 'An ABC Guide to Business Process Re-engineering', *Industrial Engineering*, May, 52–53.

Pascale, R T (1990) *Managing on the Edge: How Successful Companies Use Conflict to Stay Ahead*, Penguin, Harmondsworth.

Shillingford, J (1992) 'Offices Follow the Factory's Example', *Financial Times*, 19 March, p. 20.

Short, J E and Venkatraman, N (1992) 'Beyond Business Process Redesign: Redefining Baxter's Business Network', *Sloan Management Review*, Fall, 7–21.

Stewart, T A (1993) 'Re-engineering, the Hot New Management Tool', *Fortune*, 127, 23 August, 41–48.

Venkatraman, N (1991) 'IT-Induced Business Reconfiguration', in Scott-Morton, M(ed.), *The Corporation of the 1990s: IT and Organizational Transformation*, Oxford University Press, Oxford, pp. 122–158.

Warren, L (1993) 'Streamlining From the Outside In', *Informatics*, May, 23–28.

Wheatley, M (1994) 'De-engineering the Corporation', *Industry Week*, 18 April, 18–26.

Wilkinson, R (1991) 'Re-engineering: Industrial Engineering in Action', *Industrial Engineering*, August, 47–49.

Willmott, H (1993) 'Strength is Ignorance; Slavery is Freedom: Managing Culture in Modern Organizations', *Journal of Management Studies*, 30, 515–552.

3

BUSINESS PROCESSES: THEIR NATURE AND PROPERTIES

Alan Harrison, Warwick Business School

What is a process? This apparently simple question is providing a wide range of answers, especially amongst the rash of new books which are currently being published under the Business Process Re-engineering (BPR) theme. A selection of seven 'definitions', six from recently published American textbooks and one based on the MIT 90s programme, is given in the appendix to this chapter. It is apparent that no clear picture emerges, and that there is a wide variety of responses to the above question. Processes are variously defined in terms of activities, tasks and functions or steps which may lead to business success, output of value to a customer or simply a result. This lack of clarity casts some doubt on the credentials of BPR and its ability to deliver quantum leaps in performance. If you cannot get the basics right, then how can you do the more difficult things?

DEFINING A PROCESS

Operations management is a useful place to start in the quest for a definitive answer. This is not simply because the author happens to belong to that discipline, but because the whole subject is based on the concept of managing the transformation process. 'Process' refers to the conversion of inputs (resources) into outputs (goods and services). Figure 3.1 is a model of the transformation process which we have used at Warwick Business School in the UK (Slack *et al.*, 1995).

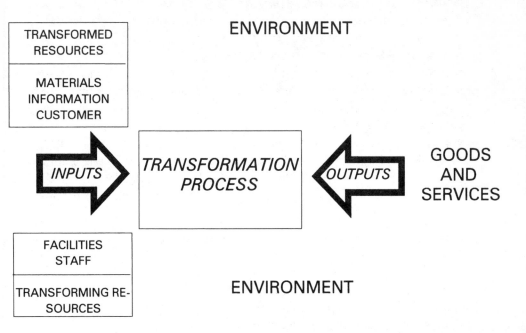

Figure 3.1   A model of the transformation process

Inputs to the Transformation Process

These can be classified as either

- **Transformed resources**: the resources which are converted in some way. Usually, they are some combination of materials, information and customers themselves. For example, a bank primarily processes information, although materials (money, statements) and customers (advice, cash transactions) may also be transformed.
- **Transforming resources**: resources which act upon the transformed resources. The two key inputs here are facilities (hardware like buildings and equipment) and staff who operate, maintain, plan and manage the operation.

Both types of input are needed in any transformation process.

The Transformation Process

The transformation process uses transforming resources to convert the transformed resources. Transformation may follow a number of different routes.

- Materials may be converted *physically,* such as steel strip into car bodies, or their *location* may be converted, as in the case of postal delivery. There may be a change in *possession* as in retailing, or a *storage* process may be involved, as in warehousing.
- Information may be *reconfigured,* such as in financial services, or its *location* may be converted, as in telecommunications. There may be a change in *possession*, as in education, or a *storage* process may be involved, as in meteorology records.
- Customers may be converted *physically,* such as hairdressing, or their *location* may be altered, as in airline or rail travel. *Accommodation* may be involved, as in overnight hotels. Customers may also be converted *physiologically* (as in health care), or *psychologically* (as in entertainment).

A relatively small number of transformation routes (physical change, locational change, storage, etc) emerges. In practice, transformations are often combinations of two or more of these basic types. In the same way that operations management must be capable of explaining transformations in a wide variety of environments, so should BPR principles be applicable to any business environment.

Outputs

Outputs of the transformation process can be characterized by two extremes:

- **Goods**: which are tangible, storable and transportable. Quality from the customer viewpoint is basically product-related
- **Services**: which are intangible and cannot be stored or transported. They are typically produced simultaneously with their consumption. Quality depends not only on the outcome of the service, but also on the customer's perception of the delivery system.

Again, outputs from many transformation processes are combinations of the two.

Business Processes

Operations should be viewed as one example of a business process. The key feature of this type of business process is that the transformed resources originate from *outside* the boundaries of the organization, and that outputs in the form of goods and services *leave* the boundaries of the organization. Operations is an example of an *end-to-end business process* – distinguished by starting with inputs to the business boundary and finishing with outputs from the business boundary. *Networked business processes* go on to consider inter-business processes – see, for example, ICL (1990).

There are not many examples so far of organizations which have 'started with a clean sheet of paper' in carrying out BPR. Work at Alcoa in the UK has been in this category (Thomas, 1993), and yet re-engineering produced only four 'business processes'. These are illustrated in Figure 3.2.

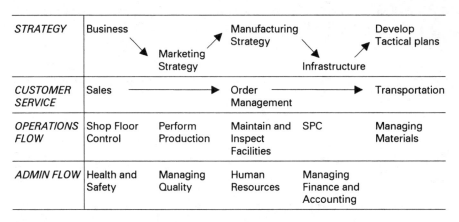

Figure 3.2   Redefining business processes: outcome of a
BPR excercise

Source: Courtesy Alcoa

- **Strategic flow:** to develop strategy to ensure long-term profitability and to optimize tactical business performance
- **Customer service:** to respond effectively to customer needs as a total business system.
- **Operations flow:** to produce cost-effective quality product
- **Administration flow:** to assure support and development of all processes.

Development is carried out elsewhere in the company, so it would be necessary to add this business process in many organizations. However, it is surprising how simple the new organization is after re-engineering, as indicated by Figure 3.2. A hypothesis for further research is that it is possible to group processes in an organization into a small number of business transformations.

The Alcoa experience illustrates a second 'end-to-end' business process: customer service, which covers the sequence from order input to order delivery. It also illustrates two other types of business process.

- **Funnel business processes:** 'Strategic flow' compiles long-term plans and operationalizes them by breaking them down into short-term tactical plans. The development process (essentially comprising the conversion of concepts for new products into product and process specifications) is strikingly similar. Such business processes are characterized by iteration and by redundancy (many potential solutions are scrapped). These are referred to as 'funnel' business processes because they move from the general to the particular.

- **Composite business processes:** 'Admin flow' is effectively a composite of the processes which are left. There is little logical connection between them, and it is quite possible that they will be subsequently redistributed. This is a typical interim solution, and in no way devalues the significance of these processes to the business. The processes do not fit into the current vision of broadly connected business processes, perhaps due to personnel constraints or to other limitations of what can currently be achieved.

BREAKING DOWN BUSINESS PROCESSES

Managing business processes needs to take into account their aggregate nature. A hierarchical structure is needed in the same way as project management needs a work breakdown structure to allocate tasks (work packages) to project teams. (The analogy with project management is further reinforced by the changes envisaged by BPR – from functional departments to process teams (Hammer and Champy, 1993: 65).) Figure 3.3 shows a proposed 'business process breakdown structure'.

Using the Alcoa work to illustrate, the names given to the levels in the hierarchy can be explained as follows:

- **Process elements:** are the major elements into which a business process can best be organized. For example, the Customer Service business process was allotted three process elements: Sales, Order Management and Transportation

- **Activities:** process elements can in turn be broken down for ease of management into recognizable activities. In the case of the Sales process element, just two activities were defined: Manage Customer Accounts and Claims Processing

- **Tasks:** finally, activities can be broken down into tasks which are written up as standard operating procedures for individual 'process owners' to carry out.

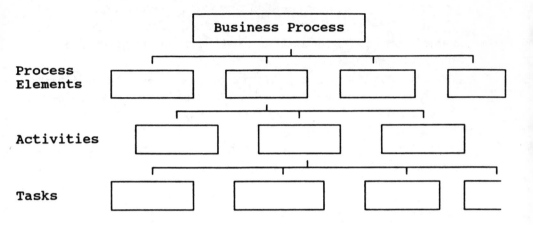

Figure 3.3   Breakdown structure for a business process

The four levels in the hierarchy share the process characteristics which were identified in the first section above. They are all transformations, but differ only in scale and that the majority of process elements, activities and tasks are internally rather than externally supplier/customer focused. It is only necessary to carry out the breakdown in order to achieve a concise, manageable and defined series of tasks so that overall business process objectives may be met. Therefore, the number of levels should be kept as small as possible, and the number of processes at each level should also be kept as small as possible. For example, Alcoa needed only 17 process elements to cover the whole business (see Figure 3.2). Progress in re-engineering over time should reflect process reduction.

PROPERTIES OF PROCESS ELEMENTS

Having postulated the nature of business processes, and that they can be broken down into a hierarchy of smaller processes which share the same characteristics, this section reviews what we have learned about properties of processes.

These properties are grouped under six headings. Again, the perspective is that of operations management.

- **Value chain**. Process elements comprise both value added and non-value added activities. The latter are often referred to as 'waste'. Major improvements in performance of process elements can be made by cutting out waste.
- **Variability**. All processes are variable. This means that the output of a process can never be exactly repeated. Distinguishing between special

causes of variability (outside causes) and normal causes (inherent in the process) has been very helpful in bringing processes under control (Deming, 1986), and then improving them. Once a process is in control, statistical methods can be used to predict the outcome, monitor the process, etc.

- **Measurement.** All processes can be measured. Some of the most important measures are customer-related, which helps in the reorientation of process thinking to serving the customer. This in turn can be used to integrate processes by sharing measurements which are aimed at 'building a chain of customers' (Schonberger, 1989).

- **Networked.** The business process breakdown structure proposed in the previous section shows how it should be possible to develop a logical set of relationships between processes within the organization. Each should have defined objectives and scope, and be strategically coordinated. The same thinking promotes process-oriented thinking beyond the boundaries of the organization to encompass external interfaces with suppliers, customers and so on. The process network should be as simple as possible: a major re-engineering challenge. Composite business processes are more difficult to network than the other types identified in the first section.

- **Ownership.** Processes benefit from ownership, whether this be through a process champion (for higher level processes), or through process owners (for tasks). Ownership assures that the process is at the centre of the organization's efforts. Processes can always be improved – especially after radical restructuring!

- **Automation.** Schonberger exhorts us to 'automate incrementally, when process variability cannot otherwise be improved' (Schonberger, 1992). Process automation should follow process simplification and integration rather than be the motor for change in itself. BPR proponents such as Hammer and Champy (1993: 83ff) refer to IT as an enabler.

Another hypothesis then is that these properties apply to all processes at all levels in the hierarchy.

CONCLUSION

Defining a 'process' is no simplistic task. Like defining 'quality', there are many interpretations and there has been much confusion. We need to tighten up on our understanding of the term 'process', if only because it is at the centre of BPR! Perry and Denna (1994) state that 'the principal reason BPR has lost its identity is the lack of a clear definition of business processes'. Below are the key conclusions of this chapter.

- A process may simplistically be defined as a transformation of inputs (resources) into outputs (goods and services).
- There are three types of business process within an organization (intra-organizational business processes):

- *end-to-end business processes* take inputs from outside the boundaries of the organization, and produce goods and services for delivery to customers outside the boundaries of the organization
- *funnel business processes* move from broad, long-term inputs (strategy, concepts) to defined outputs (specifications, tactical plans)
- *composite business processes* act as a holding category for processes which cannot be fitted into the other two until further rationalization can be made. Meanwhile, inputs and outputs are also composite, and do not form a logical sequence like the other two.

Business processes in a re-engineered organization are few in number – perhaps only four to six. Networked business processes connect organizations together (inter-organizational business processes).

- Other processes can and indeed should be ordered hierarchically under business processes. There should be few levels (four are proposed), and the fewer the better.
- Processes at any level in the hierarchy share similar properties: are a mix of value added and non-value added, have inherent variability, are capable of being measured, are logically linked with each other (networked), benefit from ownership, and should be automated after being re-engineered.

The subject is in urgent need of standard terminology and a better coordination of the lessons which have been learned. BPR, like project management, is a cross-disciplinary subject and demands cooperation across a broad front.

APPENDIX: PROCESSES AND BUSINESS PROCESSES – SOME SAMPLE DEFINITIONS

Business Processes: sequences of tasks and functions which together produce outcomes that contribute to the (business) success of an organization. (ICL, 1990)

Process: consists of policies, procedures, steps, technology and personnel needed to carry out a significant segment of operations within an organization. Usually, a process will cut across several organizational boundaries within an operating unit and require coordination across those boundaries. (Evans and Lindsay, 1993: 14)

Process: a structured, measured set of activities designed to produce a specified output for a particular customer or market. It implies a strong emphasis on how work is done within an organization, in contrast to a product focus's emphasis on what. ... a specific ordering of work activities across time and place, with a beginning, an end, and clearly identified inputs and outputs: a structure for action. (Davenport, 1993: 5)

Business Process: ... a collection of activities that takes one or more kinds of input and creates an output that is of value to the customer. (Hammer and Champy, 1993: 35)

A business process is a series of steps designed to produce a product or service. Some processes (such as the programming process) may be contained wholly within a function. However, most processes (such as order processing) are cross-functional, spanning the 'white space' between the boxes on the organization chart. (Rummler and Brache, 1990: 45)

Process: any activity or group of activities that takes an input, adds value to it and provides output to an internal or external customer. Processes use an organization's resources to provide definitive results.

Production process: any process that comes into contact with the hardware or software that will be delivered to an external customer, up to the point the product is packaged.

Business process: all service processes and processes that support production processes...[it] consists of a group of logically related tasks that use the resources of an organization to provide defined results in support of the organization's objectives. (Harrington, 1991: 9)

A process is most broadly defined as an activity carried out as a series of steps which produces a specific result or related group of specific results. (Morris and Brandon, 1993: 38)

REFERENCES

Davenport, T (1993) *Process Innovation: Re-engineering Work through Information Technology*, Harvard Business School Press, Boston, Mass.

Deming, W E (1986) *Out of the Crisis*, Cambridge University Press, Cambridge.

Evans, J and Lindsay, W (1993) *The Management and Control of Quality*, West.

Hammer, M and Champy, J (1993) *Re-engineering the Corporation: A Manifesto for Business Revolution*, Nicholas Brealey Publishing, London.

Harrington, H J (1991) *Business Process Improvement: The Breakthrough Strategy for Total Quality, Productivity, and Competitiveness*, McGraw-Hill, New York.

ICL (1990) *A Window on the Future: An ICL Briefing on the Findings of the Management in the 1990s Research Programme*, International Computers Ltd, London.

Morris, D and Brandon, J (1993) *Re-engineering Your Business*, McGraw-Hill.

Perry, L T and Denna, E L (1994) *Re-engineering Redux: An Agenda for Next-Generation BPR*. Paper presented to the Strategic Management Society, September.

Rummler, G and Brache, A (1990) *Improving Performance: How to Manage the White Space on the Organization Chart*, Jossey-Bass, San Francisco, Calif.

Schonberger, R J (1990) *Building a Chain of Customers: Linking Business Functions to Create the World Class Company*, The Free Press, New York.

Schonberger, R J (1992) *Operations Management: Serving the Customer*, Irwin.

Slack, N, Chambers, S, Harland, C, Harrison, A and Johnston, R (1995) *Operations Management*, Pitman, London.

Thomas, J (1993) *Business Process Re-engineering: Reinventing the Business Enterprise*. MBA thesis, University of Warwick.

4

A CONCEPT FOR THE MARKET-ORIENTATED EVALUATION OF BUSINESS PROCESSES

Christof Hauser and Rainer Eisele, University of St Gallen, Switzerland

BOTTOM LINE RESULTS COUNT

The redesign of business processes has become one of the top issues in management today. In order to regain or maintain competitiveness the reconsideration of the entire corporate structure and resource allocation is propounded. The organization should totally focus on internal and external customers. To do so, cross-functional business processes are to be improved dramatically by a breakthrough attempt rather than by trying to optimize performance within corporate functions. Information technology plays a key role in the re-engineering of business processes (Davenport, 1993; Hammer and Champy, 1993; Harrington, 1991; Kaplan and Murdock, 1991).

While business process redesign (BPR) has become an often suggested recipe for regaining profitability, not all attempts in that direction have proved to be successful. Empirical studies show that, although BPR led to dramatic improvements in time, costs and quality, the overall results for a business unit or an entire company in terms of profit are sometimes disappointing (Hall, *et al*, 1993). In order to avoid such deficiencies, an economic evaluation of business processes before implementation is suggested (Figure 4.1).

The expected costs and the expected market impact of a specific process design need to be evaluated before implementation. Due to the facts that the later cost and proceed drivers are determined for the most part within a BPR project and that the redesign itself requires internal and external resources, an evaluation of the bottom line results must become an inherent part of BPR.

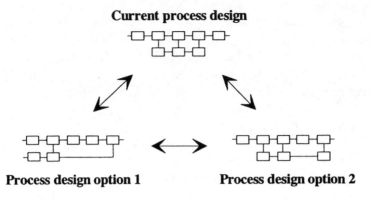

Figure 4.1 Economic evaluation of business processes

It is the objective of this chapter to outline a concept for the economic evaluation of business processes, whereby the emphasis is placed on the quantification of market-related benefits. Furthermore, it shows how to select those business processes most in need of redesign and to incorporate market orientation into BPR expressly.

QUANTIFICATION OF MARKET-RELATED BENEFITS

The most important impact of BPR may be observed on the competitive front of an organization. A successful redesign of business processes leads to improvements in time, quality and cost of products and services offered. Thus, BPR enhances an organization's ability to respond to market conditions. Moreover, it enables companies to differentiate themselves from their competitors which results in higher revenues. It must be the goal of a market-oriented evaluation to translate these market-related benefits of BPR into quantified revenue potential in order to forecast the bottom line results (Hauser, 1994).

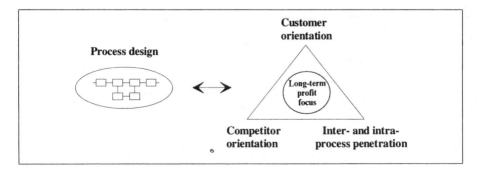

Figure 4.2 Process design and market orientation

A higher degree of market orientation is the main driver of most BPR initiatives. In order to measure the improvements, it is necessary to provide a clear definition of the term *market orientation* and to assign indicators that show the magnitude of the goals accomplished. Narver and Slater (1990) have developed a conceptual model on the content of market orientation. This model proclaims that market orientation encompasses three behavioural components: customer orientation, competitor orientation and interfunctional coordination. Both a long-term focus and profitability complement the conceptual model as decision criteria.

Customer orientation, as one building block of a market-oriented organization, is the main objective of BPR (Johannson *et al.*, 1993). Thus, methods to measure and forecast the extent of customer satisfaction which may be attributed to a given business process are required for a market-oriented evaluation. A competitor orientation presupposes knowledge of strengths and weaknesses of both current and potential competitors. Consequently, information about the competitors' capabilities has to be included into the evaluation. Market orientation is not limited to the marketing or sales department, but involves an organization-wide, coordinated effort. Thus, both the customer and the competitor orientation have to be transferred into the business processes in order to interpenetrate all corporate activities. Doing so means that information about customer requirements and market performances of competitors represent the starting point for all corporate activities and should set targets for every business process. Therefore, the terms inter- and intra-process penetration seem more suitable than interfunctional coordination as the third behavioural component for the description of market orientation (Figure 4.2).

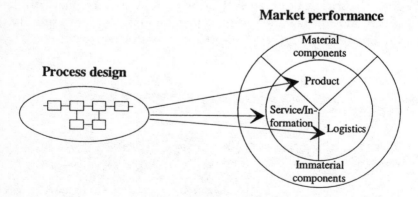

Figure 4.3   Process design's impact on market performance

In order to forecast the revenue potential of a specific process design, it is necessary to determine the impact of the new business process design on a company's overall market performance. Market performance may be defined as the total set of material and immaterial needs and wants perceived to be important by customers (Figure 4.3). This definition of market performance is analogous to the generic product notion, whereby a product is understood as a bundle of utilities (Kotler, 1990).

A company's market performance may be described in terms of key buying factors (KBF) (eg price, ease of ordering, product quality, delivery time, technical attributes or response time). A process redesign could lead to changes in KBF-performance levels, such as reducing delivery time by eliminating process steps or improving the ease of ordering through an electronic order system. These improvements, in turn, lead to an increase in customer value. The increase in customer value induced by a particular business process design could be quantified by means of a conjoint measurement (Figure 4.4).

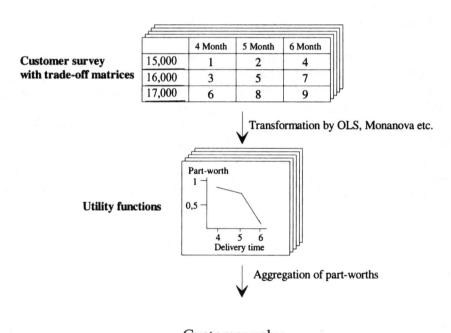

Customer survey with trade-off matrices

	4 Month	5 Month	6 Month
15,000	1	2	4
16,000	3	5	7
17,000	6	8	9

Transformation by OLS, Monanova etc.

Utility functions — Part-worth vs Delivery time (4 5 6)

Aggregation of part-worths

Customer value

Figure 4.4 Conjoint measurement and customer value

Conjoint measurement is a market research technique aiming at quantifying customers' judgements of alternative market performances. It refers to a combination of special data acquisition methods, multivariate statistical estimation and other specialized evaluation procedures. Conjoint measurement assumes that an object can be evaluated as a bundle of features or attributes. These attributes should capture all essential aspects of an object. Based on respondents' global judgements on a set of complex alternatives, conjoint measurement allows the derivation of utility functions for every attribute describing the object (Green and Wind, 1975).

In order to quantify the market effects of a new business process design, suitable KBF describing a company's market performance are to be selected. Categories are assigned to each KBF representing different levels of performance. Based on the KBF and their assigned levels, respondents are asked to evaluate several alternative market performances in terms of their desirability. Two approaches for the acquisition of such data within the context of a conjoint measurement exist. In the trade-off approach, the respondent is required to arrange all performance level combinations of two KBF in terms of their preference. The full-profile approach requires the respondents to make paired comparisons by selecting their preferred KBF combinations, each characterized by a single performance level for every KBF. Based on these ratings, a utility contribution per KBF-level or a utility function for each KBF respectively, may be determined. Several statistical estimation procedures (eg ordinary least squares, monotone analysis of variance or multiple dummy regression) lend themselves to calculating these utility functions (Green and Srinivasan, 1978). A utility function quantifies the relation between the respondents' overall assessment of the market performance and each KBF describing the market performance. By implementing a conjoint measurement it is possible to measure the customer value assigned to a specific process design.

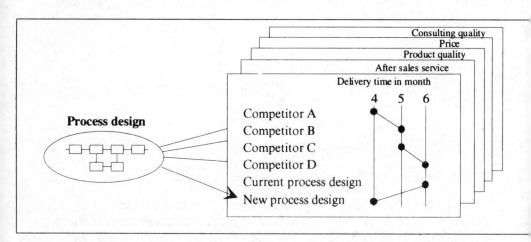

Figure 4.5   Process design and competitor performance profiles

To incorporate the second component of market orientation – competitor orientation – into the evaluation and to forecast the market potential of a new business process design, it is necessary to determine the performance levels of the competitors. This could be achieved by means of competitive benchmarking. In competitive benchmarking a company's performance is rated against the 'best-in-class'. Benchmarking can be applied to all facets of interest in a business such as products, services, business processes, strategies, procedures or methods (Camp, 1989; Watson, 1993). For the determination of performance levels, various information sources have to be considered. The required information could be provided by such different sources as customer surveys, on-line databases, reverse engineering, test orders, marketing brochures, supplier questionnaires, marketing research companies, etc. The performance level for every KBF and every relevant competitor are systematically documented by competitor performance profiles as shown in Figure 4.5. With the determination of competitor performance profiles it is possible to rank the expected KBF-performance levels resulting from a new business process design against those of the competitors and the performance level achieved by the current business process design.

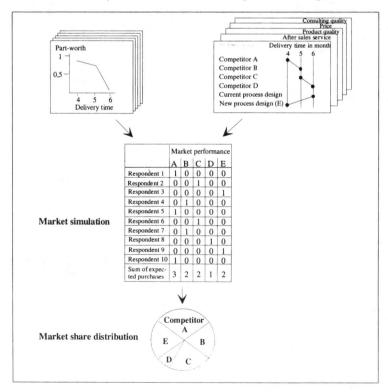

Figure 4.6 Process design and market share forecast

By transferring the derived utility functions and the competitor profiles into a simulation model, it is possible to evaluate the effects of KBF-level changes induced by BPR (eg reducing the delivery time) in terms of potential market share gains. The specification of a simulation scenario is the starting point of the market evaluation. A scenario consists of at least two market performances defined by the KBF-levels used in the conjoint measurement. Based on a certain scenario, the overall utility for each specified market performance and for each respondent is calculated. These overall utilities, in turn, build the basis for the estimation of the respondents' choice behaviour and the forecast of a market share distribution (Figure 4.6).

There are two different approaches for the estimation of choice behaviour: the maximum utility choice (MUC) rule and the Bradley-Terry-Luce (BTL) model. The MUC model assumes that a respondent will always select the market performance with the highest overall utility. In the case of the BTL model, the 'winner-takes-it-all' assumption is replaced by a probability function. Assuming that the predicted choice behaviour reflects the condition on the entire market, a market share distribution may be derived from the simulation model. The market simulation model could be calibrated against the actual market shares in order to improve the forecasts (Louviere, 1988). All said, it should be possible to assign a market share to a new business process design and, thus, transform market-related benefits into monetary figures. It should be noted that, like all forecasts, the concept is based on various assumptions and that the quality of the estimation depends on the quality of the ascertained data.

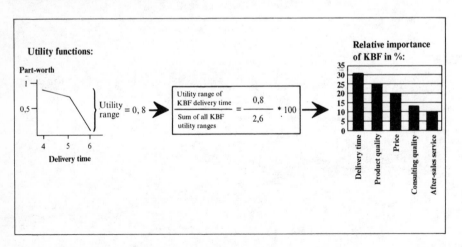

Figure 4.7 Relative importance of key buying factors

BPR should focus on those processes that are crucial for business success and promise a high improvement potential. The selection of business processes that are primary candidates for the redesign is a critical task. With the help of the conjoint measurement and benchmarking data, it is possible to provide clear guidance for the selection of those business processes most in need of redesign from a market-oriented point of view. The starting point is the calculation of the relative importance for each KBF incorporated into the conjoint measurement. The relative importance indicates the contribution of each KBF to the customer value. KBF importance is determined by dividing the difference between the highest and the lowest part-worth for one KBF by the sum of the utility ranges across all KBF (Figure 4.7).

In a second step, the impact of each business process on each KBF, ranked by their importance, is determined and documented in an impact matrix as shown in Figure 4.8. This leads to the identification of those business processes that are most important to meet customer requirements. Furthermore, the health of the business processes identified as having considerable influence on customer value is checked by comparing the current performance in terms of KBF levels with the performance levels achieved by competitors.

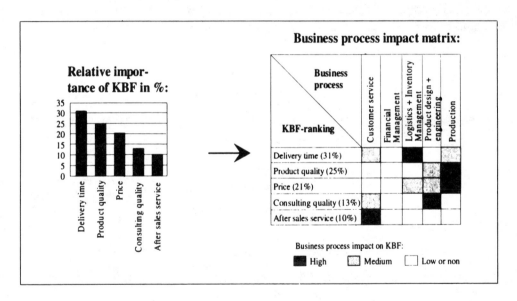

Figure 4.8 Market-oriented selection of business processes for redesign

Correspondingly, there are two decision criteria for the market-oriented selection of business processes. First, business processes with an essential impact on KBF with high relative importance should be considered for redesign. In addition to that the performance level of the KBF achieved with the current process design must be relatively poor compared with competitors. Applied to the impact matrix in Figure 4.8 and assuming that the performance profile indicates a considerably longer delivery time than that of the competitors, the business process 'Logistics and Inventory Management' should be selected for redesign. Besides market-oriented indicators, there are also internal symptoms that point to deficiencies in a business process and propose a redesign thereof, such as long cycle times or a high-cost proportion of a particular business process to total expenses.

COST ESTIMATION

As mentioned, high-cost processes are often candidates for BPR. Overhead reduction in a particular business process is an essential expectation associated with re-engineering, besides the market-related benefits. A cost estimation, as a part of the economic evaluation of business processes, has to focus on the expected resource consumption and the implementation costs of the redesigned process (eg planning costs, information technology investments and personnel training) as depicted in Figure 4. 9.

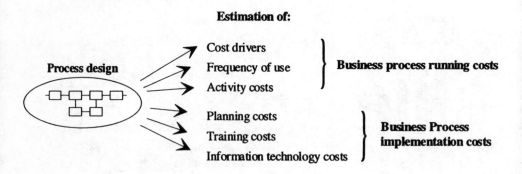

Figure 4.9 Cost estimation for a new business process design

Activity-based costing (ABC) has emerged as a new cost management concept. Activity-based cost systems focus on corporate activities as the essential resource consuming objects in an organization. Implementing ABC starts with the identification of activities (= subprocesses). Then a cost driver is assigned to each activity in order to measure the resource consumption. Dividing the total costs per activity in a specific time period by the cost driver frequency yields the costs per activity. Finally, the activity costs of all activities consumed by either a product, a customer, a process, or, more generally, any evaluation object being analyzed, are accumulated in order to determine the total object costs (Cooper, 1988). There are several extensions to the original ABC concept. To improve decision-making and to employ investment calculations based on ABC data, separating fixed and variable costs is suggested (Woods, 1992).

In order to forecast the running costs of a business process before implementation, it is necessary to assign appropriate cost drivers to the expected activities of a new business process design, forecast their frequency of use and the activity costs. Eisele and Schwan have developed a concept for the estimation of business process costs (Eisele and Schwan, 1992). The determination of implementation costs and running business process costs allows setting a budget for a specific BPR project.

DECISION SUPPORT

Having forecasted both revenues and costs, investment calculations could be employed. Thus, the potential of a new process design could be determined in terms of return on investment (ROI), payoff period or net present value. Since a BPR project competes with other projects (eg new product introduction) for the investment budget in an organization, it is possible to compare different corporate propositions by their investment ratios. Additionally, these investment ratios make it easier to initiate re-engineering efforts in an organization and allow concentration on projects that are actually contributing to overall business success. The determination of monetary figures assigned to a new process design also enables decision-makers to balance the expected benefits against implementation costs (Figure 4.10).

As outlined in Figure 4.8, the impact matrix enables the selection of those business processes that are primary candidates for BPR. For the selected business processes, redesign options are developed. These options display a particular business process after a redesign. Having more than one new design for a business process requires the evaluation of all options. Again, the market simulation and a rough cost estimation aid in selecting the preferable design.

During the design of a new process conjoint measurement data and the performance profiles could be used for deriving redesign targets. Market-oriented goals are subsequently translated into internal process targets for the new design. For example, the determination of delivery time as the most important KBF, as regarded by customers, results in a redesign target of reducing cycle time by 50 per cent in a particular process. Transferring market-oriented goals into the business processes also means implementing the third component of market orientation – inter- and intra-process penetration.

1. Selection between different types of investment projects:

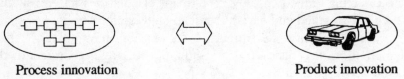

Process innovation   Product innovation

2. Selection between different business processes:

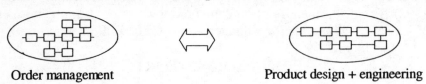

Order management   Product design + engineering

3. Selection between different business process design options:

Order management: new design 1   Order management: new design 2

Figure 4.10   Support for different types of decision

In order to establish post-implementation control of redesigned business processes, forecasted and realized figures should be compared. This indicates the degree of goal accomplishment, encourages corrective measures to be taken where necessary and builds the basis for continuous process improvement after the redesign.

REFERENCES

Camp, R C (1989) *Benchmarking – The Search for Industry Best Practices that Lead to Superior Performance*, Quality Press, Milwaukee.

Cooper, R (1988) 'The Rise of Activity-Based Costing (Part I): What is an Activity-Based Cost System?', *Journal of Cost Management*, 2, 45–54.

Davenport, T H (1993) *Process Innovation – Reengineering Work through Information Technology*, Harvard Business School Press, Boston, Mass.

Eisele, R and Schwan, Th (1992) 'CIM-Potentiale ganzheitlich bewerten', *IO Management Zeitschrift*, 5, 42–47.

Green, P E and Srinivasan, V (1978) 'Conjoint Analysis in Consumer Research: Issues and Outlook', *Journal of Consumer Research*, 103–123.

Green, P E and Wind, Y (1975) 'New Way to Measure Customers' Judgements', *Harvard Business Review*, March–April, 107–117.

Hall, G, Rosenthal, J and Wade, J (1993) 'How to Make Re-engineering *Really Work*', *Harvard Business Review*, November–December, 119–131.

Hammer, M and Champy, J (1993) *Re-engineering the Corporation: A Manifesto for Business Revolution*, Nicholas Brealey Publishing, London.

Harrington, H J (1991) *Business Process Improvement – The Breakthrough for Total Quality, Productivity and Competitiveness*, McGraw-Hill, New York.

Hauser, C, (1994) 'Market-Driven Quantification of Competitive Advantage by Means of Conjoint Measurement', *EM-Electronic Markets*, 11, April, 11–12.

Johannson, H J, McHugh, P, Pendlebury, J A and Wheeler, W A (1993) *Business Process Re-engineering – Breakpoint Strategies for Market Dominance*, Wiley, Chichester.

Kaplan, R B and Murdock, L (1991) 'Core Process Redesign', *McKinsey Quarterly*, Summer, 27–43.

Kotler, P (1990) *Marketing Management*, 7th edn, Prentice-Hall, Englewood Cliffs, NJ.

Louviere, J (1988) *Analyzing Decision Making – Metric Conjoint Analysis*. Sage University Paper Series on Quantitative Applications in the Social Sciences, Beverly Hills, Calif.

Narver, J C and Slater, S F (1990) 'The Effect of a Market Orientation on Business Profitability', *Journal of Marketing*, October, 20–35.

Watson, G H (1993) *Strategic Benchmarking – How to Rate Your Company's Performance Against the World's Best*, New York.

Woods, M D (1992) 'Economic Choices with ABC', *Management Accounting*, 12, 53–57.

5

UTOPIAN RE-ENGINEERING

Keith Grint, Templeton College, Oxford University

INTRODUCTION

The claims made for BPR or re-engineering are startling, even in a business environment long jaundiced by continuous exposure to business innovations: 'Re-engineering is new, and it has to be done' (Peter Drucker on the cover of Hammer and Champy's (1993b) book, *Re-engineering the Corporation*); and it is 'the management world's most fashionable fad' according to *The Financial Times* (22 June 1993). It is, according to its self-proclaimed progenitors Michael Hammer and James Champy, nothing less than 'a reversal of the Industrial Revolution'. 'It isn't about *fixing* anything [it] means starting all over, starting from scratch ... the alternative is for Corporate America to close its doors and go out of business.'

How did corporate America, and subsequently the rest of us, get into such a position? The argument suggests that current failure is a direct result of previous success: the extensive divisions of labour, functional divisions and economies of scale so beloved by Adam Smith, F.W. Taylor and Ford were fine in the past when demand was high, competition low and customers indiscriminate, but now all of these have been reversed and complacency has to be removed by shifting the focus from producer to consumer. In effect, the idea is to develop systems built around teams that are configured to mirror the processes that the business actually works around, rather than the functions it may use to execute these processes. It is a shift from vertical functions to horizontal processes.

Thus, to take a simple example, whereas British post office counters used to be organized along functional lines – so you had to queue three times if you wanted to buy stamps, cash a postal order and send a parcel – the redesign that occurred (many years ago now) ensured that each counter clerk could provide (virtually) anything a customer wanted: 'one-stop shopping' came of age. Naturally, there were some interesting consequences: whereas you may have been able to assume that the stamp queue would reduce by one customer every 30 seconds, the new systems meant that you may get stuck behind someone requiring a passport that could take ten minutes; hence the move to single queuing systems. Every process redesign, therefore, should be concerned with the customer rather than the producer, the process rather than the function, and a multitude of disparate things that must be amalgamated into a hybrid if the redesign is to work. This approach is simultaneously radical, holistic and novel.

This, at least, is the theory. So what of the practice? The claims are as immodest as the reliable data is to find: the new approach will, we are told:

> ... drive down the time it takes to develop and deliver new products, dramatically reduce inventory and manufacturing time, slash the cost of quality and win back market share ... The following changes are possible: 30–35 per cent reduction in the cost of sales; 75–80 per cent reduction in delivery time; 60–80 per cent reduction in inventories; 65–70 per cent reduction in the cost of quality; and unpredictable but substantial increase in market share. (Ligus, 1993: 58)

In reality, many projects (about 70 per cent is a typical estimate) seem to fail and recently some of the leading consultancies involved have begun to articulate arguments which suggest that it is not a total solution after all (if it was then presumably such consultants would soon work themselves into oblivion) but 'a component to a solution' (Treacy, quoted in Cafasso, 1993). In fact, the recent rash of 'how to re-engineer yourself' books (Obeng and Crainer, 1994; Morris and Brandon, 1993) suggest that for a few pounds most companies can make qualitative leaps in profits; for rather more pounds you can also discover why this probably will not be the case (Business Intelligence, 1994).

So what is it that has to be done? The radical claims, according to Hammer and Champy (1993a), are not driven by technical innovations, even though IT-related BPR provides the most significant examples. Rather, they concentrate on ten interrelated changes; yet each change has previously appeared in a different guise. Thus, in order:

1. 'A switch from functional departments to process teams' was the guiding light of the Tavistock development of Socio-Technical Systems as well as the motif of the original teams at Volvo's Kalmar plant.
2. 'A move from simple tasks to multidimensional work' was the original aim of the nineteenth-century Utopian socialist William Morris, and was subsequently toyed with in the Quality of Working Life movement and job enrichment schemes of the 1970s.
3. 'A reversal of the power relationship, from superordinate to subordinate empowerment' is again an element of both the above, and paradoxically suggests that superordinates simultaneously 'have' power but are unable to change organizations.

4. 'A shift from training to education' – is precisely the argument raised against standard British so-called 'education' since it began in the nineteenth century.

5. 'The development of reward systems that drop payment for attendance in favour of payment for value added' – was common in Ancient Greece, sixteenth-century England, and applied to English teachers from 1862.

6. 'A bifurcation of the link between reward for current performance and advancement through assessment of ability' – may be taken to be a 'new' history of the 'Peter Principle' of hierarchical incompetence. ('In a hierarchy every employee tends to rise to his (or her) level of incompetence' (Peter and Hull, 1970).)

7. 'The overturning of employee focus: from concern for the boss to concern for the customer' was common to, and an explanation of, low status amongst artisans in Ancient Greece, to say nothing of contemporary Japan.

8. 'Changes in management behaviour: from supervisors to coaches' was something suggested at least as far back as the Hawthorne experiments in the US in the 1930s.

9. 'The flattening of hierarchies' is an idea, again, previously attempted in the Kalmar experiments.

10. 'Changes to executive behaviour: from "scorekeepers" to leaders' suggests the Human Relations approach has been all but forgotten.

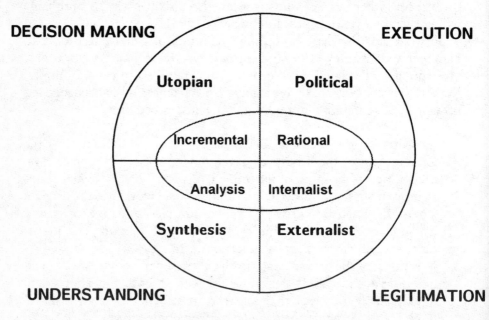

Figure 5.1 A framework for interpreting BPR

In sum there is precious little that is novel in BPR (see Grint (1994) for a more detailed review). But then two questions follow: first, why is it so popular? Second, why do so many attempts appear to fail? In what follows it is argued that one way of thinking about the high level of popularity and failure can be understood through four axes that represent different ways of understanding the world, taking decisions about it, executing those decisions and, finally, legitimizing them. The model of this interaction is represented in Figure 5.1

ANALYTIC VERSUS SYNTHETIC UNDERSTANDING

From at least the period of the Enlightenment we have traditionally sought to explain the nature of the world by a ritual system of purification. That is, by imposing boundaries between phenomena as a way of managing the complexity. Thus we distinguish between 'us' and 'them', between humans and animals, between living things and non-living things, between animals we eat and animals we do not, etc. The entire analytic method is based upon such a premise since the world is so inordinately complex the only way we can make sense of it is to impose boundaries around the phenomena – which we then take to be 'real', that is 'natural', existing *within* the phenomenon itself rather than being attributed to or imposed *upon* it by whoever has the power to construct such boundaries (Latour, 1993).

The logical end result of such an approach can best be demonstrated by considering how Treasury models of inflation 'work'. Since inflation is a complicated issue to measure, let alone predict, the analytic method deems it best to assemble an array of variables that operate relatively independently only at the level of abstract theory. Once the critical variables have been *isolated* and their *effects measured* the next trick is to combine them together into a sophisticated melting pot, known colloquially as a computer, which assesses the relative strengths of the variables and comes to a concluding number that predicts future inflationary trends. Naturally, the prediction is critical for government policy and, equally naturally, the prediction is invariably inaccurate. The typical response is to add in yet more variables, to fine tune the software, and to develop an evermore accurate predictor that strangely seems to fail yet again.

The problem, of course, is that more variables mean precisely that – more not less variance. Indeed, the whole scheme can be thrown completely off course should business 'confidence' decide to change, an intangible creature that appears completely uncontrollable. Perhaps, though, rather than accepting that we may as well count the seeds left on a dandelion 'clock' as pay computer analysts and economists vast sums of taxpayers' money, we might reconsider whether the approach itself is problematic.

Partly, it may be worth considering the extent to which analytic ways of fragmenting the world also embody forms of linear logic, in which one variable affects another in an invariant way. If the world is better described as one in which non-linear logic prevails, in which we should both, first, consider the extent to which variables are indeed independent of each other or are, in fact, construed to be independent only through our own inability to conceive of the world in more complex and interdependent ways, and second, that this interdependence introduces an element of unpredictability and instability that actually makes prediction at best a method that require more resources than is justified or, at worst, is theoretically a nonsense. A good example of this kind of problem is reconstructed by Luecke (1994) in his account of the battle of Midway which the Japanese lost as much by chance, misfortune and an overzealous adherence to linear logic, as much as by anything the Americans did.

The other aspect of the analytic approach that is problematic relates to ritual purification through boundary imposition that separates humans from all else. Hence, for example, power becomes located within humans, either individually or collectively: Napoleon won the battle of Austerlitz, while Wellington won the battle of Waterloo. Or, perhaps a little more generously, the respective commanders *and their troops* won their respective battles. Yet battles are only won through a combination of things – leaders, soldiers, guns, uniforms, transport, food, bullets, pay, ideals and many other things in between. The sight of Wellington strolling along the site of Waterloo completely naked, supported by thousands of naked, hungry, dispirited, weaponless, transportless men would hardly have won the day. Even if we establish the elements of war through a process of sophisticated analysis this does not necessarily ensure that we can explain the unfolding of events: Hitler should not, at least on a paper analysis, have been able to overcome the allied forces in France in May 1940 quite as easily as he did, but his holistic strategy compensated for his analytic weakness (Bartov, 1991). An analysis of the Mongol army at the gates of Vienna in May 1242 would have suggested that Armageddon was indeed at hand for Western Europe – but the death of Ogedai Khan led to an immediate return for the Mongol invaders (Marshall, 1993). In short, sophisticated analysis cannot compensate for the complexity of organizational life.

The consequence of this argument for re-engineering relates to the holistic nature of re-engineering – it stands or falls on the strength of the relationships it forges within the processes. Hence, just as the strength of a chain is determined by its weakest link, so re-engineering's strength lies in the novelty of its multiple linkages. One might argue that the linking of issues is precisely the innovation claimed by systems theorists, again over forty years ago (Bertalanffy, 1950), though there is a more radical interpretation available which undermines the division between the social world and natural world and speaks of the world of 'hybrids', phenomena that combine human and non-human. If we consider re-engineering's success to be rooted in this recognition and promotion of hybridization then perhaps this may explain some of its success.

The second innovative element of the model suggests a strong link between technical and organizational linkages, between non-human and human. The traditional socio-technical approach, of course, was premised upon precisely this dual axis, in which the optimal state was not necessarily one where the discrete technical and social systems were individually optimized but where they were melded together to form the optimal form of alloy. However, the promise of socio-technical systems was rarely realized and one of the reasons seems to have been the reluctance to reconstruct the technology in line with the social system rather than the more typical reconstruction of the social system to fit with the technical system.

Rather more radical are the ideas of actor–network theory (Latour, 1993; Callon, 1986; Law (ed.) 1986, 1991; Cockburn and Ormrod, 1993; Grint and Gill, 1995), in which the boundaries between elements are replaced by hybrids that dissolve boundaries; where the traditional asymmetry of explanation, in which human action is accounted for by processes that are fundamentally different from those that explain the actions of non-humans, is replaced by the principle of symmetry. In other words, and to take a single example, we should no longer consider 'interests' as an unproblematic causal variable for human action but not the action of non-humans (see Callon, 1986, for the most startling interpretation). The point here can be taken either as a claim that non-humans have interests too or that it is very dubious to attribute interests to humans for precisely the same reasons that we do not conventionally attribute interests to scallops. The resulting account of action tends to consider human actors as remarkably weak in comparison to the hybrids that unite humans and non-humans – in effect, that technology can make society more durable, that the social world is held together by more than just social ideas. Finally, and critically, that the capacity of the hybrid network – what the machine–human amalgam will do – cannot be read off from the claims of the constructors or the actants themselves but must be assessed both in the performance of the network and through the interpretive accounts of those involved in the assessment. There are problems with these approaches but they need not concern us here (see Grint and Woolgar, 1995). What is important is to note the relative utility of such an account and its potential utility in comparison to analytic models. *If*, as actor–network theory suggests, the world is composed of relatively boundary-less hybrids, and *if* the capacity of these hybrids depends upon the action and interpretation of the actants, then the stable and predictive claims of analytic and unilinear logic models are subject to severe doubt.

What re-engineering can potentially do is start from the premise that boundaries imposed between functions and between different forms of resource are precisely that, *imposed* rather than *exposed*. As soon as the analytic divisions (between human resources and marketing, between machines and people) are constructed our capacity to develop better ways of working are undermined because they impose what is essentially an artificial division between humans and non-humans. According to the model, then, we simply do not live in a world where people and things are separated: there are no humans without technological supports and there are no technologies that operate completely independently of humans. A critical advantage of the BPR approach, then, is to break down the barriers and start from the assumption that everything has to change, and change together. In effect, the approach is synthetic, that is, it synthesizes a multitude of disparate elements into an unstable but effective hybrid. (A more radical extension of this approach can be found in Latour (1993).)

INCREMENTALISM VERSUS UTOPIAN DECISION-MAKING

Although each individual aspect of re-engineering can be seen as merely a restatement of previous deliberations there is a case for asserting that the novelty of re-engineering lies in the total package not the individual elements. Re-engineering, in this account, is successful because of its *sui generis* nature: its holistic differentiation from, and superiority over, the analytic elements which have come before. This is plausible to the extent that the whole is greater than the sum of the parts. Indeed, one could argue that it is the radical extent of the change required that explains both the success *and* the failure of re-engineering. That is, that the high degree of uncertainty and risk involved unhinges the nerves of those attempting to re-engineer so that they seek more conservative and instrumental approaches to change that appear both less risky and more plausible. This, of course, is precisely the argument made over thirty years ago by Lindblom's (1959) account of 'disjointed incrementalism' or 'muddling through' and the associated 'satisficing' behaviour described by Simon (1947). These incisive critiques of rational decision-making imply that decision-makers do not approach organizational problems with a clean sheet of paper and an ideal, but with a pre-folded piece of paper and in the light of existing structures and policies (see Jabes, 1982). Re-engineering's innovation, then, may lie in its denial of this incrementalist orthodoxy that has prevailed for thirty years. Of course, day-to-day management *is* concerned with incremental change, that is change at the margin, small modifications to existing policies, procedures and methods. The bulk of the operation remains the same. The result over time, however, is a body of traditions, customs and practices that may appear to mirror the organizational sclerosis that Mancur Olson (1982) attributed to declining nation states.

In essence, the ideas imply that only an attack upon all fronts simultaneously, in which every possible institution, ritual, practice and norm is subject to critique and reconstruction, is likely to succeed. Where conventional plans for organizational change concentrate upon one or two areas (payment systems or training or customer focus or Just-in-Time and so on) re-engineering mobilizes the entire workforce in a complete and universal reconsideration and reconstruction. Moreover, not only does re-engineering require radical decisions, it also requires radically and culturally congruent decisions. That is, where decisions are made that have important consequences for the way an organization operates it makes little sense to generate wildly disparate decisions, for instance to promote teams rather than individuals but simultaneously to generate a pay and reward system that recognizes only the efforts of individuals. In short, only those organizations that re-engineer corporate strategy, management methods, reward systems and organizational structure in a congruent fashion are likely to succeed (Business Intelligence, 1994).

The premise of the argument, therefore, is that incrementalism is itself a barrier to change. This does not mean that *all* attempts to change should be Utopian in their scale and direction but rather that Utopian thought should be considered rather differently from its traditional role as fit only for dreamers, fit for 'nowhere' (Grint and Hogan, 1994a; Grint and Hogan, 1994b).

Re-engineering is a particular form of Utopian thought – it does not attempt to improve the way business currently operates (though some of the re-engineering focus upon business processes implies this (Business Intelligence, 1994)), but to rethink the way it operates. More importantly, it asserts that the critical feature of re-engineering is that associated with re-engineering management rather than production processes (Padulo, 1994). It does not seek to enhance the efficiency of functions but to examine whether functions are the best way to run a business. Moreover, it does this against a background in which the larger danger is not in radical change but in not changing at all or not changing sufficiently radically. The danger, then, is the danger of obsolescence which, by holding to established and traditional norms, allows more innovative firms to move ahead – to adopt new technologies, markets, training and reward systems.

There are several elements of traditional Utopian thought that are worth considering in some detail. First, the traditional format, either in novels such as Huxley's *Island*, or the original *Utopia* of Thomas More, tends to constitute Utopias as islands of perfection in an imperfect world. The isolation is important in that it ensures an impenetrable barrier against worldly corruption and facilitates social experimentation. Marx regarded Utopian socialism in exactly the same way, as islands of dreams that might serve as demonstrations that the world could be otherwise but as ultimately doomed unless the ideas and the practice spread rapidly across the boundaries. For re-engineering we might consider the extent to which similarly radical experiments in alternative organizational forms tend to occur within organizations that are considered to be on the brink of collapse, and the minds of the doomed inhabitants have their attention focused on survival. Alternately, where organizations do not appear to be in immediate crisis, re-engineering experiments are often executed within a delimited and heavily monitored 'island': should the experimental Utopia fail little has been sacrificed; should it succeed the success can be used to persuade others of the need for radical change. Paradoxically, in the latter case, the Utopian island must simultaneously demonstrate that it can work – but only if the rest of the organization does not 'infect' it. Yet if it, in turn, does not 'infect' the rest of the organization then it will be deemed to have failed. In other words, the boundaries around the Utopia must be permeable – but not in both directions.

The second element of Utopian thought is to demonstrate, paradoxically, its eminently practical essence. One particular form of Utopian thought is akin to the anthropological mode of research *defamiliarization* – making the world strange as a device to scrutinize the existing world – as opposed to detailing an alternative. This shifts the debate from prescription (and there are enough of these around at the moment) to estranged (re)description. There is no specified end project in this form of Utopian thought but merely an examination of the present in the light of potential, and plural, alternatives.

How does this work in practice? First, detail another organization, not to suggest that it is better than the current one but to focus attention back on the first by comparison. This may seem equivalent to the current vogue of benchmarking best practice, but it can be used in this guise for two different purposes: first, to demonstrate the contingency of the current world or organization; second, to avoid considering Utopias as idle speculation or daydreams: the alternative may not be here but it must be hypothetically possible. Hence estrangement, or defamiliarization, serves to provide an alternative that is not as detailed as current 'reality' but that is useful as a device for critically examining it and engendering the realization that the present can be changed in favour of a better alternative but not necessarily the one on offer.

It may be, then, that re-engineering requires the kind of Utopian thought discussed but much of the practice of re-engineering still rests upon the traditional practices of incremental thought. Both Utopian and incremental skills are necessary, the latter for ensuring the newly re-engineered organization operates effectively and can be altered to suit the particular conditions it faces at the time, but to get to this stage requires Utopian thought.

There are, of course, dangers in Utopian thought and decision-making too – indeed, Utopia in the political world has traditionally had a bad press though the criticism has tended to take two rather different forms: one rooted in a fear of the inevitable consequences of failure; the second rooted in a fear of the unintentional consequences of success. The case *for* Utopian thought and the significance of its application in re-engineering rests on two principles through which an attempt is made to transcend the case *against* Utopian thought.

In the first case Utopia is quite literally unrealizable, and hence thinking about it is not just a waste of resources but it raises expectations that can never be met and must subsequently be managed. This is particularly appropriate for re-engineering where the claimed improvements are qualitatively different from, and in advance of, the kind of claims made for less radical policies of change. Where the re-engineered, but not revitalized, organization results, the deflated and frustrated Utopian thinker and practitioner must, to use an old sociological term, be 'cooled out' to prevent the depression either becoming progressively worse or becoming endemic to the organization. In effect, Utopian thought here is regarded as essentially destructive, it is a regressive, negative and corrupting concept that is always looking to some far off romantic past or future that never really did or could exist. This philosophy suggests that, since we have to live in the present and plan for the future, we should avoid Utopias, including re-engineering, like the veritable plagues they necessarily bring down on all who attempt to think or implement them.

To challenge this lack of 'realism' we can turn to Utopian theorists Frederick Jameson and Ernst Bloch. In Jameson's *The Political Unconscious*, Utopia is conceived of as *fantasy grounded in reality* (see Grint and Hogan, 1994a, 1994b, for a fuller account of this). That is, although Utopian thought always exists 'outside of time' and might therefore rightly be considered as divorced from reality, history and society, the articulation of Utopia itself occurs within specific time and place. In effect, the expression of Utopian desire is always contextualized and can therefore be developed for that specific time and place. In other words, Utopian texts and ideas should be seen as cultural constructs, not as ahistorical and acultural phenomena.

Relatedly, Bloch's *Principle of Hope* considers the significance of the German term 'noch nicht'. This translates as both 'not yet' implying a future orientation, and 'still not' rooted in the present. The 'still not' focuses attention upon the steps taken towards an alternative – or not taken as the case may be – in the present. The 'not yet' focuses upon the ultimate future goal: the Utopian vision. In managerial discourse this might be translated as the difference between vision and mission. The vision is the ultimate goal while the mission is the path. The juxtaposition of present and future, absence and potential presence, draws attention to current shortcomings and therefore acts as a necessary step to change (Levitas, 1990: 85). In Bloch's terms, it creates an 'anticipatory consciousness' – a precondition for, not an inhibition of, change. Hence, Utopias are not normally unrealistic but merely different from the existing reality: a potential reality waiting to be made real. Utopian thought, then, only makes sense – and especially practical sense – if it is considered as a way of thinking about an alternative but achievable reality. This kind of approach can be demonstrated in the development of Disneyland. Had Walt Disney not had the 'Utopian' dream of Disneyland, it would not exist. Or to quote the popular story, the issue is not that it was a shame that Disney did not live to see Disneyland, but that it wouldn't exist without him seeing it in his Utopian imagination.

The second argument against Utopian thought is not that it is inherently unrealizable but the very opposite: that the danger lies in its realization – the Utopia becomes Dystopia. Where our first principle suggests that we should all free up our thought processes, our second principle does not deny the danger of Dystopia but rather attempts to transcend the problem by avoiding the cause. The fear of Dystopia has enough solid historical support to warrant serious concern. Indeed, such concerns can be summarized in the phrase: 'the road to hell is paved with good intentions'. For management, such Utopias may be the CEO's latest dream that involves all members of staff wearing the same uniform or watching endless 'corporate vision' videos that ought to come with a plain wrapper to avoid scaring the children. Here Utopia becomes a straight-jacket that warrants no deviation, that considers all protest as a sign of indiscipline or conspiracy or worse; it becomes the nightmare rather than the dream because it implies that the originator of the dream has a universal wisdom that simply cannot exist.

In the business field we can consider a litany of gods that failed, or at least failed to revolutionize our businesses on a *permanent* basis: Taylorism, Fordism, Management by Objectives, Measured Day Work, Payment by Results, Collective Bargaining. We might even note how these gods recur in time when today's executives forget yesterday's Utopias.

For example, individual payment systems were an essential principle for F.W. Taylor and they were tried and found wanting in the inevitable tendency to decay which appears to undermine all such schemes. That they are now back in favour is not the issue, but we should not expect them to last indefinitely any more than they did last time.

The implication of this, and a possible explanation for the high failure rate – though it appears to be no higher than anything else – is that the very radicalism of re-engineering, that is its Utopian essence, is simultaneously what makes it so difficult to achieve but, when achieved, makes its productivity achievements so high (see Hall, et al, 1993). In effect, re-engineering has to be Utopian to work at all, and if it is Utopian then it is possible to achieve the results hitherto regarded as impossible. But, since we know that all previous management revolutions have ultimately proved less and less viable over time, we should recognize that this organizational atrophy implies that the only permanent revolution is exactly that: permanent revolution.

EXECUTION

The third aspect of the circle is often regarded as the point at which the Utopian dreams of the revolutionaries and re-engineers become impaled upon the spikes of reality; where idealistic decisions are progressively deracinated into pragmatic compromises: it is the place of execution. Yet, paradoxically, much of the failure to execute decisions lies not in the irrationality of the decisions but rather in the irredeemably political context in which the execution of decisions occurs.

It has been a convention of Western thought since the Enlightenment that the same rationality that persuaded us to think in analytic rather than synthetic terms also operates to persuade us rationality, rooted in reasoned individual action and the application of scientific principles, is the means by which individuals are persuaded to execute decisions made by others or to change their opinion, their attitude or their behaviour. Indeed, if one opens up most textbooks on management behaviour they will almost all suggest that persuasive accounts are those which are deemed to be rational. Yet when we get close to organizations they appear to operate along political or moral lines rather than lines that we might otherwise recognize as rational.

The original responsibility for this confusion lies at the feet of Adam Smith whose work captured and promoted the transformation of an economy run along moral lines to one run along market lines. The traditions that made up the moral economy have a very long history and involved fines for overpayment of wages or overpricing of goods, prohibitions on the export of materials for making cloth (including the emigration of skilled workers) and a whole host of regulations covering industry (see Grint and Woolgar, 1995; Bland *et al.* (eds), 1933).

One historical illustration will suffice for our purposes here. Smail (1987, 1991), for instance, has argued that the 1806 British Parliamentary Committee appointed to consider the state of the woollen industry at the time was a seminal point in the development of a new discourse through which the old moral economy, articulated through what he calls a 'corporatist discourse' was displaced by the new laissez-faire economy, articulated through what he terms an 'industrial discourse'. As Smail notes, the old discourse is nicely reproduced in the 1555 *Act Touching Weavers*: 'No Woollen Weaver using or exercising the feate or Mistery of Weaving ... shall have or kepe at any one time above the number of Twoo Wollen Loomes' (quoted in Smailes, 1987: 53), whereas the new discourse inverted the concern from collective to individual and supported: 'The right of every man to employ the Capital he inherits, or has acquired according to his own discretion, without molestation or obstruction' (ibid.). It would seem that Smail has probably exaggerated the significance of this single episode (see Randall, 1990), but the point is that the committee does represent the increasing influence of the new discourse and by the trial of the Luddites in York, six years later, the *argument* that technical development represents rational progress appears to have become common sense for the establishment. For the Luddites, and those who followed in their resistance to economic and technical changes, the old discourse (which had prevailed for some five hundred years) that talked of moral obligations, reciprocity between all and the protection of craft rights, was decreasingly effective against the new discourse of the factory entrepreneurs. This new mode of thought sought to strip out the morality from the economy, divest itself of all taint of collective interests, and facilitate the unfettered pursuit of private interests. This old discourse never actually died (and its persistence can be seen in the work of Noble (1983)), but after the Luddites it became progressively less influential amongst the establishment and, perhaps equally significant, amongst the representatives of the working class.

When one considers the significance of this argument to the present day it is reasonable to consider the difference between what the texts say about organizations and what managers say about organizations as the difference between the official line and the unofficial line on organizations. The former sees organizations as rational bodies driven by the rational desire for profit maximizing and executed by rational individuals acting rationally in pursuit of rational organizationally defined objectives. This is quite different from the unofficial line where organizations are considered as political institutions run by Machiavellian Princes in pursuit of what appears to many to be their own private interests. Hence, decisions are effectively executed by (successful) political infighting, by (successful) networking, by making the right friends and the right enemies, by going to the right school and university, by choosing the right parents, gender and ethnicity and by a whole host of related aspects that have precious little to do with any form of rationally legitimated criteria for ensuring success.

If this is the case in organizations, and if this approach – which is political and moral rather than rational – is extended away from explaining managerial behaviour and success, then it might seem viable to consider how this impacts upon attempts by managers to introduce organizational change. Under this approach the desperate search for explaining the failure of yet another management initiative at the doors of inadequate consultation or communication or whatever is missing the point. If managers operate politically rather than rationally in their lives – and succeed or fail on political rather than rational criteria – then we might consider the extent to which change programmes, such as re-engineering, succeed or fail on the same grounds. In effect, explaining the rational implications of continuing the traditional way of doing things and the rational effects of a re-engineered process may be considerably less effective than setting out to achieve the same ends through a political process. In short, this might mean moving from a campaign to persuade people through an appeal to their minds to a campaign to enrol people through an appeal to their hearts.

Despite this, most conventional perspectives on organizational decision-making are predicated upon a very traditional theory of power. These tend to imply that where organizational power is in the hands of an individual or a small elite, then power emanates from the centre to the periphery with the causal influence similarly centrifugal (see Handy, 1985). In short, a leader's power *causes* others to act, that is to enact the decisions of others.

We can clearly see this in the way Mrs Thatcher, the most powerful British politician of the 1980s, *caused* others to do things for her. Yet, if Mrs Thatcher was indeed the most powerful politician of the day, and did *have* power, then it becomes difficult to explain how the effects of an attacking speech by Geoffrey Howe, previously described by Dennis Healey as equivalent to being mauled by a dead sheep, should lead to a series of events that led to her removal from power very shortly afterwards. How can a leader who *has* power *lose* it?

In practice, of course, leaders do not 'do' very much in terms of actually performing the acts required to secure change. On the contrary, leaders generally get others to do the performing. Thus, when such a leader does 'exert power' it is subordinate others, not him or herself, which actually engage in action. Now here is the rub – *if* the subordinates do not act then the leader has no power; only as a *consequence* of subordinate actions can leaders be deemed to have power. Power, in this perspective, therefore, is contingent upon the production and reproduction of a network of associations that facilitates 'acting at a distance' (Latour, 1986). Thus, power is a consequence of action, rather than a cause of action. Perhaps the difference is best appreciated by comparing the cause of a 'domino collapse' – that is where the act requires just one human action to initiate the action – with the cause of a 'human wave' – that is where every member of the wave is involved in reproducing the effect.

This shift from the 'principle' of power to the 'practice' of power, as Latour (1986) calls it, also implies that subordinate action only occurs through the interpretation of self-advantage by the subordinate: subordinates obey because they consider it to be in their self-interest to obey. In turn, it is likely that the command of the leader will become distorted through what Latour calls the 'translation' process: not only are leaders dependent upon their subordinates but a subordinate's translation of the edict may well prove to be a distortion of the leader's intention. The implication of this is that rather than the rays of power spreading out from the centre to the periphery in a determinate and unmediated fashion they are both highly contingent and the subject of constant interpretation and renegotiation. Such a revision in this context implies that the existence of policies or rules does not ensure the enacting of such policies or commands. Thus the chain of command from Prime Minister down does not, *in and of itself*, secure the execution of the policy.

Instead, all policy implementation is critically dependent upon the self-interested – and contingent – action of others. It is precisely because of this that 'working to rule' implies that nothing gets done. Rule-based execution is perhaps *the* most rational variant of methods of execution; it is premised upon the assumption that subordinate initiative undermines policy execution, yet we can never have enough rules to determine all our actions. Indeed, for this to occur we would need rules to tell us which rule to apply, a theoretical impossibility in the face of the complex processes that face decision-makers. The consequence is that superordinates are forced to rely upon the very initiative on the part of subordinates that they sought to remove through rule-bound execution.

However, the reversal of a causal explanation of execution does not account for the way certain forms of decisions appear to derive their legitimacy from sources beyond the appeal to logic. In other words, the way that organizations work and the direction in which they move and change appears to depend as much upon changing fashions as upon any evolutionary or linear progression towards better ways of managing. The final section considers the last dichotomous axis of the re-engineering debate and assesses the extent to which the predominance of the rational has prevented us from assessing the degree to which the success of approaches to organizational change can be linked to the predominance of resonances which the new vogue appears to set up between itself and other, related, ideas.

LEGITIMATION

It has already been argued above, at length, that there is a problem with assuming that the internal rationality of an idea is sufficient to ensure its acceptance let alone execution. Here it is not the intention to rerun the problems of rationality but to consider the extent to which we might focus upon the congruence of 'new' organizational or management ideas, such as re-engineering, with other, ostensibly unrelated ideas beyond the world of business – that is, the way new approaches render an account of the problem and solution that sets up sympathetic 'resonances' with related developments. BPR's or re-engineering's popularity, according to this approach, also lies in the resonances it 'reveals' between old and new business systems previously right but now inappropriate. Hence:

> [It] 'isn't another imported idea from Japan ... [it] capitalizes on the same characteristics that made Americans such great business innovators: individualism, self reliance, a willingness to accept risk and a propensity for change ... unlike management philosophies that would have 'us' like 'them', [it] doesn't try to change the behaviour of American workers and managers. Instead, it takes advantage of American talents and unleashes American ingenuity. (Hammer and Champy, 1993b: 1–3)

To arrive at this conclusion a certain amount of cultural manipulation is required if the resonances between the idea and the particular culture concerned are to be clear. For example: BPR is supposed to be about teamwork not (American) individualism; it is supposed to be about starting to risk change – so how can change be an element of the US culture? It is supposed to be about radically increasing the level and content of supportive social networks, not about American individual self-reliance. In effect, what counts as important aspects of culture can be interpreted afresh by those who seek to change it – an important note for BPR consultants eager to work outside the US.

It also resonates with the increased power of transnational corporations (TNCs) in the age of globalization: to compete with the Japanese, Western TNCs must generate similar levels of loyalty, increasingly disembedded from the concerns of nations or nationalities. This is particularly so in light of the collapse of old stabilities such as the Cold War and US political and economic domination, and the political and economic turbulence that appears to increase daily. One way to restabilize the present is by reinterpreting the past such that radical (and the word 'radical' no longer bears the left-wing political resonance it once had) innovations prosper when marketed as the way to return to former glories.

In effect, then, since all the elements have been around for varying amounts of time the issue is not so much whether the elements are novel but whether the packaging, and selling of the package, is what makes re-engineering different. This is the equivalent of subordinating internalist accounts to externalist accounts – that is, to concern ourselves less with whether the *content* of re-engineering is radically different *and* demonstrably superior to anything that went before (which it appears not to be from the analysis above), and rather more with *why* the package is effective in its particular envelope of space and time. In other words, why has re-engineering taken off at the very end of the 1980s and early 1990s and why is it so popular in the US rather than anywhere else?

Clearly, if the re-engineering approach failed to convince its target population that its analysis of the problems was accurate, then its prescriptive advice would probably not be heeded. But the intention is to argue here that the persuasive utility of re-engineering, the reason for its popularity, rests not in the objective validity of the constitutive elements or the whole, the internal novelty and validity of re-engineering as it were, but in the way the rendering of the problem and solution provided by re-engineering generates a resonance with popular opinion about related events, an external explanation as it were. This does not mean that the ideologies are functional responses to the requirements of capitalism, or anything else for that matter. Rather my argument is that these ideas and practices have to be read as plausible by those at whom they are targeted, and for this 'plausibility' to occur the ideas most likely to prevail are those that are apprehended as capturing the *Zeitgeist* or 'spirit of the times'.

There are precedents for this in the popularity of previous managerial philosophies (see Rose, 1990). For example, Taylorism and Fordism can be understood in relation to the contemporary development of social statistics: the rise of the eugenics movement in the US and its attempted legitimation through scientific measures of IQ (Kamin, 1977; Karier, 1976a, 1976b); the high point of pre-1914 beliefs in the efficacy of scientific rationality – soon to be radically disturbed by the events of 1914–18 (Pick, 1993); in light of the changes in disciplinary and temporal schemas adopted originally in armies and prisons (Foucault, 1979); and, of course, in the development of assembly line systems, or rather disassembly line systems, in the Chicago slaughter houses then 'processing' 200,000 hogs a day (Pick, 1993: 180). One might want to go further here and suggest that the kind of mechanical tactics adopted by the British Army, at the battle of the Somme in 1916 for example (Winter, 1979;

Ellis, 1993), are precise replicas of scientific management displaced from the factory to the killing fields of Flanders. Relatedly, the Human Relations reaction to Taylorism and Fordism can be read as a shift from the 'rational individual' to the 'irrational group' as the development of Communism and Fascism appeared to be explicable only through an assumption about the fundamentally irrational needs of people to belong to groups and to construct their group identity through the destruction of 'the other'. In the military field, again, the 'new' common sense that began to prevail towards the end of the Second World War was that, as in the factory so in war, group cohesion and the solidarity of a relatively small 'primary group' was what motivated people (Shils and Janowitz, 1948), a claim subsequently disputed by Bartov (1991) who suggests that the Wermacht's cohesion on the Eastern front, beyond the barbarism of the military system itself, was the result of a powerful organizational culture – another resonance from the present.

The defeat of Fascism and the arrival of the Cold War provided fertile ground for the reconstruction of Neo-Human Relations in the form of democratic individualism; the 'Evil Empire' was neither of these, and, particularly in the UK (Donovan, 1968), the informal primary group, so long propounded by the Human Relations school, appeared to be the cause of the problem of economic malaise, not the solution. This time the alternative was written in the language of Lewin's democratic leadership, or McGregor's Theory Y version of responsible employees, and Maslow's and Herzberg's quest for self-fulfilment through work. Finally we can posit the arrival of the fourth wave, the cultures of excellence approach where the limits of modernism and Fordism are perceived as the stimulus to change. Re-engineering, in this perspective, is the summation of this fourth wave (see Grint, 1994, for a more detailed account).

Re-engineering, therefore, provides what can be considered as a new discourse with which contemporary developments can be simultaneously explained and controlled. The language of re-engineering renders opaque developments clear, not by providing a more objective analysis of the situation and the solution but by providing a persuasive rendering of them. Moreover, part of the persuasive essence lies in the resonances that it 'reveals' between the old and the new, particularly between American past glories and future conquests. However, for this to be achieved successfully the world has to be conveyed in ways that make re-engineering appear as an appropriate response.

Re-engineering's historical narrative, at least that provided by the originators of the term, Hammer and Champy, asserts that the current business systems were not always wrong but are no longer appropriate. To assert that what America has been doing was always wrong both fails to explain why it has become such an economically successful economy and implies that American culture was and is inappropriate. It is clearly advantageous to argue that blame for the current state of affairs lies in the actions of 'the other' (ie foreign competition) if one is intending to persuade one's own customers of the viability of change. The second manoeuvre, having persuaded Americans that they were right the first time, is to suggest that the current conditions, although responsible for the problems facing American business, are, paradoxically, ideally suited to turning the tables on 'the other'. Thus the two major problems in such an account are transcended. American industry is weak now *because*, rather than despite the fact that, it was so strong before; and American industry will be strong again *because* of, rather than despite, American culture.

We can assume from this rhetoric that re-engineering is not only a way of fending the attacks of 'the other' (ie Japan), but also a mechanism that will allow America to regain authority over 'the other' – primarily because the American culture is uniquely suited to the re-engineering approach. The Japanese, already under attack in such books as Tolchin and Tolchin's *Buying into America: How Foreign Money is Changing the Face of Our Nation* to Michael Crichton's *Rising Sun*, may be emulated but they must not be imitated.

This obviously poses related problems for other cultures and suggests that only American corporations are likely to experience the full benefit of re-engineering. Unless, of course, re-engineering can be reconfigured in such a way that its resonances lie not so much with cultural changes that restrict its utility but with changes that expand its utility beyond the US shoreline.

Nor is it coincidental that the rise of functional accounts of organizations, and subsequently integrated systems approaches to organization, developed at a time of organizational, especially business organization, stasis, or even more appropriately the long boom which survived from the end of the war to the oil crisis of 1974. When growth is considered strong and the future appears secure what hope for the management guru who wants to experiment with radical innovations? But when old stabilities like the East–West conflict crumble in the Berlin Wall collapse; when American, and even Western, economic domination withers under pressure from Japan and the Asian Tigers; and when the long boom turns into the long collapse, the conditions for organizational radicalism are set fair. This is particularly so when, in the absence of the Soviet 'Evil Empire' the legitimacy of the 'victor' rests on much less stable grounds. The reconstruction of national boundaries, then, may, if anything, make the 'foreignness' of economic competitors even more significant and the search for radical remedies more frenetic.

The response by the US has been twofold. On the one hand, the global competition now threatening the US has seen first President Bush and now President Clinton warning their fellow citizens that America can no longer fend off the competition alone and must itself join trading blocs, such as the North American Free Trade Agreement (NAFTA) currently under discussion. The possibility of US-based corporations exporting what the AFL-CIO call 'millions' of jobs to Mexico to take advantage of cheaper labour and laxer health and safety legislation has provoked a storm of criticism and considerable public outcry at the potential loss of, or slur on, American identity (Tisdall, 1993).

On the other hand, the fall of the 'Evil Empire' has freed some of the language of change, such that 'radical' change no longer implies shifts to the political left, and talk of giving power to the employees no longer embodies the failure of management or capitalism. Hence, where several prior attempts at organizational change have concentrated upon partial and very specific aspects of the organization: total quality or human resources, etc, re-engineering gains strength from its radicalism. Where these have been tried and found wanting or, even more appropriately, found wanting because they are not just partial solutions but *foreign* partial solutions, then the time is ripe for radical overhauls.

However, a crucial aspect of temporal resonances is that there must be a juxtaposition of the old and the new. That is, although an element of novelty is critical, this must not be regarded as a complete break with all that has gone on before – thus Hammer's concern to remind potential American customers that the novelty element is actually a historically rooted part of American culture. Success can be achieved not through breaks with tradition but through a radical return to tradition. This paradoxical juxtaposition is itself hardly novel. Max Weber makes a strong argument for precisely this enmeshing of the present and future in the past in his analysis of charismatic leadership, particularly that associated with Jesus Christ. Weber argues that it was only because the apparently radically innovative ideas of Christ's message were so deeply embedded in Jewish culture over a long period of time that they found any resonances with the population (Weber, 1978: 630–4; Cavalli, 1987). The parallel with re-engineering and American culture is clear: radical innovations prosper best when they are marketed as methods to return to former glories. Moreover, the return of this former glory will be constructed in a re-engineered environment which is ideally suited to American culture: it will comprise powerful corporations that vie with nation states for supremacy; it will require individual dedication and loyalty to an ideal of a kind which many other nationalities may find difficult to achieve; it will require the construction of new identities from across many boundaries where origin and history are less important than an attitude of mind; and it will be a land of opportunity for bootstrappers. The re-engineered future is not the land of the sullen or lethargic employee but of the dedicated corporate warrior; it is a re-engineered neo-feudalism, a total way of life.

CONCLUSION

This chapter has disputed the analytic claims to novelty espoused by re-engineering's supporters but accepts that the holistic and, in particular, the hybrid nature of re-engineering's approach implies that there is something different about it. By dividing the way managers operate into four segments (the analytic revenge?) it suggests that re-engineering is most likely to fail where it is construed as a method and goal of change that is premised upon rational analysis, where the decision-making is incremental, where the methods of execution depend wholly upon assumptions about rational individuals, and where its legitimizing characteristics are regarded as self-evident and lie in its internal and objective value. Re-engineering, it is argued, might be better configured as a Utopia, and it embodies the same kind of possibilities and problems that Utopias throughout history have manifested. In effect, the chapter argues that for re-engineering to work as a radical and long-term change the focus should be more about re-engineering the way managers think and work as about re-engineering the way processes operate. Furthermore, the methods by which re-engineering might be achieved have to be more firmly rooted in the current cultural climate.

To summarize, whatever the concerns over the uniqueness of re-engineering – and the development of a holistic account that locks human and non-human hybrids into complex networks is certainly an interesting way of considering re-engineering, even if it is not something re-engineering supporters articulate – the main point is not to suggest that the lack of novelty implies re-engineering is mere hype, nor that it will fail because it is not novel. On the contrary, novelty is no guarantee of success and, anyway, many of the ideas embodied in re-engineering do, so its adherents claim, facilitate greater levels of efficiency. Rather, the concern is to suggest that we look beyond the content of re-engineering if we wish to understand why it appears to have taken parts of the US by storm and why it has done this at a particular time. For those seeking to encourage British or Japanese or any other form of industry to re-engineer, the appropriate strategy may be to reinterpret the national culture so that it resonates with those aspects allegedly required by re-engineering.

As part of this process it is suggested that Utopian thought should be brought back in from the cold, especially since the ending of the Cold War has taken the chill off many Utopias. Utopian thought is destructive but only in the sense of creative destruction that is necessary to change the present in and through imagining a better future. There is little doubt that historically many people have suffered at the hands of Utopians whether within business enterprises that required almost religious adherence to the corporate code of a Utopian CEO, or within the confines of a Dystopian political system where the future starts with Year Zero. However, Utopian thought can serve as a valuable heuristic mechanism through which the status quo can be considered in a much more reflective way. Here, Utopia becomes the estranging device that marks out the problems of the present and offers an array of potential alternatives without the usual prescriptive coercion beloved of those peddling or seeking simplistic solutions. Utopia does not have to mean Nowhere in the sense of never existing, and it can mean Nowhere in the sense of nowhere *yet*. The point is not that we should strive for the unrealizable but that we might consider 'what might be' as a first step towards 'what will be'.

If the world is in a constant flux then the issue is whether we should respond by abandoning the dreams of a better future or suffer the consequences of attempting permanent change. The danger of somnambulism, sleepwalking through life when all around is changing rapidly, appears to us as much more of a risk. One only has to consider the proportion of organizations that survive by remaining static and immune to change to know that this is a recipe for disaster: the danger is not moving slowly but not moving at all.

But where does this leave the average manager, or indeed the average person? We suggest that four things should be borne in mind. First, change and stasis are the responsibility of each one of us: to believe otherwise is to be guilty of 'bad faith' – the illegitimate denial or displacement of responsibility. Second, managers might try a thought experiment which can be extremely useful in provoking new avenues of imagination: imagine what your perfect job and perfect organization might look like – and then compare them with your account of reality: are there gaping holes between the two that might be filled, or at least reduced, by practical measures taken or suggested by you? Third, don't get hung up on the practical details of the Utopia; the critical issue is to use the Utopian ideal to make the current situation appear strange and in need of justification so that improvements might be made.

In short, BPR's success can hardly be explained by the novelty of its individual ideas but it may have something to do with the holistic and synthetic hybrid amalgamations of them. It might also be explained by the resonances that can be established with related events and movements elsewhere. Indeed, I would argue that probably the most important aspect of successful organizational change is getting people to read the world in a different way, persuading them that Utopia is both possible and necessary. However, to get there the drive for re-engineering will need to stop concentrating upon re-engineering the operational processes in isolation from the way management thinks and works: the Utopia is one where management is re-engineered. Only then would what Trotsky (1969), in a different context, called 'The Permanent Revolution' occur.

REFERENCES

Bartov, O (1991) *Hitler's Army*, Oxford University Press, Oxford.

Bertalanffy, L (1950) 'An Outline of General System Theory', *British Journal of Philosophical Science*, 1, 134–165.

Bland, A E, Brown, P A and Tawney, R H (eds) (1933) *English Economic History: Select Documents*, Bell & Sons, London.

Bloch, E (1986) *The Principle of Hope*, Blackwell, London.

Braudel F (1973) *Capitalism and Material Life*, Weidenfeld & Nicholson, London.

Business Intelligence (1994) *Re-engineering: The Critical Success Factors*, Business Intelligence/Financial Times, London

Cafasso, R (1993) 'Re-engineering: Just the First Step', *Computer World*, 19 April.

Callon, M (1986) 'Some Elements of a Sociology of Translation', Law, J (ed.), *Power, Action and Belief*, RKP, London.

Caulkin, S (1993) 'Leaner, Faster, Cheaper', *The Observer*, 3 October.

Cavalli, L (1987) 'Charisma and Twentieth Century Politics', Whimster, S and Lash, S (eds), *Max Weber, Rationality and Modernity*, Allen & Unwin, London.

Cockburn, C and Ormrod, S (1993) *Gender and Technology in the Making*, Sage, London.

Donovan Commission (1968) *Report of the Royal Commission on Trade Unions and Employers' Associations*, HMSO, London.

Ellis, J (1993) *The Social History of the Machine Gun*, Pimlico, London.

Ellwood, W (1993) 'Multinationals and the Subversion of Sovereignty', *The New Internationalist*, 246, August.

Foucault, M (1979) *Discipline and Punish*, Penguin, Harmondsworth.

Giddens, A (1990) *The Consequences of Modernity*, Polity Press, Cambridge.

Gray, R (1987) 'The Languages of Factory Reform in Britain, 1830–1860', Joyce, P. (ed.), *The Historical Meanings of Work*, Cambridge University Press, Cambridge.

Grint, K (1994) 'Re-engineering History', *Organization*, 1(1), 179–202.

Grint, K and Gill, R (eds) (1995) *The Gender–Technology Relation*, Taylor & Francis, London.

Grint, K and Hogan, E (1994a) *Utopian Management*, Management Research Paper, Templeton College, Oxford.

Grint, K and Hogan, E (1994b) *Fatalism and Utopia: Construction of an Index of Possibilities*, Management Research Paper, Templeton College, Oxford.

Grint, K and Woolgar, S. (1995) *Deus ex Machina*, Polity Press, Cambridge.

Guest, D (1990) 'Human Resource Management and the American Dream', *Journal of Management Studies*, 27, (4), 377–397.

Habermas, J (1971) *Towards a Rational Society*, Heinemann, London.

Hall, G, Rosenthal, J and Wade, J (1993) 'How to Make Re-engineering *Really* Work', *Harvard Business Review*, November/December, 119–131.

Hammer, M (1990) 'Re-engineering Work: Don't Automate, Obliterate', *Harvard Business Review*, July–August, 104–112.

Hammer, M and Champy, J (1993a) 'Re-engineering the Corporation', *Insights Quarterly*, Summer, 3–19.

Hammer, M and Champy, J (1993b) *Re-engineering the Corporation: A Manifesto for Business Revolution*, Nicholas Brealey Publishing, London.

Harvey, D (1989) *The Condition of Postmodernity*, Blackwell, London.

Jabes, J (1982) 'Individual Decision Making', in McGrew, A G and Wilson, M J (eds), *Decision Making: Approaches and Analysis*, Manchester University Press, Manchester.

Kamin, L (1977) *The Science and Politics of IQ*, Penguin, Harmondsworth.

Karier, C J (1976a) 'Business Values and the Educational State', in Dale, R *et al.* (eds) *Schooling and Capitalism*, RKP, London.

Karier, C J (1976b) 'Testing for Order and Control in the Corporate Liberal State', in Dale, R *et al.* (eds) *Schooling and Capitalism*, RKP, London.

Kolind, L (1994) 'Thinking the Unthinkable', *Focus on Change Management*, 3, 4–7.

Latour, B (1988) '*The Prince* for Machines as well as Machinations', in Elliott, B (ed.), *Technology and Social Process*, Edinburgh University Press, Edinburgh.

Latour, B (1993) *We Have Never Been Modern*, Harvester Wheatsheaf, Hemel Hempstead.

Law, J (ed.) (1986) *Power, Action and Belief*, RKP, London.

Law, J (ed.) (1991) *A Sociology of Monsters*, Routledge, London.

Leucke, R A. (1994) *Scuttle Your Ships Before Advancing*, Oxford University Press, Oxford.

Levitas, R (1990) *The Concept of Utopia*, Simon Schuster, Hertford.

Ligus, R G (1993) 'Methods to Help Re-engineer Your Company for Improved Agility', *Industrial Engineering*, January.

Lindblom, C (1959) 'The Science of Muddling Through', *Public Administration Review*, 19, 79–99.

Marshall, R (1993) *Storm from the East*, BBC, London.

Morris, D and Brandon, J (1993) *Re-engineering Your Business*, McGraw-Hill, New York.

Mitchell, J and Parris, H (1983) *The Politics and Government of Britain*, Open University Press, Milton Keynes.

Noble, D (1983) 'Present Tense Technology', *Democracy*, Spring, 8–27.

Obeng, E and Crainer, S (1994) *Making Re-engineering Happen*, Pitman, London

Olson, M (1982) *The Rise and Decline of Nations*, Yale University Press, New Haven, Conn.

Padulo, R (1994) *Re-engineering Management Learning*, Templeton College Management Research Paper.

Peter, L J and Hull, R (1970) *The Peter Principle*, Pan Books, London.

Pick, D (1993) *War Machine: The Rationalization of Slaughter in the Modern Age*, Yale University Press, London.

Randall, A J (1990) 'New Languages or Old? Labour, Capital and Discourse in the Industrial Revolution', *Social History*, 15(2), 195–216.

Roethlisberger, F J & Dickson, W J (1947) *Management and the Worker*, Harvard University Press, Cambridge, Mass.

Rose, N (1990) *Governing the Soul*, Routledge, London.

Shils, E A & Janowitz, M (1948) 'Cohesion and Disintegration of the Wermacht in World War II', *Public Opinion Quarterly*, 12, 280–315.

Simon, H A (1947) *Administrative Behaviour*, Macmillan, New York.

Smail, J (1987) 'New Languages for Labour and Capital: The Transformation of Discourse in the Early Years of the Industrial Revolution', *Social History*, 12(1), 49–71.

Smail, J (1991) 'New Languages? Yes Indeed: A Reply to Adrian Randall', *Social History,* 16(2), 217–222.

Smith, A (1974) *The Wealth of Nations*, Penguin, Harmondsworth.

Tisdall, S (1993) 'America Wrestles with Its Identity', *The Guardian*, 18 September.

Trotsky, L (1969) *The Permanent Revolution*, Pathfinder Press, New York.

Wallerstein, I (1983) *Historical Capitalism*, Verso, London.

Weber, M (1978) *Economy and Society*, University of California Press, Berkeley, Calif.

Zuboff, S (1989) *In the Age of the Smart Machine: The Future of Work and Power*, Heinemann, London.

6

RETHINKING BUSINESS PROCESS RE-ENGINEERING: A SOCIAL CONSTRUCTIONIST PERSPECTIVE

Ranjit Tinaikar, Amir Hartman and Raghu Nath,
University of Pittsburgh

INTRODUCTION

Given the rapidly changing environment, the organizations of today are forced to generate equally fast responses in order to survive and prosper. What is needed, it seems, is a view of planned change that makes the organization more responsive to environmental shifts. Business Process Re-engineering (BPR) is propounded by many as the solution to this fundamental need. In the past few years BPR has come to take an increasingly prominent position in the practitioner's world. It is touted by many as the panacea to the problems of the 'new' organization. As such it behoves us – the academic community – to cast a critical eye on BPR before jumping onto the proverbial bandwagon.

In this chapter we first present an analysis of contemporary BPR literature to justify our allegation of its narrow Tayloristic perspective and lack of theory. Then we argue for a broader and more balanced approach through a social constructionist perspective, and offer an alternative definition of BPR through the same. Finally, we discuss the implications of such a broader definition of BPR.

ANALYSIS OF BPR LITERATURE

That BPR is a 'hot topic' is an understatement. Over the past three years there has been a plethora of articles dealing with this subject. To provide a basis for the analysis of the BPR phenomenon, we undertook an examination of the articles dealing with the topic in the three years, 1991 through 1993. In an attempt to better understand the vast amount of literature on the subject, we characterized the articles along the following dimensions

- **Attitude towards BPR:** In what light did the author(s) view BPR? Was BPR seen to be a positive or negative endeavour, or were the authors more cautious and neutral in their advocacy? (*Positive/Neutral/Negative*)
- **Values of BPR:** What were the values privileged by BPR? This was measured by categorizing the objectives and constraints of BPR as stated by the author(s). (*Technical/Social*)
- **Role of information technology:** Did information technology play an integral part of the BPR effort? (*Yes/No*)
- **Voice of article:** In what voice does the article present BPR? (*Academic/Practitioner*) and (*Normative/Narrative*)

For us to get a fair sampling of contemporary BPR literature we referred to the widely used database of ABI/Inform. We searched the database on the keywords 'Business Process Re-engineering', 'Business Process Redesign' and 'Process Innovation' and obtained a preliminary list of 468 articles. However, 70 were found to be duplicates, which left 398 articles for analysis. Of these 398 articles, 150 were screened out of our analysis as they were found not to be pertaining to BPR – 14 out of the 150 were book reviews and the remaining did not deal with the subject of Business Process Re-engineering. The remaining 248 articles were then coded by content analysing their abstracts along the dimensions listed above.

The articles were content analysed independently by two of the authors. Seventeen of the articles generated disagreement between the two coders. Further discussions and joint analysis were conducted under the purview of a third person to arrive at a commonly understood characterization of these articles. Through such analysis, a number of interesting facts were brought to light.

1. The number of articles published each year has increased exponentially from 18 in 1991, to 43 in 1992 and 187 in 1993. This is evidence that BPR is being increasingly accepted and advocated by the corporate world. However, the fact that only two of the 248 articles seemed to be in the academic tradition (Grover *et al.*, 1992; Henderson and Venkatraman, 1993) reaffirms the need for a greater effort on the part of academics to participate in an issue seemingly so important to the practising world. The lack of a concerted theory-building effort in BPR is a problem given the fact that one of the primary objectives of the academic business community is to describe and prescribe business practice, or more precisely, to be of some social value.

2. The articles were further analysed along a normative/narrative dimension. Our analysis showed that BPR literature was evenly split between narrative and normative (55.25–44.75 per cent). Most of the narrative articles were cases (88 per cent) which included case histo-

ries and anecdotal experiences of real organizations serving as exemplars – or more accurately propaganda – promoting BPR. The normative articles consisted predominantly of checklists of guidelines for success.

3. Another useful finding was the overwhelmingly positive attitude towards BPR: 98.8 per cent of the articles presented BPR in a positive light. Phrases such as 'Businesses should be "re-engineered," and the power of modern information technology should be used to redesign business processes to achieve dramatic improvements in performance' (Hammer, 1990: 104) were quite common. This unquestioned acceptance of the utility of BPR, along with the above finding, begs for a more circumspective and theoretical work in the future.

4. Information technology was commonly promoted as the harbinger of hope in many of the discussions: 51.2 per cent of all the articles referred to the role of IT in BPR as integral to success. Although the importance of IT in BPR cannot be contested, the role and the impact on the human agent seems to have taken a back seat.

5. Perhaps the most striking issue is that of the values (social and/or technical) most privileged in BPR. Almost all of the articles (95.9 per cent) portray BPR as being concerned with only technical issues. The few articles discussing social issues such as empowerment of the lower levels, resistance to change, etc, focused primarily on the managerially relevant benefits of BPR. Cost-cutting through technology and downsizing, or the politically correct 'rightsizing', were some of the most common themes. However, the implications of this potential job loss through BPR were singularly neglected. The cumulative tradition of academia should play a very crucial role in helping to provide a more equitable balance.

In the light of the above findings we made the following conclusions regarding the who, why and how of BPR. BPR is a purely *top-down* approach to restructuring organizations in order to increase *efficiency* on the basis of *technical* design criteria. In this sense the principles of BPR are no different from the principles of Scientific Management espoused by Frederick Taylor in the early part of this century.

CONTRASTING THE IMAGES OF ORGANIZATIONAL PROCESSES

The great change that organizations are witnessing requires modern managers and researchers to free themselves of restrictive norms of tradition. However, in spite of the wealth of evidence pointing towards a rapid transformation in business activity, contemporary management thought still stays restricted by the dogma of technocracy. The process revolution, which was introduced as one of the answers to the rapidly transforming environment, is in no way free from this dogma. In fact, through BPR we seem to be reinforcing it.

The Tayloristic approach to processes, which seems to be guiding contemporary process thinking, is derived from disciplines such as Industrial Engineering, Cybernetics, Decision Theory, Communications Theory, Economics and Artificial Intelligence, which are heavily steeped in rationalism. It emphasizes the task-related aspects of processes and ignores the human performing the task. The task comes before the human and any discussion of the human is relevant only in his [*sic*] capacity to perform the task. This total lack of consideration of the 'human' aspects of organizational processes serves to mechanize the activities involved in a process, and trivialize human agency. Though Hammer and Champy (1993) briefly discuss the importance of culture, they conveniently leave it to the discretion of the knowledgeable 'softer' scientist.

In what follows below, we contrast technocracy with a more humanistic social perspective, and show how the latter provides a richer and more realistic conceptualization of organizational processes. This in turn will be used to introduce a broader definition of BPR.

TECHNOCRACY AND ORGANIZATIONAL PROCESSES

The instrumental bias which is predominant in BPR literature leads to an inflexible characterization of organizational processes and creates particular technical images of the process – *process as a converter of commodities* and *process itself as a commodity*.

Process as a Converter of Commodities

This view holds the process as a conduit for the conversion of commodities. Organizational processes are a well-defined sequence of activities involved in the attainment of certain well-defined goals (Scherr, 1993). These commodities may be either tangible (widgets) or intangible (information). Either way, they are assumed to have an objective existence. The process itself has a passive existence, in that it serves as an instrument to convert the inputs into outputs.

This view of processes has its origins in Taylor's *Principles of Scientific Management* (1914) and has culminated into the guiding principles of modern day Industrial Engineering. Davenport and Short (1990) in fact describe BPR as the forerunner of the modern-day industrial engineering. Re-engineering processes on these tenets gives primacy to design and tends to ignore implementation practicality. For it is assumed that all individuals performing the various tasks involved in the process, share the unitary goals laid down by the management and operate under conditions of high certainty while performing their tasks. This leads to viewing the process as a linear sequence of antecedent–consequent relationships (Boland, 1979). It is conveniently forgotten that the humans performing the tasks may derive certain meanings and satisfaction for the tasks they work on.

A technocratic vision of the process leads to efficiency as the basic criterion driving the role of the process re-engineer, a fact that is clearly seen in our analysis of the literature. As such, the process re-engineer's role gets reduced to looking for the most efficient conversion path and the primary constraint faced is the capacity of the technology used (Davenport, 1993). We argue that such an approach emphasizes the needs and expectations of only one of the social stakeholders – the upper management who initiate the re-engineering project. Using efficiency as a primary criterion for re-engineering may lead to disastrous results in implementation success. This may perhaps explain the fact that nearly 80 per cent of all BPR projects end in failure (Bashein *et al.*, 1993).

Process as a Commodity

This view treats the process itself as a commodity with a value that can be objectively measured. This perspective assumes a commonly understood purpose for the process. The process is then valued on the extent to which it is effective in attaining this goal. Thus effectiveness becomes the primary criterion for the evaluation of a process. This view is echoed by Davenport (1993) when he identifies the various process selection criteria:

> We have identified four criteria that may guide process selection: 1) the process's centrality to the execution of the firm's business strategy, 2) process health, 3) process qualification, and 4) manageable project scope. (Davenport, 1993: 32)

As seen, all the criteria seem to have an objective existence and imply a commonly understood goal for the process. In fact, one may also notice that all the criteria seem to have a managerial top-down perspective with no consideration for the human actually performing the task. In fact Davenport (1993) explicitly calls for a top-down implementation of the process vision. The consideration of the human if any is only as an object of control – another element in the cybernetic system. However, organizational processes often help embody many of the social needs of organizational members and may have different and even conflicting values to various stakeholders.

SOCIAL CONSTRUCTIONISM AND ORGANIZATIONAL PROCESSES

We have so far argued for the lack of consideration of the 'human' aspects in BPR. We choose to make salient these human aspects through the social constructionist perspective. As an approach to the study of the 'social', social constructionism (SC) represents an important tradition. It is a tradition in the social sciences which encompasses many a 'theory', such as ethnomethodology, hermeneutics, symbolic interactionism and others. We use the term SC to mean a perspective rather than a theory or method of enquiry. Fundamentally, SC describes the way reality is created and maintained by social actors, as opposed to the traditional view that reality objectively exists in nature and that we must simply discover it. The view of organizational processes as socially constructed gives rise to quite a different image of processes: *process as socially constructed*.

Process as Socially Constructed

Berger and Luckmann (1966) are often credited with crystallizing this school of thought. They see social construction to be made up of three processes: externalization (the process by which social understandings are concretized through normative determination of performance, behaviour and other social artefacts), objectification (the process by which these understandings are given an objective and unquestionable status in society), and internalization (the process of maintenance of these realities through socializing mechanisms like education, incentives and sanctions, etc) (Quaid, 1993).

Although SC has its fair share of diversity and disagreement regarding these 'tenets', it is generally agreed upon that meaning or reality creation is seen to be a social act. That is not to say that reality is only a social construction by humans – there are theorists within the SC community that accept the reality of tangible, physical and structural constraints (Fine, 1984) – but rather that meanings or realities have a large social aspect to them. Within the administrative sciences, similar perspectives have been used (Smircich, 1983; Boland, 1979). Such foundational concepts as constructed or negotiated meaning, structural and physical constraints, and symbol, afford us with a perspective for the study of organizations. And given SC's concentration on how meanings are created, maintained, and possibly differ between various stakeholders, it seems ripe for use in the study of organizational change such as BPR. With such premises in mind, an SC perspective leads to quite a different image of organizational processes.

From the SC perspective, organizational processes are socially constructed. In other words they are defined in terms of the meanings attributed to them by the social actors. While most of BPR thinking seems to focus on the technical core of the process, they ignore that the process lies in a certain social context which varies across and within organizations. The humans interacting with the process make sense of it on the basis of this context and construct – so to speak – an outer shell of meanings round the inner technical core of the process. And it is this constructed process through which the organizational members appropriate symbolic meaning.

Re-engineering organizational processes invariably changes the patterns of social interactions and thus changes the inherent meaning carried by the process. Therefore the process re-engineer's role and the extent to which other organizational members interpret their actions puts them at the centre of organizational accountability. More than anyone else, they must understand and take advantage of the organization's structure of shared meanings (Boland, 1979).

Given the state of knowledge in the area of BPR, and the focus on technocratic values, it is obvious that an overall framework or model that organizes our view of the subject is needed. The notion of organizational processes as socially constructed and not simply technical systems leads to an alternative view of BPR. The objective of this effort was not to develop an explicit theory of BPR but rather to provide a conceptual basis for driving future research and practice. In the following section we shall present an alternative definition of BPR.

REDEFINING BPR

In the light of the above discussion, we propose that:

> BPR is the *reconstruction* of organizational processes through a *mutually integrated effort* by various organizational coalitions to achieve and maintain *negotiated improvements*.

Reconstruction emphasizes that BPR is an intentional effort to restructure or change a 'constructed' process. It highlights the social dimensions involved in the creation and maintenance of organizational processes, ie relationships of processes, technology, people, objects, etc, and how change in such relationships impacts much more than organizational efficiency. Reconstruction also broadens the notion of design variables beyond the technical/objective sense-making mechanisms of the managerial control system to the other more social/subjective sense-making mechanisms used by the workers performing the task. While we are not maintaining that meanings can or should be arbitrarily controlled, we do feel that there is an added dimension, the social construction of reality, which the constituents must be sensitive to.

BPR literature tends to view the process management goals as the sole driving force behind business process re-engineering. The decision to re-engineer is, in this sense, more or less unilateral and is accepted by the rest of the organization with little or no questioning. Our definition, on the other hand, broadens the social world beyond just the management, the re-engineer and the customer to include the worker who, arguably, is most impacted.

Mutually integrated effort acknowledges the existence of a greater diversity of perspectives to be considered in the re-engineering effort. It should not simply be initiated and adopted unilaterally by the top management with no consideration of the workers' needs and expectations. Since BPR not only impacts on the managers and customers of the process but also on the participating workers, it should be an effort planned for, agreed upon and undertaken by all those who will have a stake in the matter.

This mutually integrated effort should move towards what we call *negotiated improvements*. Different coalitions construct different meanings for processes. Management tends to evaluate processes on much more instrumental and 'objective' criteria such as profitability, efficiency, cycle time, etc, while the process worker will evaluate it in terms of more 'subjective' criteria such as satisfaction, self-esteem, quality of work life, stress, etc. Furthermore, process re-engineering involves social disruptions which may range from the moderate (change of work structures) to the acute (loss of job). Therefore the new process design and design objectives should find an acceptable compromise between managerial objectives and workers' expectations through the negotiation of divergent 'meanings' and language.

DISCUSSION AND RESEARCH IMPLICATIONS

SC contends that social interactions mediate what is and what is not meaningful to the social actors. These commonly understood meanings thus provide the forces of cohesion within a social coalition. People often times, especially within an organization, belong to more than one social coalition at any time, and just as the meanings serve to coallesce social actors, the diversity of meanings among the various social coalitions may also be the source of many conflicts. BPR, to a large extent, is a result of the social interactions between three social groups or coalitions – workers, re-engineers and management. It should be noted that although organizational roles and authority structures may play an important role in deciding the members of these coalitions, our description of the coalitions goes beyond the formalized duties. Given this new perspective, important questions arise.

What is the Role of the Process Re-engineer?

The process re-engineer as depicted in contemporary BPR literature is expected to assume the role of a technocratic systems expert who implements the managerially mandated process vision. Hammer and Champy (1993) even go on to coin the term re-engineering *Czar* – a clear indication of a top-down (almost dictatorial) approach. However, the re-engineer may choose to take a completely antithetical stance and assume an emancipatory role to further the cause of the workers so as to give greater credence to the workers' social realities (Hirschheim *et al.*, 1991). We advocate that the re-engineer should play the role of an 'integrator' between the workers working close to the process, who use more subjective sense-making mechanisms, and the more distant managers.

The contention of this chapter has been that the process designer has an ethical obligation not to subject the workers in business processes to excessive stress due to the disruption of the meaningful environment in which (s)he operates (Boland, 1979).

What Does this Mean for Process Re-engineering?

The technical view of organizational processes described throughout this chapter, has given birth to an overly rationalistic approach to BPR methodologies. This is reflected in the unnatural distinction between the design and implementation phases in BPR (Davenport, 1993; Hammer and Champy, 1993).

From the perspective of the 'constructed' process, none of the various steps involved in these frameworks can be sequentially separated from each other. Since an integrated re-engineering effort considers the needs and expectations of both the workers and managers, the resulting design will be a negotiated compromise between all the parties concerned. In this sense, implementation issues will need to be considered during the design phase. Consequently, re-engineering methodologies which allow for greater democratic interaction between the workers, managers and the re-engineers will be needed throughout the process.

CONCLUSION

This chapter provides a perspective on BPR which may not be as glamorous as the one propounded by Hammer and Champy (1993) and Davenport (1993), but which does provide some recommendations which may reduce BPR failures in the future. We have shown that BPR, as described by its proponents, is in many ways similar to Scientific Management as propounded by Taylor some 80 years ago. Furthermore, we have tried to make the case for a more well-grounded or theoretical foundation to BPR. In summary, we should note that this is not a righteous call for the total rejection of BPR, but rather an attempt to encourage a more balanced approach through greater circumspection to the study and practice of process redesign. The perspective of social constructionism is but an attempt to encourage the consideration of alternative perspectives in BPR. It is a call for re-engineering 'Re-engineering'.

REFERENCES

Bashein, B J, Markus, M L and Riley, P (1993) *Business Process Re-engineering: What Does the Literature Say?*, Information Science Application Center, The Claremont Graduate School.

Berger, P and Luckmann, T (1966) *The Social Construction of Reality*, Doubleday, Garden City, NJ.

Boland, R (1979) 'Control, Causality and Information Systems Requirement', *Accounting Organizations and Society*, 4, 259–272.

Davenport, T H (1993) *Process Innovation: Re-engineering Work Through Information Technology*, Harvard Business School Press, Boston, Mass.

Fine, G A (1984) 'Negotiated Orders and Organizational Cultures', *Annual Review of Sociology*, 10.

Grover, V, Teng, J T C and Fiedler, K D (1993) 'Information Technology Enabled Business Process Redesign: An Integrated Planning Framework', *Omega International Journal of Management Science*, 21(4), 433–447.

Hammer, M (1990) 'Re-engineering Work: Don't Automate, Obliterate', *Harvard Business Review*, July–August, 104–112.

Hammer, M and Champy, J (1993) *Re-engineering the Corporation: A Manifesto for Business Revolution*, Harper-Collins, New York.

Henderson, J C and Venkatraman, N (1993) 'Strategic Alignment', *IBM Systems Journal*, 32(1), 4–16.

Hirschheim, R J, Klein R, Newman (1991) 'The Four Paradigms of Information Systems Development', *Communications of the ACM*, September.

Pfeffer, J (1981) 'Management as Symbolic Action', in Cummings, L L and Staw, B M (eds), *Research in Organizational Behavior*, Vol. 3, Greenwich, Conn.

Quaid, M (1993) 'Job Evaluation as Institutional Myth', *Journal of Management Studies*, 30(2), 239–260.

Scherr, A L (1993) 'A New Approach to Business Processes', *IBM Systems Journal*, 32(1), 80–98.

Smircich, L (1983) 'Organizations as Shared Meanings', in Pondy, L, Frost, P, Morgan, G and Dandridge T (eds), *Organizational Symbolism*, JAI Press, Greenwich, Conn.

Taylor, F W (1911) *Scientific Management*, Harper, New York.

7

IT AND ORGANIZATIONAL CHANGE: WHERE DOES BPR FIT IN?*

R D Galliers, Warwick Business School

INTRODUCTION

Contrast, if you will, the views expressed by proponents of Information Technology (IT), enabled business process redesign (BPR) or business innovation and those successful chief executive officers (CEOs) who have set in place the vision and strategy to achieve major change and improved results for their companies – sometimes quite dramatically – in the global marketplace. The contrast is an enlightening one which should help us to understand the crucial issues associated with strategy formation and implementation – the management of change in other words – and to locate the role of IT in that change process.

In an interview with the Whirlpool CEO David Whitwam, reported in a recent edition of the *Harvard Business Review* (Maruca, 1994), the major components of change in 'going global' are identified as: defining and communicating a vision; objectives and market philosophy combined into a unifying focus worldwide leading to common processes and systems; a focus on the customer; a realization that were we to stick 'to the path we were on, the future would be neither pleasant nor profitable' (p.137), and a *slow* process of communication and persuasion to get managers to buy into globalization 'thinking global but acting local'

> You can't expect it to happen overnight. Bear in mind that we have many, many employees in our manufacturing plants and offices who have been with us for 25 or 30 years. They didn't sign up to be part of a global experience ... Suddenly we give them new things to think about and new people to work with. We tell people at all levels that the old way of doing

---

*   A version of this chapter is to appear in W Baets and R D Galliers, eds, *Information and the 21st Century Organization: Organizational Innovation and Transformation*.

business is too cumbersome. Changing a company's approach to doing business is a difficult thing to accomplish in [a single country], let alone globally. (Maruca, 1994: 139–140)

Ways of achieving such major change include helping employees own both the change itself and the process of change, by giving them authority and responsibility to see through aspects of the overall change, and to compensate them based on their performance in so doing.

Note that the emphasis is on understanding customer requirements, defining a new vision, and communicating and implementing it through people. Changed processes and systems in all the different company locations – greater commonality – are part of the process (and an integral part at that), but the focus is on people. There is hardly a mention of IT in the whole interview.

Contrast this with the following extracts from Davenport's (1993) book *Process Innovation: Re-engineering Work through Information Technology.* While acknowledging that 'information and IT are rarely sufficient to bring about process change; most process innovations are enabled by a combination of IT, information and organizational/human resource changes' (p.95), the central role of IT in the process is virtually unquestioned. For example, '... the use of IT for process innovation [is] a virtual necessity' (p.44) and 'although it is theoretically possible to bring about widespread process innovation without the use of [IT], we know of no such examples. IT is both an enabler and implementer of process change' (pp.300–301).

This chapter attempts to locate an appropriate role for IT in BPR. While recognizing that it may well have a role to play, along with other drivers for change, this chapter questions IT's centrality in the process. For BPR to be taken seriously, for the proportion of BPR success stories to improve from the current low level of 30 per cent or so, a more balanced, holistic stance has to be taken. This is the contribution that this chapter attempts to make: to present a case for a more holistic and even–handed stance on BPR which sees the process as a learning experience requiring ongoing assessment and review, which emphasizes the need to develop and communicate a shared vision, leading to a review of existing structures and processes, but which takes account of customer requirements and the values, expectations and viewpoints of those whose job it will be to implement the change.* In a nutshell, the argument is for a refocusing of our attention from strategy formulation to strategy *implementation* and from IT-induced business change to the *incorporation* of IT considerations, in a more balanced way, into that change process.

---

* This argument has since been echoed by Julian Watts in an editorial to the journal *Business Change and Re-engineering* (Watts, 1993)

The chapter looks first at the question of radical versus incremental change and places BPR in the context of developments in our thinking regarding business strategy. Given the much vaunted radical new thinking which, or so it is claimed, underpins BPR, the outcome of the following analysis may come as a surprise. Our analysis suggests that BPR, as currently practised and discussed in the literature, far from being a new departure, is in fact a reversion to the classical school of strategic thinking popularized in the 1960s.

In line with the above arguments, the chapter then presents a holistic framework for BPR which incorporates IT considerations but does not place IT centre stage. As a result of this analysis, it presents a process by which business innovation may be achieved. The process should not be seen as a prescriptive methodology, but is introduced more as an *aide-mémoire* for the kind of considerations that should be incorporated into change projects of this kind. Any thought that all innovation should take precisely the same route should be banished from one's thinking at the outset. Each situation we face is unique and should be treated as such. The kind of issues we need to incorporate into our treatment of the topic can be identified, however, and this chapter aims to do just that.

RADICAL VS INCREMENTAL CHANGE

Davenport (1993), in arguing for radical change rather than incremental change, suggests that this is the only means of obtaining the order-of magnitude improvements necessary in today's global marketplace. In the face of intense competition '… quality initiatives and continuous, incremental improvement, though still essential, will no longer be sufficient'(p.1). In addition, he discounts existing approaches as being unable to deliver the scale of improvement necessary: ' Existing approaches to meeting customer needs are so functionally based that incremental change will *never* yield the requisite interdependence' (p.4, emphasis added).

Both these central tenets of his argument are highly contentious, as we shall see. First, let us consider the question of radical versus incremental change. Davenport (p.11) provides a summary of what he sees as the key distinguishing features of the two philosophies. This is reproduced as Table 7.1.

The first point of contention is the starkness of the contrast presented by Table 7.1. One could certainly question whether it is indeed the case that all incremental change is characterized by a focus on existing processes, a short period of intervention and a bottom-up, functionally-based approach, all informed by statistical data and motivated by a perceived need for greater control. Quinn's (1980) theory of logical incrementalism, for example, suggests that while we need to take account of the current circumstances in effecting change (as does BPR for that matter), we do not have to use as a basis for our analysis existing processes or structures.

Table 7.1 The characteristics of process improvement and process innovation compared

	Improvement	**Innovation**
Level of change	Incremental	Radical
Starting point	Existing processes	Clean slate
Frequency of change	One time, continuous	One time
Time required	Short	Long
Participation	Bottom-up	Top-down
Typical scope	Narrow, functional	Cross-functional
Risk	Moderate	High
Primary enabler	Statistical control	IT
Type of change	Cultural	Cultural, structural

Amended from Davenport 1993: 11

Similarly, Checkland's (1981) soft systems methodology enables us to base our analysis on the processes (he uses the term activities) that are required to achieve a defined objective (formulated in what he terms a root definition) which can represent a minor or major departure from the current situation, depending on what is perceived as relevant and appropriate. In addition, it is often the case that the scope of the analysis is broad and almost certainly cross-functional because, almost by definition, a narrowly-focused, functionally-based analysis is likely to be asystemic!

In addition, Senn (1992) reminds us that it is often the case that, in situations where IT has been the catalyst for change, radical improvement in competitive standing may have risen from *incremental* change in *existing* information systems (IS) or their application. Clemons (1986) questions the sustainability of any competitive advantage that may have been brought about by IT, unless it is accompanied by improved skills and knowledge on the part of the firm concerned, with the IS being embedded into new business practice, thereby rendering it more difficult for competitors simply to replicate what has been achieved.

A second point of departure from the analysis of many an advocate of BPR is that radical change will be required in every case. Notwithstanding evidence that suggests radical improvements can be achieved through incremental change (Senn, 1992), it appears to be almost self-evident that periods of change need to be followed by periods of relative stability during which time the change is being put into effect. Lewin's ('unfreezing', 'change', 'refreezing') analysis is apposite in this context (Lewin,

1951). This is not to say that no change should occur in the refreezing era; organizations will always need to adapt to the changing circumstances and environments in which they operate.

But there is an even more subtle, but no less crucial, point about the nature of change and stability that seems to have been overlooked in the rush to BPR:

> Change is ubiquitous. Or is it? In the micro-events which surround our particular lives and in the daily trumpetings of the media change has an ever-present illusion of reality. Yet observe other men consciously attempting to move large and small systems in different directions, or attempt it yourself, and one sees what a difficult and complicated human process change is. And there is the problem of perspective. Where we sit not only influences where we stand, but also what we see. No observer of life or form begins with his mind a blank, to be gradually filled with evidence. Time itself sets a frame of reference for what changes are seen and how those changes are explained. The more we look at present-day events the easier it is to identify change; the longer we stay with an emergent process and further back we go to disentangle its origins, the more we can identify continuities. Empirically and theoretically, change and continuity need one another ... Change and continuity, process and structure, are inextricably linked. (Pettigrew, 1985: 1)

BPR IN THE CONTEXT OF BUSINESS STRATEGY

In one of the more thoughtful contributions to the topic of business strategy, Whittington (1993) identifies four major schools of thought which have characterized developments in our understanding of the topic since the 1960s. These he labels classical, processual, evolutionary and systemic. He locates the four generic approaches on the kind of two-by-two grid (Figure 7.1) now all too familiar to us all.

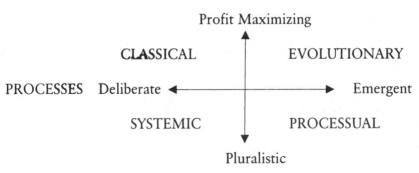

Figure 7.1   Four approaches to business strategy

The underlying philosophy of the *classical* approach is the kind of self-interest identified by Adam Smith in his *Wealth of Nations*. Formal, deliberate plans are the result of rational analysis. Competition is the watchword. Similarly, the *evolutionary* approach has as its objective, survival in the jungle that is the marketplace. It takes a more fatalistic view of the world: organizations are unable to anticipate and respond to environmental changes, it is the market itself that makes the choices. The best one can hope to do is optimize the current fit between one's organization and the business environment, and hope that this will lead to survival. The *processual* school also takes a fairly pragmatic view of the world. Here, the argument is that strategy emerges, not from the marketplace, but as a result of individual actions, which are themselves a series of compromises. Given the complexity of the environment, all that one can hope to do is to adapt to changing circumstances and to pursue an objective of satisficing. The *systemic* school of thought is more recent, and more optimistic in its outlook. While it recognizes the plurality in desired outcomes, it also recognizes that these are sociologically sensitive, that cultural influences will play a major part in their determination. Table 7.2 provides an overviewing of the key features of the four generic approaches to strategy.

Table 7.2 Key aspects of the four schools of strategic thought

	Classical	Processual	Evolutionary	Systemic
Strategy	Formal	Crafted	Efficient	Embedded
Rationale	Profit maximization	Vague	Survival	Local
Focus	Planning	Internal politics	Environment	Culture, society
Processes	Analytical	Bargaining, learning	Keep options open	Social fit
Key influences	Economics	Psychology	Economics biology	Sociology
Key period	1960s	1970s	1980s	1990s

Amended from Whittington 1993: 40

If we analyse the underlying philosophy of BPR, we can see immediately that it fits most closely with the classical school. Profit maximization is the key; little thought is given to more pluralistic outcomes; there is little concern for cultural, contextual issues other than to deal with them as obstacles to change; the process is a deliberate one – a rational analysis (undertaken by senior executives) of the key business processes in line with a shared business vision that meets customer requirements.

It seems, then, that our radical new departure from the staid approaches of yore is in fact more of a rerun of the classical approaches of the 1960s! And given that the major features that, or so it is claimed, distinguish BPR from existing approaches turn out to be not so clear-cut after all, one is left to ponder whether there is anything special or even helpful about the process, especially when so little is provided in terms of advice regarding the *implementation* of the (radical) change.

BPR IN CONTEXT: TOWARDS A HOLISTIC FRAMEWORK

But let us not 'throw out the baby with the bathwater'. If we take into account its limitations and place BPR in the context of current thinking on both strategy and change, we can utilize the most useful features of the approach to good effect. If, at the same time, we remember to incorporate information and IT into our consideration of the topic, we might avoid the myopia that all too often exists when treating strategy and change from the sole perspective of marketing and strategic management on the one hand, or organizational behaviour on the other.*

One way of placing BPR in this broader context is to reflect on the lessons brought to us by the socio-technical school (eg the work of the Tavistock Institute of Human Relations soon after the end of the Second World War) and by Leavitt (1965). Leavitt's so-called 'diamond' reminds us that any change in process, for example, is likely to have an impact elsewhere in the socio-technical system framework that can be used to describe an organization. An amendment to the original framework proposed by Leavitt which takes into account the cultural issues brought to our attention by proponents of the *systemic* school of strategic thinking (eg Granovetter, 1985; Whitley, 1991) is provided as Figure 7.2.

---

* It is so often the case that our treatment of the subject of strategy and change is considered from the perspective of a particular discipline only. We seem to be imprisoned in our own disciplinary base. Strategy is, or so it is often argued, the domain of marketing; change that of organizational behaviour. In addition, when reading any well-known text on strategy or organizational change, how often do the topics of information and IT get considered? And if they are considered, the treatment is likely to be either superficial or, at the other extreme, filled with hyperbole, with IT being seen as the key to organizational success! A more balanced, multidisciplinary view (something that the BPR literature is beginning to hint at) is rare indeed.

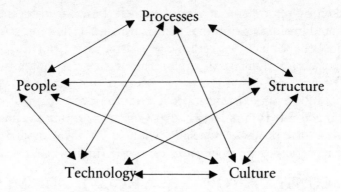

Figure 7.2 Amended version of Leavitt's 'diamond'

What this analysis suggests is that BPR should be seen as but one aspect of the socio-technical approach implied by the early work of Leavitt (1965). Our focus should not be on process alone, neither should it depend solely on the opportunities provided by new technology. The assessment should certainly take these into account, but in addition should understand the cultural context in which strategy is being formulated and change is to be implemented. It also needs to take into account the art of the possible ... and this understanding will come in part from an assessment of the implications for organizational structure and the attitudes and beliefs of all relevant stakeholders, both internal to the firm and outside of it.

A SOCIO-TECHNICAL APPROACH TO BPR

Given the above analysis, a socio-technical approach to business strategy formation and organizational change which incorporates IS considerations and aspects of the BPR philosophy but does not place IT centre stage, nor assumes that change will be necessarily radical and processual, would seem to hold out some promise. The approach is summarized as Figure 7.3.

While the approach might at first sight be placed towards the deliberate half of the horizontal spectrum of Figure 7.1, it nevertheless attempts to incorporate emergent thinking in addition. In the context of the vertical spectrum, it is located towards the pluralistic pole rather than meekly assuming that the outcome is purely about profit maximization.

The approach also incorporates the kind of thinking championed by de Gues (1988) among others in that it views the strategy formation and implementation process as being concerned with learning (as a result of a review of both the intended and unintended impacts of previous actions – planned and unplanned), and uses the creation of scenarios as a means of considering alternative actions, and reviewing taken-for-granted assumptions about the business and its environment (see also Schnaars, 1987; Galliers, 1993).

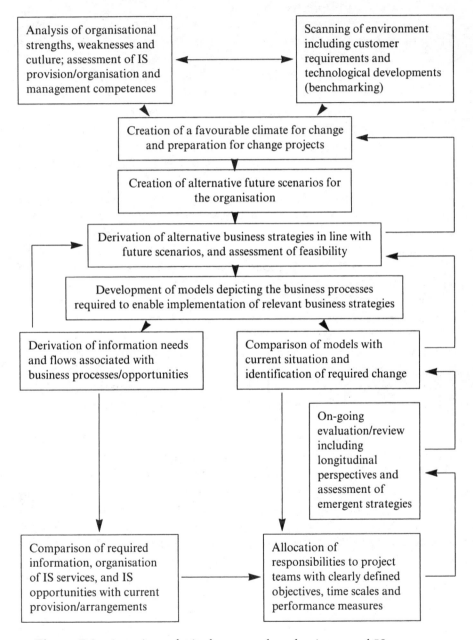

Figure 7.3 A socio-technical approach to business and IS strategy formation and the management of organizational transformation
Source: Amended from Galliers 1993: 206 and 1994: 6

Based on the work of Checkland (1981), the approach described below also takes into account Lewin's (1951) analysis that a period of change requires the creation of a favourable climate in which change *can* take place ('unfreezing'), followed by a period in which the required change is set in place ('freezing'). A number of feedback loops have been incorporated into the process in order to indicate that it is essentially an iterative one which builds upon past experiences and an evaluation of both intended and unintended consequences of the changes that are being implemented, and the changing nature of the business (and technological) environment in which the organization is operating. The iterative nature of the approach assists the recognition that strategy is, to some extent at least, emergent (cf. Figure 7.1). As a result, the process is designed to aid the kind of organizational learning advocated by Argyris and Schön (1978).

As we have seen, key stakeholders have to be favourably disposed to change for change strategies to have any real chance of success. There is a tendency in much of the BPR literature to view BPR as a process instigated by senior executives and often orchestrated by external consultants. This is not the only mode of operation, nor is it always likely to lead to a motivated workforce should the change include – as it often does – downsizing and forced redundancy. Indeed, we should be aware that in many firms, the anticipated economic and organizational benefits of downsizing have failed to materialize and that any 'reductions in headcount need to be viewed as part of a process of continuous improvement that includes organizational redesign, along with broad, systemic changes designed to eliminate [redundant processes], waste, and inefficiency' (Cascio, 1993: 95). Downsizing as a sole objective of BPR is likely to be unsuccessful.

The approach being advocated herein has been used to good effect as part of a series of workshops rather than relying on individual interviews. The benefits to be gained from workshops of this kind are well documented (see, for example, Hardaker and Ward, 1987, and Galliers *et al.*, 1994), and include the opportunity to debate contrasting views as an integral part of the process of gaining a shared vision, ie rather than waiting to raise points of debate as an outcome. In the latter instance, such issues remain as obstacles to implementation. In the former, attitudes may well change, and even if they do not, implementation issues can be identified as part of the very process of strategy formulation.

Nevertheless, it is as well to prepare for these workshops in terms of clarifying the nature of such roles as project champion, project manager and facilitator, carefully selecting a team from a range of functional backgrounds, and deciding on the membership of a steering committee (see, for example, Ward, 1990).

A climate in which change is eagerly anticipated is likely to be achieved by a realization that all is not well, for example that competitors are making inroads into one's markets, that key customers are becoming increasingly discontented with one's products and/or services, and that personnel are becoming increasingly frustrated with the way business is conducted. This perceived need for action can be reinforced and harnessed by the process advocated herein. The very analysis of organizational strengths and weaknesses and environmental opportunities and threats, when undertaken by key executives with the involvement of personnel who are responsible for key day-to-day operational activities, can often lead to concerted action and, properly handled, an enthusiastic response to ways and means of dealing with the problems that have thereby been uncovered.

The analysis of the internal and external environments can usefully utilize such tried and tested techniques as SWOT (analysis of strengths, weaknesses, opportunities and threats), PEST (analysis of political, economic, social and technical environments), Porter's (1980; 1985) five forces and value chain analysis, and the like. In addition, however, it is worthwhile, especially in the context of understanding the nature of the IS/IT agenda in all of this, to take stock of the quality of IS provision and the full range of issues associated with the management of IS services.

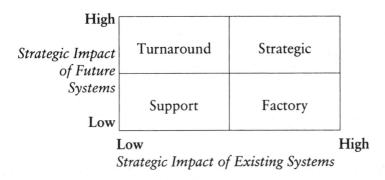

Figure 7.4   McFarlan's (1984) IT strategic grid

The extent to which an organization is dependent on IS can be estimated by the application of McFarlan's (1984) so-called strategic grid, as depicted in Figure 7.4. In addition, an assessment of the appropriateness of an aggressive competitive strategy with respect to the utilization of IS/IT can be made using a similar grid developed by McLaughlin *et al.* (1983), as shown in Figure 7.5.

As indicated by Figure 7.4, having undertaken the kind of analysis advocated by Porter and Millar (1985), for example, it is possible to estimate the value adding potential to the firm of IS/IT. An assessment of the quality of IS resources also needs to be undertaken, however. Organizations with sound IS resources and good business opportunities from the application of IS/IT are clearly in a position to adopt an aggressive stance. Those that have identified only limited opportunities are likely to be relatively safe from attack by competitors even if their IS resources are weak. Conversely, those in a similar position but with sound IS resources may wish quietly to explore the situation further as the business/technological environment changes and/or they uncover a previously hidden opportunity. Should a firm identify considerable value adding potential from IS/IT but have relatively poor resources, there is a requirement to act with due urgency. Such an enterprise is currently in a 'Catch 22' situation, being damned if they do and damned if they don't. An aggressive strategy is likely to be become unstuck since they are likely to lack the capacity – both in technological and human terms – to see it through to a successful conclusion. Inaction is likely to lead to the firm coming under attack from the competition.

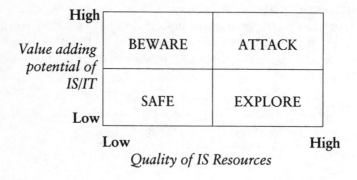

Figure 7.5 Choosing an appropriate IT-based business strategy
Source: McLaughlin et al., 1983

How then can a firm make an assessment of the quality of its IS resources and decide what urgent action it should take? This is not simply an assessment of the strategic impact of IS as in McFarlan's (1984) analysis. A broader evaluation is required and this can be achieved by a development on the well-known 'stages of growth' concept (Gibson and Nolan, 1974; Nolan, 1979) which incorporates the so-called '7S' analysis pioneered by McKinsey and Co. (see, for example, Pascale and Athos, 1981). This broader 'stages of growth' model is described in detail in Galliers and Sutherland (1991) and lessons from its application are recounted in Galliers (1991). It is illustrated in outline in Figure 7.6.

As with other aspects of the approach, we have found that the revised model is best used in a workshop environment where key stakeholders can debate their different perceptions about the current state of affairs since there almost certainly will be different perceptions expressed! It is almost always the case that certain elements of the 7S framework will be at different stages of growth. The resultant profile will help to identify where particular urgent action is required.* In addition, it is almost bound to be the case that different parts of the organization (eg functions, SBUs, sites) will find themselves at different stages of growth and this may well point to different solution/initiatives in different parts of the enterprise.

Placing the current company profile in relation to the profile that existed, say, five years, three years and one year ago can be particularly insightful, as this gives an indication of the rate of progress that has been made, if any. This is an important point. There is no God-given right for firms to move towards the later stages of growth as implied by earlier models. Indeed, it can often be the case that firms may revert to earlier stages. Discussion on the reasons for lack of progress or reversion to earlier stages is particularly enlightening.

Having taken stock of the current (and recent past) situation, it is useful then to consider possible future scenarios (Schnaars, 1987; de Gues, 1988) for the organization as a precursor to considering alternative business strategies that appear to be appropriate in these different contexts. A helpful technique in this aspect of the approach is one developed by the SEMA Group. This considers the future in terms of 'facts' (those elements that are considered to be relatively stable within the planning period), 'heavy trends' (those trends that are thought very likely to continue during the planning period), and 'issues' (those elements over

---

*   For example, in a large multinational chemical company, it was apparent that its current situation could best be described as passing between stages 3 and 4 of the model – except for the fact that a board-level IT director had recently been appointed. In the discussion which ensued, it became clear that his board colleagues had assumed that his appointment was practically all that was needed to move the company rapidly ahead in terms of its strategic use of IT, and to deal with the residual relationship problems between the IS/IT function and the business units typical of stage 3. As a result of the workshop, expectations of the new IT director were revised downwards, and a joint approach, with other members of the board taking responsibility for a number of initiatives, was agreed. The CEO confided later that, had the model not been discussed in the workshop, it would have been highly likely that very little would have been achieved and that the IT director's career would have been in jeopardy within a matter of months! The joint approach that resulted led to a series of initiatives that have already borne fruit.

which there is disagreement or considerable doubt). By building up alternative scenarios by altering the 'issues' while keeping the 'facts' constant and making minor alterations to the 'trends', it is possible to consider alternative strategies in the light of the differing 'futures' thus constructed. It also proves useful to include a counter-intuitive 'future' (ie altering key 'facts') to identify what the firm might do in such unforeseen circumstances.

STAGE ELEMENT	I	II	III	IV	V	VI
STRATEGY	ACQUISITION OF IT (SERVICES)	AUDIT OF IT PROVISION	TOP-DOWN ANALYSIS	INTEGRATION, COORDINATION	STRATEGY LINKAGE	INTERACTIVE PLANNING COLLABORATION
STRUCTURE	INFORMAL	FINANCE CONTROLLED	CENTRALIZED DP DEPT	INFORMATION CENTRE(S)	DEPARTMENTAL COALITIONS	COORDINATED COALITIONS
SYSTEMS	AD HOC, OPERATIONAL ACCOUNTING	GAPS/ DUPLICATION: LARGE BACK-LOG: HEAVY MAINTENANCE	UNCONTROLLED END-USER COMPUTING VERSUS CENTRALIZED SYSTEMS	DECENTRALIZED APPROACH, SOME EXECUTIVE INFORMATION SYSTEMS	COORDINATED CENTRALIZED AND DECENTRALIZED IS; SOME STRATEGIC IS	INTER-ORGANIZATIONAL SYSTEMS: IS/IT-BASED PRODUCTS & SERVICES
STAFF	PROGRAMMERS, CONTRACTORS	SYSTEMS ANALYSTS, DP MANAGER	IS PLANNERS, IS MANAGER, DATABASE SPECIALISTS	BUSINESS ANALYSTS, INFORMATION RESOURCE MANAGER	BUSINESS & IS PLANNERS INTEGRATED	IS/IT DIRECTOR (BOARD LEVEL)
STYLE	UNAWARE	'DON'T BOTHER ME (I'M TOO BUSY)'	ABROGATION, DELEGATION	PARTNERSHIP: BENEFITS MANAGEMENT	INDIVIDUALISTIC (PRODUCT CHAMPION)	MULTIDISCIPLINARY TEAMS (KEY THEMES)
SKILLS	INDIVIDUAL: TECHNICAL LOW LEVEL	SYSTEMS DEVELOPMENT METHODOLOGY: COST-BENEFIT ANALYSIS	IS AWARENESS PRODUCT MANAGEMENT	IS/BUSINESS AWARENESS	ENTREPRENEURIAL MARKETING	LATERAL THINKING (IT/IS POTENTIAL)
SHARED VALUES	OBFUSCATION	CONFUSION	SENIOR MANAGEMENT CONCERN, DP DEFENCE	COOPERATION	OPPORTUNISTIC	STRATEGY MAKING & IMPLEMENTATION

Figure 7.6 Assessing the quality of an organization's information systems management: a revised 'stages of growth' model
Source: Amended from Galliers and Sutherland 1991: 111

Having agreed on a small number of scenarios following discussion of a range of alternatives (three or four is fairly normal), one can begin to consider an appropriate business strategy in each context and the potential role that IS/IT might play in each. Questioning the key assumptions on which these strategies are based is an important route to the identification of strategic information.

A comparison of the processes that go to make up such models, and their interrelationships, especially when the potential of IS/IT is being considered at the same time, often leads to the realization that some of the current business processes which until this time were considered to be key to business success can actually be streamlined or even omitted altogether. Conversely, processes that *are* crucial may not be in place or may be undertaken poorly.

It is important to remember that the models are based on *required* processes and do not relate to existing organizational arrangements nor to current functional boundaries. An information architecture based on key information needs and flows *as these relate to required, not existing, processes*, is a natural outcome of this kind of thinking. Key information can be identified by using such techniques as the critical success factor (CSF) approach (Rockart, 1979), augmented by its corollary, critical *failure* factors (Galliers, 1993) and the critical *assumptions* upon which the strategies are based. Ongoing assessment of the impact of change projects is assisted by the collection of information of this kind.

CONCLUDING REMARKS

This chapter has attempted to answer the question as to where BPR fits into our thinking and practice regarding business/IS strategy formulation *and* implementation, and what role IT might play in organizational change. It has cast doubt on the novelty of the BPR approach, classifying it with the more traditional strategic approaches that were popularized in the 1960s. Having said that, it has not dismissed it out of hand but has attempted to incorporate some of its more useful features into current thinking on business strategy and the management of change. What is more, the chapter identifies a common omission in much of the BPR literature, ie the lack of guidance regarding *how* one might go about implementing the conclusions drawn from the analysis. In other words, it provides a means by which the kind of discontinuous thinking advocated by Hammer (1990) can actually be achieved.

The comparison of what is needed in the context of alternative future scenarios may lead to a decision that radical change is required – and, just as likely, that it may not! Discontinuous thinking and radical change may well not be synonymous. Incremental change may well be more appropriate, for example during a period following rapid change (cf. 'freezing') or where the analysis suggests that this change is either unnecessary or foolhardy.

IT can often be a catalyst in this process and IT opportunities for new or enhanced products and services should certainly not be overlooked. Having said that, an aggressive competitive strategy with IT at its heart is only likely to yield benefits when the firm's IS resources (human as well as infological and technological) are sound. Organizations should be wary of the hyperbole surrounding the topic of competitive advantage arising from IT, especially those without a sound IT and IS management track record.

The approach that has been described above gives equal weight to internal as well as external concerns. Customer – potential as well as current – requirements are highlighted, as is the changing competitive, political, economic and technological environment. A fresh review of what might otherwise be seen as essential internal business processes is also at the heart of the analysis. Above all, however, concern needs to be focused – as part of the process itself – on the propensity of key stakeholders for change and on the implementation issues. A more balanced, socio-technical perspective is what seems to be necessary.

One final word on the process is that it is meant to be applied flexibly and on an ongoing basis so that it contributes to organizational learning. The techniques that have been incorporated into it in this chapter, for the purposes of ensuring greater understanding, are meant to be illustrative rather than prescriptive. While they have been found to be extremely helpful in a range of BPR projects, it is more than likely that other techniques can be applied as successfully. The approach described in this chapter should not be applied rigidly – rigid application leads to rigid thinking and that is certainly *not* what is required!

REFERENCES

Argyris, C and Schön, D (1978) *Organizational Learning*, Addison-Wesley, Reading, Mass.

Cascio, W (1993) 'Downsizing: What Do We Know? What Have We Learned?', *Academy of Management Executive*, 7(1), 95–104.

Checkland, P B (1981) *Systems Thinking. Systems Practice*, Wiley, Chichester.

Clemons, E K (1986) 'Information Systems for Sustainable Competitive Advantage', *Information and Management*, November, 131–136.

Davenport, T H (1993) *Process Innovation: Re-engineering Work through Information Technology*, Harvard Business School Press, Boston, Mass.

Davis, G B and Olson, M H (1984) *Management Information Systems: Conceptual Foundations, Structure and Development*, 2nd edn, McGraw-Hill, New York.

de Gues, A (1988) 'Planning as Learning', *Harvard Business Review*, 66(2), March–April, 70–74.

Galliers, R D (1991) 'Strategic Information Systems Planning: Myths, Reality and Guidelines for Successful Implementation', *European Journal of Information Systems*, 1(1), 55–64.

Galliers, R D (1993) 'Towards a Flexible Information Architecture: Integrating Business Strategies, Information Systems Strategies and Business Process Re-design', *Journal of Information Systems*, 3(3), 199–213.

Galliers, R D (1994) 'Information Systems, Operational Research and Business Re-engineering', *International Transactions on Operational Research*, 1(2), 1–9.

Galliers, R D and Sutherland, A R (1991) 'Information Systems Management and Strategy Formulation: The "Stages of Growth" Model Revisited', *Journal of Information Systems*, 1(2), 89–114.

Galliers, R D, Pattison, E M and Reponen, T (1994) 'Strategic Information Systems Planning Workshops: Lessons from Three Cases', *International Journal of Information Management*, 14(1), February, 51–66.

Gibson, C and Nolan, R L (1974) 'Managing the Four Stages of EDP Growth', *Harvard Business Review*, 52(1), January–February, 76–88.

Granovetter, M (1985) 'Economic Action and Social Structure: The Problem of Embeddedness', *American Journal of Sociology*, 91(3), 481–510.

Hammer, M (1990) 'Re-engineering Work: Don't Automate, Obliterate', *Harvard Business Review*, 68(4), July–August, 104–112.

Hardaker, M and Ward, B K (1987) 'How to Make a Team Work', *Harvard Business Review*, 65(6), November–December, 112–120.

Leavitt, H J (1965) 'Applying Organizational Change in Industry: Structural, Technological and Humanistic Approaches', in March, J G (ed.), *Handbook of Organizations*, Rand McNally, Chicago.

Lewin, K (1951) *Field Theory in Social Science*, Harper & Row, New York.

McFarlan, F W (1984) 'Information Technology Changes the Way You Compete', *Harvard Business Review*, 62(3), May–June, 98–103.

McLaughlin, M, Howe, R and Cash Jr, J I (1983) 'Changing Competitive Ground Rules – The Impact of Computers and Communications in the 1980s'. Unpublished working paper, Graduate School of Business Administration, Harvard University, Boston, Mass.

Maruca, R F (1994) 'The Right Way to Go Global: An Interview with Whirlpool CEO David Whitwam', *Harvard Business Review*, 72(2), March–April, 135–145.

Nolan, R L (1979) 'Managing the Crises in Data Processing', *Harvard Business Review*, 57(2), March–April.

Pascale, R T and Athos, A G (1981) *The Art of Japanese Management*, Penguin, Harmondsworth.

Pettigrew, A M (1985) *The Awakening Giant: Continuity and Change in ICI*, Basil Blackwell, Oxford.

Porter, M E (1980) *Competitive Strategy: Techniques for Analyzing Industries and Competitors*, Free Press, New York.

Porter, M E (1985) *Competitive Advantage: Creating and Sustaining Superior Performance*, Free Press, New York.

Porter, M E and Millar, V E (1985) 'How Information Gives You Competitive Advantage', *Harvard Business Review*, 63(2), March–April, 149–160.

Quinn, J B (1980) *Strategies for Change. Logical Incrementalism*, Richard D. Irwin, Homewood, Ill.

Rockart, J F (1979) 'Chief Executives Define Their Own Data Needs', *Harvard Business Review*, 57(2), March–April, 81–93.

Schnaars, S P (1987) 'How to Develop and Use Scenarios', *Long Range Planning*, 20(1), 105–114. Reprinted in Dyson, R G (ed.) (1990) *Strategic Planning: Models and Analytical Techniques*, Wiley, Chichester, 153–167.

Senn, J A (1992) 'The Myths of Strategic Information Systems: What Defines True Competitive Advantage?', *Journal of Information Systems Management*, Summer, 7–12.

Ward, B K (1990) 'Planning for Profit', in Lincoln, T (ed.), *Managing Information Systems for Profit*, Wiley, Chichester.

Watts, J (1993) 'The Future of Business Process Re-engineering', *Business Change and Re-engineering*, 1(3), Winter, 4–5.

Whitley, R D (1991) 'The Social Construction of Business Systems in East Asia', *Organization Studies*, 12(1), 1–28.

Whittington, R (1993) *What Is Strategy – and Does It Matter?*, Routledge, London.

8

BUSINESS PROCESS RE-ENGINEERING: DEFINITIONS AND MODELS REVISITED

Hean Lee Poh and Wan Wan Chew,
National University of Singapore

INTRODUCTION

'Take a clean sheet of paper' was the title of an article that appeared in the 1 May, 1993 issue of *The Economist*. Indeed, Business Re-engineering or Business Process Redesign, as advocated by some researchers and consultants, involves starting with a clean sheet of paper to design the processes of a company without referring to the existing processes or modes of operation. The practice of Business Re-engineering is not new. What is new is the jargon of Business Re-engineering believed to have been coined and popularized by Michael Hammer, an MIT computer science professor turned management consultant. Ever since the 'invention' of re-engineering, there has been an exponential increase in the number of researchers and consultants working in this field. However, not everyone defines re-engineering in the same way, and not everyone agrees on what re-engineering should do and deliver. In fact, a blurry solution space is an axiom of re-engineering according to Cypress (1994).

The aim of this chapter is thus to discuss some of the definitions and models proposed by researchers and see how these concepts relate to Michael Hammer's definition and model. In the modelling area, Michael Hammer's re-engineering model is also compared with the earlier popular models of Michael Porter, Scott Morton, and John Rockart. A framework for conducting re-engineering is proposed which deviates somewhat from the 'clean sheet' approach in that it allows systematic and incremental changes to be made to an organization in a given condition. Rules for re-engineering can be spelled out and the execution can be automated.

DEFINITIONS

Business Re-engineering as defined by Michael Hammer (Hammer and Champy, 1993) is 'the fundamental rethinking and radical redesign of an entire business system – business processes, job definitions, organizational structures, management and measurement systems, values and beliefs – to achieve dramatic improvements in critical measures of performance (cost, quality, capital, service, speed).' Hence, Business Process Re-engineering (BPR) is just a subset of Business Re-engineering (BR) according to Hammer and Champy (1993).

What is a Business Process?

A business process, according to Hammer and Champy (1993), is a 'collection of activities that takes one or more kinds of input and creates an output that is of value to the customer'.

The definition of a business process by Davenport and Short (1990) is most similar to that by Hammer and Champy (1993), with 'a collection of activities' being replaced by 'a set of logically related tasks', and the crossing of organizational boundaries being highlighted. Both deviations are, however, implicit in the definition by Hammer and Champy (1993). Davenport's (1993) subsequent definition of a process is also close to that of Hammer and Champy (1993). A process as defined by Davenport (1993) is a specific ordering of work activities across time and place, with a beginning and an end, and clearly identified inputs and outputs: a structure for action. The structure for action that is emphasized here is also implicit in the Hammer and Champy (1993) definition, if the assumption of structured actions leading to valuable output for customers is valid.

What is Business Process Re-engineering?

Business Process Re-engineering, as defined by Tapscott and Caston (1993), is 'a fundamental revaluation/redesign of a company's business processes and organizational structures in order to achieve dramatic improvements in its critical success factors – quality, productivity, customer satisfaction and time to market etc.' This definition is most similar to that of Hammer with the exception that it refers to a process in particular.

According to Morris and Brandon (1993), re-engineering is an approach to planning and controlling change. Business re-engineering means 'redesigning business processes and then implementing the new processes.' In this definition, the purpose of the change is not explicitly stated, but the implementation of the change is highlighted.

The AT&T Quality Steering Committee (1991) defines re-engineering as 'the redesign and implementation of a process or a major part of a process to meet new customer requirements or achieve significant improvements in process performance.' Again, this is another Hammer 'look-alike' definition, though the focus is on process only, and the objective of the change is not specified in greater details such as cost, quality, capital, service and speed.

Hall, Rosenthal and Wade (1993) also regard re-engineering as 'the redesign and improvement of business processes both in depth (roles and responsibilities, measurements and incentives, organizational structure, information technology, shared values and skills) and breadth (activities to be included) which can lead to long-term profits.' Again, the focus here is on business processes. However, the 'things' to be changed are discussed in detail. One of the objectives highlighted was long-term profits.

Davenport (1993) takes it one step further. According to him, business re-engineering, or business process redesign, is only part of what is necessary in the radical change of processes. The term 'process innovation' was suggested by him to encompass the envisioning of new work strategies, the actual process design activity, and the implementation of change in organizations involving human beings and technology. Hence, his definition is the most dynamic one of all the above.

The list of different definitions with different foci goes on. The following definition of business re-engineering captures the essence of all the definitions above. The definition is illustrated in the form of a framework (see Figure 8.1).

There are four levels of interactions in the framework: At the bottom level, the *individual level*, there are the people of an organization. At the next higher level, the *internal system and structure level*, there are job definitions, organizational structure, beliefs and values, measurement and management systems, and any other concepts or systems that determine the relations between people. The third level is then the *process level* which consists of activities or actions which transform several inputs into an output. The highest level, or the fourth level, is the *objective level*. The objectives of an organization can include such things as the (dramatic) improvement in the critical measures of performance (cost, quality, capital, service, speed) from the organizational as well as client's perspectives, thus leading to long-term sustainable profits.

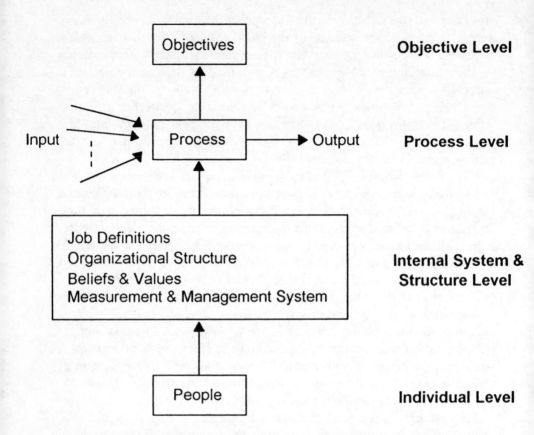

Figure 8.1 A four-level framework leading to the definition of BPR

Business Re-engineering hence involves the redesign/replanning of each of the four levels on an ongoing basis. Business Re-engineering is used synonymously with Business Process Re-engineering, even though 'process' is only one of the levels in the framework. The acronym BPR will thus be used throughout the chapter to refer to Business Re-engineering as defined here.

A comprehensive definition for Business Re-engineering can be reworded as follows:

> Business Re-engineering is a total replanning and redesign of manpower consisting of individuals, internal system and structure, and processes in direct or indirect response to external forces, in order to achieve some objectives which are usually not easy to achieve given current conditions of an organization.

The above definition is consistent with the three levels of the organizational performance improvement approach proposed by Rummler and Brache (1990), namely *organization*, *process* and *job* (individual), whereby the *organizational* level encompasses the objective level and the internal system and structure level of the definition. By defining the goals, design and management guidelines of each of the three levels, Rummler and Brache (1990) provide a 'blueprint' or the tools for change in organizations.

UNIFICATION OF HAMMER'S MODELS WITH OTHER MANAGEMENT MODELS

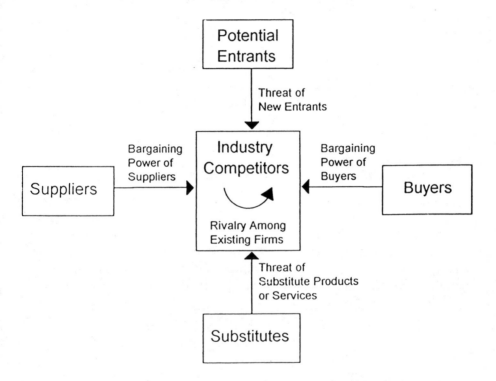

Figure 8.2 Porter's (1980) five forces model

Reprinted with the permission of The Free Press, a Division of Simon & Schuster Inc, from *Competitve Strategy: Techniques for Analyzing Industries and Competitors* by Michael E Porter. Copyright © 1980 by The Free Press.

Before looking at some frameworks for business re-engineering, the forces affecting an organization will be considered first. These include economic forces, social, cultural, demographic, geographic, political, governmental and legal factors, as well as technological and competitive forces. In particular, the *industry competitive forces* have been analysed in detail by Porter (1980). He classified them into five categories – the rivalry among existing firms, the bargaining power of suppliers, the bargaining power of buyers, the threat of new entrants, and the threat of substitute products or services. The latter four forces also have an impact on the competitors which form the first force. These are the external influences that an organization will have to take into consideration when making marketing decisions such as the determination of prices, the design of product lines, the selection of sales channels and the planning of advertising and promotion (see Figure 8.2).

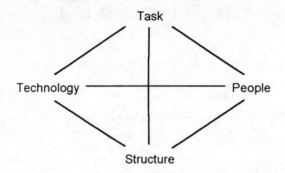

Figure 8.3 Leavitt's (1965) model of the organization

The internal influences are captured by Leavitt's model of the organization (Leavitt, 1965) (see Figure 8.3). He described task, structure, people and technology as the main components of the organization, and he placed them at the corners of a diamond, to bring across the point that a change in any one factor will affect and bring about changes in the other factors so as to retain the shape of the diamond.

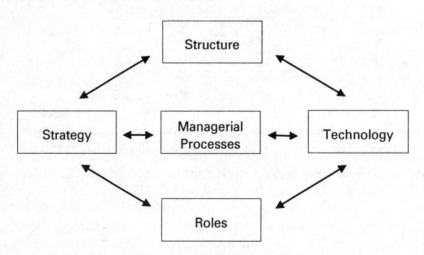

Figure 8.4 Leavitt's adjusted model as modified by Scott Morton and Rockart

Leavitt's model was later modified by Scott Morton and John Rockart (see Figure 8.4) and reported in Rockart (1988). They replaced 'Task' with the broader concept of the organization's 'Strategy' and added 'Management Processes' as well. They noted that management processes help hold the organization together, and have a central controlling function. The representation of the internal influences is thus more complete.

Scott Morton (1991) presented the MIT 90 framework in which an organization is thought of as comprising five sets of forces or components (management processes, structure, strategy, individuals and roles, technology) in dynamic equilibrium among themselves, even as the organization is subject to influences from the external environment.

In fact, the internal and external organizational influences have been integrated. An organizational boundary has been drawn, and the internal components can be thought of as interacting with the organization's external environment. Additionally, the existence and the importance of the organization culture has been recognized.

Hammer introduced a framework to guide organizations to re-engineer their businesses too. His framework is a causal representation of the organization, with 'strategy' being identified as playing a directing role. Figure 8.5 can be explained as follows

- The external forces (customer needs, competitor actions, technological and environmental factors) and internal factors (assessment of internal capabilities) influence the formulation of the organization strategy, which in turn determines the design of the business processes.
- The business processes then interact with (enabled by and determine) the jobs, people, organizational structure, management and measurement systems, values and beliefs, and infrastructure, to determine the internal capabilities of the organization.

Hammer and Champy's model thus fits quite well into the four-level framework of our definition. The objectives are implicit in the strategy because a strategy is always devised with some objectives in mind, though not always explicitly. Apart from that, level 1 and 2 of the definition framework are integrated in Hammer and Champy's model too.

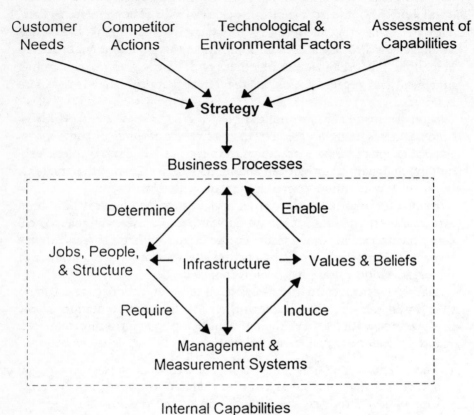

Figure 8.5 The diamond in context – Hammer and Champy's
(1993) model

From *Reengineering the Corporation: A Manifesto for Business Revolution* by
Michael Hammer and James Champy, Nicholas Brealey Publishing Ltd,
London, 1993.

Comparison between Hammer and Champy's Model and Porter's Model

In Hammer and Champy's model as depicted in Figure 8.5, the first
competitive force of Porter's model, the buyers, determines the customer
needs. Four of the five competitive forces (buyers, suppliers, potential
entrants, substitutes) determine the competitor's actions. Technological
and environmental factors are not explicitly mentioned in Porter's model
of five competitive forces. The assessment of (internal) capabilities are
not mentioned as well. To achieve competitive advantages, a firm should

place emphasis on cost advantages and product differentiations, according to Porter. One of the motivations of BPR is customer orientation. With the change due to BPR, an organization strives to understand the customer needs better, and to achieve product (including service) differentiations. This entails a reorganization of work and organizational processes, thus improving cost advantages at the same time. Hence, the BPR concept by Hammer and Champy is also consistent with the competitive advantage concept proposed by Porter (1985).

Porter (1985) also introduced the concept of the *value chain* as a way of achieving competitive advantage, via cost reduction, differentiation and/or the linkages of value activities (optimization, coordination). The value chain can be viewed as a way of representing the interactions between the business processes and the internal components of the organization in the Hammer and Champy model. However, it is only a subset of Hammer and Champy's model, and is at a much 'lower' level of representation, getting to the functional units of operations or marketing etc, whose division is supposed to break down under the BPR concept.

In conclusion the Porter (1980) model on competitive forces captures most of the external forces influencing the strategy in Hammer and Champy's model. The Porter (1985) model on competitive advantage, on the other hand, partly explains the interactions between the business processes and the internal structure and systems of the organization, though functional division is avoided or de-emphasized in Hammer and Champy's model.

Comparison between Hammer and Champy's Model and the MIT 90 Framework

The MIT 90 framework, compared to the Porter (1980) model, focuses more on the internal elements of an organization. In mapping the framework on the Hammer and Champy model, one notices the obvious absence of the 'technology' factor. However, 'technology' is implicit in the interaction between the business processes and the infrastructure of the organization in Hammer and Champy's model.

Another obvious difference is the existence of causal relationships in Hammer and Champy's model but not in the MIT 90 framework. The MIT 90 framework is an interactive representation of an organization in the 1990s with no specific theme in mind, whereas the Hammer and Champy model stresses the business processes, and thus the interaction of the various elements of the internal structure and systems leads to a common *cause* – the achievement of certain objectives.

In conclusion, the MIT 90 framework maps well onto Hammer and Champy's model. In fact, we can even consider Hammer and Champy's model as a special case of how an organization in the 1990s should look – technology is implicit in the 1990's as an enabler of business processes; change or re-engineering is also important for an organization of the 1990s to achieve some objectives.

A FRAMEWORK FOR EXECUTING BPR

One of the purposes in having re-engineering frameworks is to guide organizations in achieving sustainable competitive advantage. However, Hammer and Champy's model focuses more on what the factors and components influencing and affecting one another are, rather than on how to improve the organization.

Hence, a framework for sustainable business competitiveness will be introduced here to fill the missing gap (see Figure 8.6). The framework is at a 'lower' level or a more detailed level than Hammer and Champy's model. It takes into consideration the influencing factors outlined in Hammer and Champy's model, and focuses on the steps to be taken to achieve sustainable business competitiveness. It illustrates how one step leads to and interacts with the other steps, so as to guide the growth of the organization. The model is a dynamic one, as illustrated by the feedback loops at multiple points. The model also distinguishes between the continuous improvement of the business processes and business re-engineering. It recognizes that, depending on the situation, the organization may opt for incremental improvement, multiplicative improvement, or a hybrid of both.

In Hammer and Champy's model, the strategy formulated for the organization determines the structure of the business processes. This idea has been expanded in the proposed model. It uses steps common in information and business systems planning models, such as 'understand the business', 'identify business processes', and 'assess process performance'.

In the proposed model, an 'organization' is thought of as being a subset of the whole 'environment'. It accepts inputs from the environment and, being part of it, influences it as well. To grow in the environment, it is necessary to first *Understand the business* – to determine the position the organization occupies. This requires an analysis of the 'competitive forces' affecting the organization, as well as an inspection of the state of the organization – its performance, resource structure, values and beliefs. Porter's five competitive forces (industry competitors, potential entrants, substitutes, suppliers and buyers) can be used as a guideline during the analysis of the competition faced by the company. Attention should also be paid to the special skills and know-how that the company possesses, for these can serve as a foundation upon which future business can be built. On the whole, this first exploration should 'just' reveal the company's strengths, weaknesses, opportunities and threats and, as a by-product, an appreciation of the business organization the company is involved in ('just' – so as not to consume too many resources, and not to 'lock' the planners into the way the business is currently being carried out).

The next two steps, *Invent strategy* and *Identify business processes*, can be carried out simultaneously. Inventing a strategy is very important because the chosen strategy sets the direction for future growth of the organization. It requires a careful analysis and forecast of the environmental trends, and an appreciation of the company's strengths and weaknesses. Such an exercise is a difficult one, and calls for a lot of innovation and creative thinking. Identifying business processes is important too, because the new organization is structured around business processes. Care should thus be exercised to ensure that the identifiers are not 'locked' into a functional perspective of the organization. Once the visions are defined as a result of strategy invention and the business processes identified, the process owners, the process objectives, and the process performance measures can be determined during the *Plan for business processes* step.

The process owner is in charge of the whole process, while the process objectives, strategies and performance measures are used to help determine how to *Manage business processes*. Managing the processes involves a decision on whether to improve the process performance incrementally, or to re-engineer the process (called business re-engineering, because it affects the whole business). Besides, if more than one process are identified as candidates for re-engineering, then it may be necessary to further prioritize or coordinate the projects due to the high demand that such projects place on resources and senior management commitment and their widespread effects. One way to prioritize the processes to be re-engineered is to assess the impact of the change in consultation with the senior management.

A process orientation is adopted during the management of the business, with the view that the processes would significantly shape the IT architecture, organization structure, management and reward systems, values and beliefs, and job definitions as implied in the Hammer and Champy (1993) model. However, this does not mean that they can be left to evolve and develop by themselves. Rather, an active change management process should be in place to smooth and guide the transition.

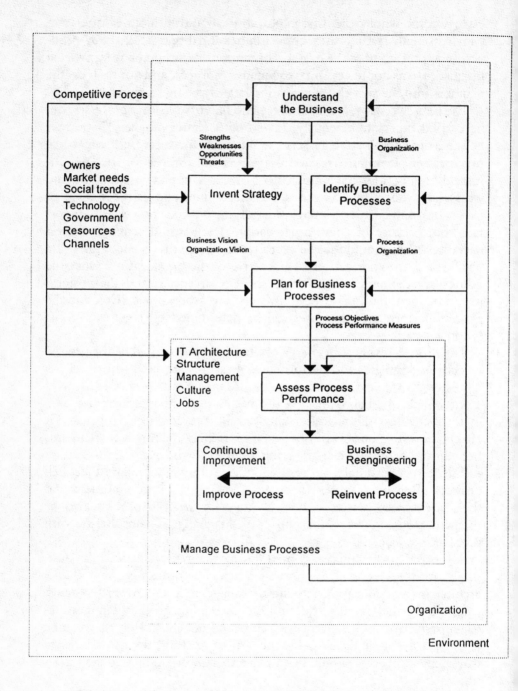

Figure 8.6 A framework for sustainable business competitiveness

After process improvement, the new performance results would be used for assessment in the *Assess process performance* step, and a decision would be made as to whether to continue employing the existing process design, or to opt for business re-engineering. If the existing process design is to be maintained, then efforts should be made to continuously improve the 'quality' of the process. Quality can be measured by the degree to which the process produces the desired outcome meeting the objectives.

When some major changes occur in the environment, or when the business processes have achieved their objectives, or when some flaws are found in the plans, or simply after a reasonable time interval, the plans for the business processes would have to be revised. The processes would then be managed according to the revised set of objectives, strategies and measures. Different processes may have their plans reviewed at different times. Sometimes, it may also be necessary to re-identify the business processes, or even re-understand the business again. The steps for sustainable business competitiveness thus do not terminate, but iterate forever.

CASE STUDY

The proposed model has not been tested in practice due to the recency of the proposal and the long time that would be required for testing. Nevertheless, the model can be mapped to the experiences of companies that have successfully re-engineered their businesses to illustrate its applicability.

For example, the well-known case of Ford Motor Company, which instituted 'invoiceless processing', thereby achieving dramatic improvement for its order fulfilment process is used as an example (Hammer, 1990).

At the point in question, Ford should have already understood the business ('Understand the business') and decided upon a strategy ('Invent strategy'). It should also have identified its business processes ('Identify business processes'), defined objectives and performance measures for them ('Plan for business processes') and was then managing them ('Manage business processes').

When the American automotive industry was in a depression ('Understand the business'), Ford's top management decided to review the organization in search of ways to cut costs ('Invent strategy'). While planning for its accounts payable department, Ford looked at Mazda, and figured that its own accounts payable organization was five times the size it should be. Hence Ford managers decided that accounts payable would perform with many hundreds fewer clerks ('Plan for business processes'). Since the difference between the performance and the objective was great ('Assess process performance'), continuous improvement would not be adequate, and thus it decided to re-engineer the business ('Business re-engineering').

While analysing the existing system ('Understand process'), the purchasing department and the material control department (which received the ordered goods) were also examined ('Identify business processes'), as the managers realized that looking at the accounts department alone would not enable them to get to the root of the problem. It was discovered that the accounts payable department spent most of its time on mismatches, instances where the purchase order (from the purchasing department), the receiving document (from the material control equipment) and the invoice (from the vendor) disagreed. In these cases, an accounts payable clerk would investigate the discrepancy, a long and tedious procedure in itself.

One way to improve things might have been to help the accounts payable clerk investigate more efficiently, but a better choice would be to prevent the mismatches in the first place ('Redesign and test'). To this end, Ford instituted 'invoiceless processing' ('Implement'). When the purchasing department initiates an order, it enters the information into an on-line database. When the goods arrive at the receiving dock, the receiving clerk checks the database to see if they correspond to an outstanding purchase order. If so, the clerk accepts the goods and enters the transaction into the computer system. Payment is then made based on the goods that have been received.

Ford opted for radical change, and achieved not the 20 per cent reduction in head count that it would have got with a conventional programme, but a 75 per cent reduction ('Measure and review'). Since its performance has been brought to a level comparable to its objectives ('Assess process performance'), it would now be appropriate to manage the process by seeking continuous improvement.

UNIFICATION OF SOME BPR MODELS WITH THE UNIFIED FRAMEWORK

Some published frameworks will now be examined, to see if they have identified anything that is overlooked in Hammer and Champy's model and the 'framework for sustainable business competitiveness' presented earlier.

In Schnitt's 'strategic re-engineering' (Schnitt, 1993), the use of critical success factors are emphasized (see Figure 8.7). These can be thought of as the objectives in the 'framework for sustainable business competitiveness'. Information systems have also been highlighted, as the context of the framework is to re-engineer the organization using information technology.

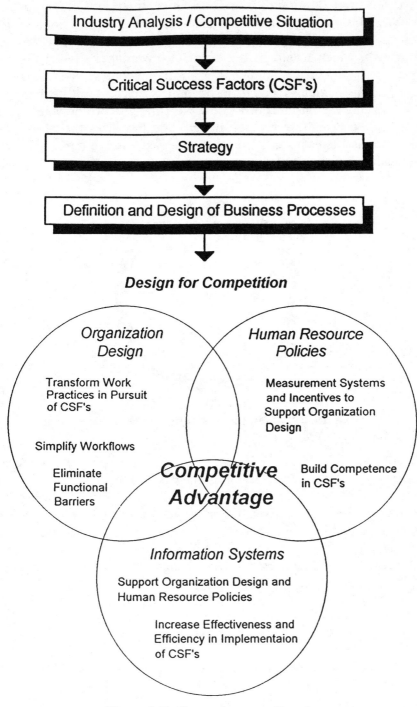

Figure 8.7 Strategic re-engineering

Source: Schnitt 1993

The Gemini Consulting's framework as reported by Gatermann and Krogh (1993), on the other hand, maps more to the methodology for re-engineering (see Figure 8.9). 'Revitalizing' identifies new opportunities for growth, which would be the result of inventing a strategy for the organization and understanding the business process. 'Restructuring' more efficiently employs the existing resources, which would be the result of redesigning the business processes. 'Reframing' repositions the management system, culture and job design, and mobilizes the people for action, while 'Renewing' signifies the implementation of the new system and quality management.

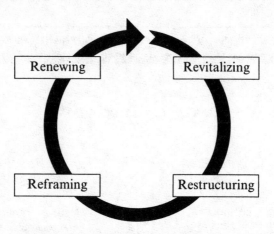

Figure 8.8   Gemini Consulting's framework
Source: Gatermann and Krogh 1993

Similarly, in Tapscott and Caston's transitioning framework (Tapscott and Caston, 1993), 'Reimage' refers to the reinventing of the organization strategy, 'Reshape' refers to the redesign of the business processes, 'Realize' refers to the implementation of the new designs, while 'Renew' refers to the continual improvement of the business process (see Figure 8.10). As the business is re-engineered, the information architecture and information systems support must be changed too. Again, information technology has been emphasized. The context in which the framework was set revolves around the new promises of information technology. These have been expressed, though not as explicitly, in Hammer and Champy's model and the 'framework for sustainable business competitiveness'.

Hence most of the frameworks map well into either the Hammer and Champy model or the 'framework for sustainable business competitiveness', with some deviations in focus.

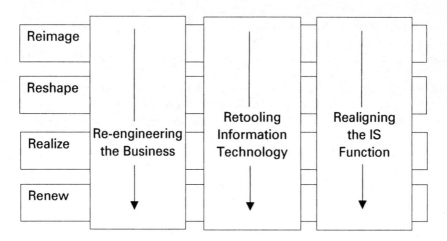

Figure 8.9 The transitioning framework
Source: Tapscott and Carson 1993

CONCLUSION

A comprehensive definition for BPR was developed in this chapter. The unification of Hammer and Champy's model with some popular management models was also carried out. This provided a theoretical foundation for the development of a BPR framework based on Hammer and Champy's model. The framework brought the BPR concepts one step closer to the practitioners. As further research, a BPR system support tool could be developed based on the 'framework for sustainable business competitiveness', and then tested on real-world primary cases for the verification and enhancement of the framework.

REFERENCES

AT&T Bell Laboratories (1991) *AT&T Re-engineering Handbook*, AT&T Quality Steering Committee.

Cypress, H L (1994) 'Re-engineering', *OR/MS Today*, February, 18–29.

Davenport, T H (1993) *Process Innovation: Re-engineering Work through Information Technology*, Harvard Business School Press, Boston, Mass.

Gatermann, M and Krogh, H (1993) 'Special Report on Re-engineering' (German), *Manager Magazin*, 12, 117–213.

Hall, G, Rosenthal J and Wade J (1993) 'How to Make Re-engineering Really Work', *Harvard Business Review*, Nov–Dec, 119–131.

Hammer, M (1990) 'Re-engineering Work: Don't Automate, Obliterate', *Harvard Business Review*, July–August, 104–112.

Hammer, M, and Champy, J (1993) *Re-engineering the Corporation: A Manifesto for Business Revolution*, Harper Collins, New York.

Leavitt, H J (1965) 'Applying Organizational Change in Industry: Structural, Technological and Humanistic Approaches', in March, J G (ed.), *Handbook of Organizations*, Rand McNally, Chicago.

Morris, D and Brandon, J (1993) *Re-engineering Your Business*, McGraw-Hill, New York.

Morton, M S S (1991) *The Corporation of the 1990s: Information Technology and Organizational Transformation*, Oxford University Press, Oxford.

Porter, M E (1980) *Competitive Strategy: Techniques for Analysing Industries and Competitors*, Free Press, New York.

Porter, M E (1985) *Competitive Advantage: Creating and Sustaining Superior Performance*, Free Press, New York.

Rockart J F (1988) 'The Line Takes the Leadership – IS Management in a Wired Society', *Sloan Management Review*, Summer, 57–64.

Rummler, G A and Brache, A P (1990) *Improving Performance: How to Manage the White Space on the Organization Chart*, Jossey-Bass, San Francisco, Calif.

Schnitt, D L (1993) 'Re-engineering the Organization Using Information Technology', *Journal of Systems Management*, January, 14–20, 41–42.

Tapscott D, and Caston, A (1993) *Paradigm Shift: The Promise of Information Technology*, McGraw-Hill, New York.

Part Three

LEARNING FROM EARLIER IMPROVEMENT PHILOSOPHIES

One of the issues which has been explored by the authors in Part 2 is whether BPR is a fundamentally new management philosophy which offers valuable insights and opportunities or whether it is nothing more than old philosophies repackaged – a case of 'old wine in new bottles'. Like many such questions, the answer which appears to be emerging is 'yes' and 'no'! The general consensus of opinion seems to be that BPR provides a fresh perspective within which it draws together existing bodies of knowledge and lessons from earlier improvement philosophies.

Of course, this makes sense – after all, these earlier philosophies have proved their value over time. But as each new prescription comes and goes it is important to distil the valuable lessons, so that subsequent philosophies can build on that body of experience. The main purpose of the chapters in this part is to distil these lessons by exploring the similarities and differences between BPR and earlier philosophies and approaches to organizational improvement. From these explorations, the authors draw valuable lessons which should help BPR practitioners.

In the first chapter of this part, Chapter 9, Joe Peppard and Ian Preece first position BPR using Andrew Pettigrew's framework of context, content and process. By examining the intellectual inheritance of BPR, they illustrate how its antecedents have influenced its development. By considering the context within which BPR is undertaken, they emphasize that BPR is concerned with performance improvement and that it has highlighted the essential fact that organizations are composed of three ingredients: business processes, technology and people. They maintain that any organization must strive to ensure that it achieves the optimal balance between these three elements. In analysing the process of undertaking a BPR initiative, they present a framework within which they position existing tools, methods and techniques. They conclude that BPR is an amalgamation of previous theories and practices of organizations, systems and management thinking. What BPR offers over and above these previous theories is a holistic approach to combining a range of tools and methods that can be matched to the organization context and problem.

In Chapter 10, Chris Morgan compares TQM and BPR. Using a number of dimensions he identifies few areas of agreement. He argues that TQM is essentially a normative theory that seeks to change people's attitudes, and through this organizational efficiency. In contrast, he contends that BPR, as currently portrayed, is a structuralist theory that seeks to change processes and through this organizational efficiency.

In Chapter 11, Enid Mumford discusses and compares BPR with the socio-technical approach developed by researchers at the Tavistock Institute of Human Relations from the 1950s onwards. Socio-technical design argues that when new work systems are being designed equal weight should be given to social and technical factors. It places great emphasis on improving the quality of working life. By contrast, she sees BPR placing most emphasis on gaining competitive advantage. She argues that these two approaches are similar in their procedures although, in her view, socio-technical design has a better theoretical basis and a stronger methodology.

Many commentators have suggested that BPR has its inheritance grounded in operations management. Building on this theme, Colin Armistead and Philip Rowland draw on lessons learned from philosophies in the operations management discipline in order to improve the chances of success of BPR. In Chapter 12, they suggest that the adoption of the process paradigm for managing enterprises creates new challenges of reconciling the relative roles of functions and processes within an organization. While these issues have yet to be resolved, there are other aspects of BPR concerned with activities to improve performance which may have many similarities with existing concepts and techniques in the domain of operations management. They argue that there is a danger that the learning in areas of quality management, just-in-time, and simultaneous engineering may be disregarded or hidden from those engaged in BPR programmes. They indicate where such knowledge lies and identify some of the lessons learned from these improvement methods so that they may be applied to BPR.

Moving beyond the boundaries of a single organization, Fred Hewitt in Chapter 13 suggests that an organization's whole supply chain is in fact a business process. He argues that supply chain process management has a long history and the lessons from it are applicable to other process types. He addresses the concepts of process efficiency and effectiveness and makes a distinction between business process management (BPM) and BPR. He sees BPM as being concerned with the maximization of efficiency and effectiveness of existing business processes. He argues that looking at those few companies with integrated intra- and inter-company supply chain process management yields a better understanding of both BPR and

BPM in this particular process area. The final sections of the chapter present panel consensus from a 'supply chain roundtable' with over 30 successful supply chain redesign practitioners. He concludes that the view of the supply chain as a 'process' differs from the conventional 'logistics network' view primarily by simultaneously addressing all aspects of the operation of the supply chain, including work practices, information flows and authority/decision-making structures.

9

THE CONTENT, CONTEXT AND PROCESS OF BUSINESS PROCESS RE-ENGINEERING

Joe Peppard, Cranfield School of Management, and Ian Preece, Mercury Communications Limited

---

Managers of today are under increasing pressure to improve the competitive position of their organization, either to steal a march on their competitors or to simply keep up with the ever accelerating pace of competition. They are constantly in search of new ideas and concepts which will enable them to achieve competitive excellence. At the same time they are presented with new approaches and prescriptions which claim to provide the solutions they have been seeking. The re-engineering of business processes is considered by many academics and practitioners alike as a possible path to salvation.

Despite the considerable interest in business process re-engineering (BPR), there is confusion over what exactly is BPR, what role it might play in organizational design and how it can be successfully implemented. Literature searches by the authors have revealed only limited discussion on the synthesis of these themes (Preece and Peppard, 1993; Shah *et al*, 1994). This paper attempts to redress this deficiency by presenting an analysis of BPR centred around Pettigrew's (1987) model to guide research in the area of strategy and, in particular, strategic change. He contended that formulating the content of any new strategy inevitably entails managing its context and process. We believe that this framework is a powerful tool in examining BPR and its role in strategy, organizational design and change management.

The paper begins by looking at the content of BPR, addressing the intellectual inheritance of the concept in relation to the history of organizational, management and systems thinking in the twentieth century. This is done by analysing the concept of process, a fundamental cornerstone of the BPR philosophy, which allows us to explore the implications for those elements of an organization which we are interested in managing or redesigning. It also allows us to understand what, if anything, is new about BPR and where it draws inspiration from.

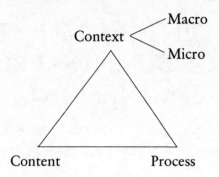

Figure 9.1   Content, context, and process.

In examining context, we position BPR in relation to strategy formulation and the development of an infrastructure for continual renewal and learning. We consider the role BPR plays in understanding and shaping the organization's capability to support its own strategy and the organizational context required to support a re-engineering initiative. For BPR to be successful there is a clear need for organizational processes to be linked to strategic objectives (Edwards and Peppard, 1994b). However, strategy formulation does not necessarily entail the re-engineering of business processes. Equally, BPR may indicate the need for changes in the organization that are not part of the re-engineering project but are essential to sustain the redesigned processes.

Having addressed content and context we then examine the process of BPR. Based on theoretical and practical research, we identify the potential stages which organizations are likely to go through during a re-engineering initiative. At each of these stages a set of questions need to be addressed and resolved. The broad span and scope of a BPR project, from concept to implementation and from chief executive to shop floor, demands a wide variation in thought process and personal style. Understanding and managing this balance is key to managing the progression of work through the project and in selecting the appropriate techniques and methodologies which can potentially support a re-engineering initiative.

CONTENT

All theories of organizations are founded upon a philosophy of science and a theory of society, whether the theorists are aware of it or not (Burrell and Morgan, 1979, p 119)

Drawing on this statement by Burrell and Morgan (1979), understanding the content of BPR requires considering both the philosophical and practical dimensions which underlie the concept. We believe that it is only through an appreciation of the relationship between these two aspects that one can begin to understand the relevance of BPR to the practising organization and to formulate an appropriate approach for implementation. In other words, to determine 'how' to do BPR we need to know 'what' it is. This section of the chapter addresses this issue by attempting to clarify the epistemological and metaphorical assumptions which underlie BPR.

While most writings stress the necessity and indeed substantial rewards of BPR, few have addressed its underlying philosophy and concepts (Preece and Peppard, 1993). The majority of the literature appears to agree that BPR focuses on the need to improve the effectiveness and efficiency of business processes in response to an increasingly volatile, competitive and global business environment. However, a commonly recurring debate is whether BPR is fundamentally different or merely a case of 'old wine in new bottles'. We believe that this is a polarized and, to some extent, a redundant debate.

Most writers would agree that what separates BPR from previous improvement approaches is that traditional ways of thinking about and managing organizations are becoming outdated in their ability to deal with a constantly changing business environment. This demands not only changing the way we organize and manage but also challenges assumptions about the very nature of organizations themselves.

Discussions on BPR encompass a wide range of metaphors and models, although these are not usually made explicit. There appears to be no one universally accepted perspective on what BPR is and, even less so, how to do it. This ambiguity is at one level a weakness because of the difficulty of grasping the essence of the concept. Conversely it is a strength as the lack of determinism allows the integration and adoption of many different tools and techniques dependent on the context of the organization and problem. The key aspect is understanding that the choice of metaphor must be consistent with the context and that any methods and tools selected must be chosen and used in a consistent manner. Table 9.1 describes the relationship between the change in paradigm and the underlying metaphors, methods and tools.

Table 9.1 Paradigms, metaphors, methodologies and models of BPR.

Paradigm	• Essentially pragmatic and focused on outcomes.
	• Driven by process rather than structure and organization.
	• What processes do is more important than what they look like.
	• Contingent, recognizing that there are multiple potential ways of achieving the desired objective.
	• Satisfaction of customer needs.
Metaphor	• The concept of 'process' embodies a range of different metaphors at different levels of the organization and different stages of a BPR project. Embodies: mechanistic, organic, systemic, cybernetic and cultural metaphors.
Methodology	• A non-deterministic framework that allows for the selection of different approaches to achieve the desired end.
	• Requires a clear business context and direction
	• Migration from current state to desired state requires an understanding of both.
	• Encompasses creative (divergent) thinking and analytical (convergent) thinking
Tools	• Wide range of tools and techniques are utilized. Many already exist through previous process oriented philosophies, eg total quality management (TQM). Many new ones are currently being developed, especially integrated software tools that combine design, simulation and enactment.

THE INTELLECTUAL INHERITANCE OF BPR

Research by one of the authors reveals the philosophical and practical parallels between BPR and existing process oriented philosophies, such as Fast Cycle Response and Just-In-Time (Peppard and Rowland, 1995). Summarized in Table 9.2, it highlights that there are new ideas in BPR as well as the presence of some older elements. That many of the principles of BPR are common with other performance improvement philosophies which have gone before make sense, not least because they are proven and well understood. As each philosophy has elements which have proved useful over time, so subsequent philosophies build on that body of experience. As each new 'fad' comes and goes it is important to distil the valuable elements of each and thereby assemble the appropriate 'toolkit' for improvement from

Table 9.2   Comparison of BPR with other improvement philosophies

Source: J Peppard and P Rowland, *The Essence of Business Process Re-engineering*, Prentice-Hall International, Hemel Hempstead, 1995, p 16).

ELEMENT	Total Quality Management	Just-In-Time	Simultaneous Engineering	Time Compression Management/ Fast Cycle Response	Business Process Redesign / Re-engineering
Focus	Quality Attitude to customers	Reduced inventory Raised throughput	Reduced time to market Increased quality	Reduce time (time=cost)	Processes Minimize non-value-added
Improvement scale	Continuous Incremental	Continuous Incremental	Radical	Radical	Radical
Organization	Common goals across functions	'Cells' and team working	R&D and Production work as a single team	Process based	Process based
Customer focus	Internal and external Satisfaction	Initiator of action 'pulls' production	Internal partnerships	Quick response	'Outcomes' driven
Process focus	Simplify Improve Measure to control	Workflow/ Throughput efficiency	Simultaneous R&D and Production development	Eliminate time in all processes	'Ideal' or Streamlined
Techniques	Process maps Benchmarking Self-assessment SPC Diagrams	Visibility Kanban Small batches Quick set-up	Programme teams CAD/CAM	Process maps Benchmarking	Process maps Benchmarking Self-assessment IS/IT Creativity/out of box thinking

the complete body of knowledge available to business, a view which perhaps questions whether BPR is really a paradigm shift at all.

While Table 9.1 illustrates comparisons with contemporary process oriented improvement philosophies it is more revealing to examine BPR within an historical context. In Figure 9.2 we trace a number of key developments in organizational and systems thinking over the last 150 years and attempt to illustrate the intellectual inheritance of BPR. In this figure, the concepts of metaphor, 'hard' and 'soft' thinking and the focus of organizational learning are used to draw out key similarities and differences and to provide a reference point for our discussion.

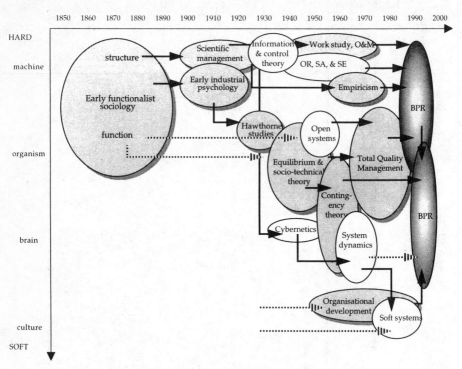

Figure 9.2   Intellectual Inheritance of BPR

Figure 9.2 illustrates the evolution of thought in both the theoretical and practical aspects of organizational understanding. From the more mechanistic ideas embodied in the functionalist specialism of Adam Smith and scientific management, we can see a path to the human interactionist models of organizational development and soft systems. Each of these disciplines embodies discreet, often conflicting, paradigms, metaphors and tools and yet lays the ground work for subsequent developments in thinking. For example, dissatisfaction with the dehumanising elements of management science lead to experiments in human interaction, through programmes like the Hawthorne studies (Mayo, 1971) to socio-technical perspectives (Trist and Bamforth, 1951) which explicitly recognize the self-determination of human systems. This is an important point when considering BPR as its value may not be in creating new techniques and approaches, rather building and integrating previous disciplines, a point also highlighted in Table 9.2.

The obvious success of science in dealing with physical problems from the renaissance to the mid-1850s led a number of leading thinkers of the time to apply scientific method to social problems. This saw the establishment of the social sciences as a discreet discipline which has become the guiding force for the majority of twentieth century thinking on organizational dynamics. The vision of people like Auguste Comte (1798-1857) was to use scientific rationality to establish a well regulated social order and to provide 'the one type of society which is absolutely valid'. Within this order scientific laws would describe absolutely the relationships between the various parts of society – 'social statics' – and the way in which they changed over time – 'social dynamics'. Other philosophers, such as Spencer (1820–1903) and Durkheim, extended Comte's work through the use of biological analogies to explore issues such as organizational evolution, diversity, integration and need satisfaction.

While much of this debate had been at a largely intellectual and abstract level, the early 20th century saw the application of these philosophies for the practical management of organizations. It is not the intention of this chapter to take the reader on an excursion through the literature on organizational and systems thinking. Excellent summaries can be found in Burrell and Morgan (1979), Morgan (1986) and Checkland (1981). What we do wish to do is position BPR in relation to previous developments. This is done through exploration of the concept of process, a cornerstone of the philosophy and practice of BPR. Table 9.3 summarizes these key developments in organization and management thinking in relation to the underlying paradigm, the dominant metaphor and the view of process which each subscribes to.

While often seen as something relatively new, the concept of process, central to the doctrine of BPR, has been with us for some time. It can be traced back to writings on early functionalist sociology in the late 19th century and a key focus of the debate at that time was whether the behaviour of a process was determined by its 'structure' or 'function'. This is a fundamental point, as the answer to this question defines which organizational aspects one is interested in studying.

During this early period in the development of organization and management thinking, there was a debate over the relative importance of structure and function to social behaviour. Simplistically, one extreme focuses on the 'social morphology' of organizations believing that structure determines how people behave in an organization. Alternatively,

Table 9.3 Paradigm, metaphor and process underlying major developments in organization and management

	Paradigm	Metaphor	Process
Functionalist sociology	Used scientific rationality to establish a well regulated social order and to provide 'the one type of society which is absolutely valid'.	Organic - mechanistic. Used biological analogies to explore issues such as organizational evolution, diversity, integration and need satisfaction	Scientific laws would describe absolutely the relationships between the various parts of society – 'social statics' – and the way in which they changed over time – 'social dynamics'. Debate over the relative importance of structure and function to social behaviour.
Scientific management	Emphasis on an internally focused structural view, believing that if you get the situation right, the appropriate human behaviour and organizational performance will follow. Freedom of expression and individual judgement are seen as dysfunctional. The belief is that there is one best way to organize and if you do it effectively the right results will be produced, regardless of the environment and people.	Machine.	Processes are driven by structure and rules to achieve optimum output. Human behaviour and interaction need to be factored out.
Industrial psychology	Organization still seen as a machine, albeit a more complex one, using science to explore the links between personal satisfaction, fatigue and monotony at work. The organizational environment dictates behaviour not people and their interactions.	Complex machine.	Essentially structural but considered the links between personal satisfaction, fatigue and monotony at work.
Hawthorne studies	Identified the informal organization and the fact that man, although part of the organization, has complex needs that are satisfied through society as a whole.	Initially complex machine, later simple organism.	Organizational 'statics' were seen to have an effect on behaviour but the way in which the organization developed was determined by the 'dynamics' of human interaction and need satisfaction.
Socio-technical and equilibrium theory	Introduction of new technology affects the social and psychological aspects of the organization. The organization is primarily reactive in striving to attain equilibrium under external pressures. The mechanism by which it achieves this is much more organic and contingent.	Organism, culture and brain.	Human dynamics and interaction affect the structure and function of the process. The role of management is to manage this balance and to minimize conflicts.

Open systems and organizations	Saw a system as a discipline that could help produce a 'unity of science'. The organization is portrayed as a living organism that maintains itself through a process of exchange with the environment 'importing' and 'exporting' material in doing so.	Organism.	Based on concepts of 'input', 'throughput', and 'output'; centred on homeostasis, with the organization regulating its behaviour to accommodate changes in the environment. Differentiation and integration of subsystems necessary to create a stable structure.
Contingency theory	Adaptation to the environment is key to survival. Different organizations are required for different environments with no one ideal organizational structure. An effective organization depends upon achieving a balance between strategy, structure, technology, the commitment and needs of people and the external environment.	Organic and brain.	Structure or form of the organization is contingent upon the demands placed upon it. May be more than one form that will satisfy the same need. Unlike previous organic models, contingency theory does not take structure as given. It is something the organization creates in its process of survival as it responds to a changing environment.
Operations research	Highly quantitative perspective focused around model building and optimization with the computer used 'as the basic tool of interior system design' focusing on 'measures of effectiveness'.	Machine.	Structural. Linear development process, the starting point of which was a defined need which could be expanded into a requirement, a series of objectives, a number of alternatives and so on.
Systems analysis and systems engineering	Defines alternatives to get from a current state to a desired state. Focuses on how you might get to where you are going and not what your goal might be. Developed from the basic principles of engineering communications and control.	Machine.	Predominantly structural. Human behaviour and interaction not accounted for.
Work study and organisation and methods (O&M)	Reductionist approach focusing on improving efficiency and optimizing organizational effectiveness. Highly analytical and quantitative.	Machine.	Predominantly structural. Human behaviour and interaction not accounted for.

Total quality management (TQM)	Improving the quality of organizational outputs through the involvement of all employees. Each employee has a personal responsibility for satisfying the customer – both internal and external.	Simple organism and culture.	Highly structural and analytical in its analysis. Human interaction considered but from a unitary perspective.
Cybernetics	Linked to information theory and the communication and control aspects of engineering. It is these control processes that prevent an organization from decaying. The organization must be able not only to learn, but to learn to learn. More contingent in approach than the classical open organistic idea.	Brain.	Views a system as a network of information where 'all control processes depend upon a flow of information in the form of instructions or constraints'.
Systems dynamics	Organizational behaviour determined by flows, feedback, cause – effect and emergent effects. Cause and effect often separated by time. It is our assumptions about these relationships which define our decision making.	Complex organism and brain.	Interested in both the 'statics' and the 'dynamics' and the relationships between these elements. This may form loops and feedback upon one another. Feedback can either be positive or negative.
Soft systems	The founding assumptions of SSM are based on human subjectivity, understanding and interaction as fundamental truths in the evolution and dynamics of organization.	Complex organism and culture.	Predominantly processual in nature. Involve human activity and understanding the relationship between two people. These are evolutionary, cannot be predicted and are fundamentally governed by human behaviour.
Organizational development	Human relations have a decisive influence on outcomes and must be the focus of an intervention in order to make any improvements. Face to face intervention is key.	Culture.	Emphasizes the interactive and essentially dynamic aspects of organizational behaviour. Human interaction and behaviour frequently differ from the behaviour implied within the organizational structure.

there was a view that it was the functions that people performed and the processes they went through that determined the shape and structure of society. In other words, the former held the view that the 'statics' of the organization defined the 'dynamics'. The latter held the opposite view that the actions and interactions within the organization defined the structure and form of the organization. This is important because each perspective defines which elements of the organization need to be examined and managed. The outcome of this debate was that structuralism triumphed and led to an 'increasing focus on "structure" [which] has led to "increasingly hard and indiscriminate application of the models and methods of the natural sciences"' (Burrell and Morgan, 1979, p 57).

Up until the Hawthorne studies the view of organizations as machines dominated organizational thinking. The key output of the Hawthorne studies was to identify the informal organization and the fact that man, although part of the organization, has complex needs that are satisfied through society as a whole. For the first time since the late 19th century the concepts of structure and process were linked and identified within a 'process of social change' (Burrell and Morgan, 1979, p 139). This was a more organic view that went some way to reconciling the differences between the structural and functional views. The Hawthorne studies also laid the groundwork for future developments of organizational thinking that have a direct bearing on the philosophy of BPR today: socio-technical systems and the process view of organizations.

The concept of the 'socio-technical system' was based largely on research by Trist and Bamforth at the Tavistock Institute and highlighted the conflicts between the needs of the individual and the characteristics of the formal organization (Trist and Bamforth, 1951). Katz and Kahn (1966) developed what is perhaps the first process view of organizations looking at the concepts of 'input', 'throughput', and 'output'. An underlying principle of this model was the concept of feedback or homeostasis, where the organization regulates its behaviour to accommodate changes in the environment. The organization, however, is still seen as primarily reactive and striving to attain equilibrium under external pressures.

The move away from mechanistic analogies and the classical command and control structure to more organic and specialized structures was seen to represent an improvement in knowledge towards a fundamental underlying structure. As with the early discussions within the functionalist sociology, there was still a debate between the concepts of structure and function. In practice, the focus on structure prevailed and the more dynamic concept of function was largely bypassed during this period.

At the same time that organizational theory was moving towards a more open and organic view of organizations, the systems movement was also developing along similar lines. Biologist Ludwig Von Bertalanfy

(1958) formalized the principle of systems thinking using the analogy of a biological organism. One of Bertalanfy's key contributions to the systems movement was the concept of the open system, with an organization portrayed as a living organism that maintains itself through a process of exchange with the environment, 'importing' and 'exporting' material in doing so.

In the contingency model, the concepts of structure and process remain separate but the process is seen to manifest itself through structural characteristics, eg technology or organizational form. The structural aspects still remain as the dominant characteristics that are researched and measured – partly because the processual nature of a system does not lend itself to meaningful study through the use of objectified social structures. Unlike previous organic models, contingency theory does not take structure as given or fixed nor as a fundamental principle of the organization. It is something the organization creates in its process of survival as it responds to a changing environment.

Despite the development of these ideas, the mechanistic principles developed from and through the natural sciences were still providing the dominant frameworks for organizational analysis. Part of this was due to the emergence of hard analytical techniques, largely influenced by developments in systems analysis and operational research. These highly quantitative techniques are based on model building, optimization and measures of effectiveness. It is these ideas that have led to the establishment of modern systems analysis and the ubiquitous systems life cycle. Although developed from the field of engineering, these disciplines have been widely used in the engineering of human systems.

In the systems arena there were a number of spin-offs from the developments in both open systems and operational research. One of these is cybernetics. Articulated by Norbert Wiener in the 1940s, the subject is linked to information theory and the communication and control aspects of the engineering functions. These principles have been linked to a metaphor, that of a brain, to help explore the nature of the adapting and self-organizing organization. With this metaphor there is more focus on establishing a corporate understanding and defining boundaries and limits for action rather than prescribed goals. Ouchi (1981) describes this as one key difference between Japanese and American cultures.

Another development in systems thinking that has implications for BPR is that of systems dynamics. Systems dynamics is very useful as it allows us to explore the dynamics of processes, more so than traditional systems analysis which focuses on the statics (see van Ackere *et al.*, 1993). That is, the same organizational structure can produce different behaviour in different people. We may therefore end up with defining different processes to those at the outset of the analysis. This last point is crucial and moves us into the more subjective areas of organizational understanding and is a cornerstone of the soft systems method (SSM).

The underlying assumptions of SSM are based on human subjectivity, understanding and interaction as fundamental truths in the evolution and dynamics of organization. This is in direct contrast to the harder disciplines which either exclude them or seek to clarify them through the application of scientific techniques. Checkland, its founding father, believed that only well structured and simple problems can be resolved by such techniques (Checkland, 1981). Unfortunately most managerial problems are not of this type and are messy, poorly structured and, essentially, soft in their nature. These invariably involve human activity and understanding. In a similar vein, the work by Schein (1988) on process consultation and organization development emphasizes the interactive and essentially dynamic aspects of organizational behaviour. His ideas were based on an understanding of human processes developed from work on group dynamics (Kurt Lewin, 1951), small group processes, applied anthropology (Chapple, 1940), sociology (Bales, 1950) and psychology (Carter *et al*, 1951). The predominant metaphor is that of a culture.

THEMES IN BPR REFLECTING ITS INTELLECTUAL INHERITANCE

Early thinking on BPR was drawn primarily from mechanistic thinking on organizational engineering (cf Davenport and Short, 1990; Hammer, 1990). Although, when one examines the framework governing the *MIT's Management in the 1990s* programme, it is clearly grounded in organistic metaphors underlying equilibrium and contingency theory (see Scott-Morton, 1991). The focus on IT enabled business change however (cf Ventrakaman, 1991; Hammer, 1990), led to an implicit inheritance of the tools and methods used to develop IT which were then applied to the analysis and design of business processes. These were often used in conjunction with other hard analytical approaches such as work study and organization and methods. This is not negative *per se*, but reflected a focus on the 'what' of BPR at an abstract and philosophical level with little attention paid to the 'how' – either at a methodological or technical level (Preece and Peppard, 1993). Earl and Khan (1994) also highlight this point, claiming that 'popular writers will admit that so far methodologies are immature and implementation more challenging than the concept'.

Although often compared to TQM, BPR is intellectually different in a fundamental way. There is an awareness with BPR that in competing and interacting with the environment, the organization itself may have to evolve and change its form. The principal focus of TQM, however, is on optimization of organizational processes, not fundamental changes in its form and function. A crucial difference is that a potential outcome of a BPR programme may be the questioning of the strategic goals of the organization, particularly where the development or capability to support that strategy is not possible or feasible, highlighting the necessity to understand the strategic context.

Most BPR models recognize the requirement to satisfy the needs of the external customer as the prime mechanism for organizational survival. This subscribes to the view of the organization as an open system coupled with the idea of measurement and feedback and is very similar to the homeostatic control processes seen within organisms and used in the open systems ideas developed by Bertalanfy. Although proposed as dynamic, many of the suggested approaches to BPR focus on mapping the structural elements of the process. Some adopt the systems dynamics ideas of process flow and offer simulation techniques but, in general, the focus is on the static elements of the process. Parallels can be seen with methods used in TQM and systems analysis – in fact many of the techniques used in BPR have been adopted from these areas.

In the more recent literature, particularly those reporting empirical research findings, cultural metaphors have become more prevalent (Ascari *et al*, 1994; Champy, 1995; Earl and Khan, 1994; Hall *et al*, 1993). Two reasons for this can be suggested. Firstly, the critical problem of implementation in any BPR initiative. Research has clearly shown that people are likely to be the greatest barrier to a successful implementation of a new process design (CSC Index, 1994; Dickson *et al*, 1994; Jarvenpaa and Stoddard, 1993). Secondly, the shift from an internal focus to an external focus, emphasizing a contingent and evolutionary approach to meeting the needs of the external environment. This latter view is more interactionist in its nature, recognizing the human element of processes, particularly in the management of change.

The concept of culture is, however, poorly developed and follows a unitary rather than a pluralistic and essentially political model. The objective is to minimize conflict, a view that does not recognize or manage politics as a core organizational mechanism. This perspective has predominated a great deal of organizational thinking, including the equilibrium and contingency models. Ideas from areas such as SSM do recognize the political dimension but offer little in the way of approaches in dealing with it. This may be one reason why so many BPR projects are seen to fail. It would appear that the methodologies we have available to deal with and manage these problems are largely based in the hard metaphors of classical management science. It may also indicate that our search for prescriptive approaches to BPR may be futile. An underpinning assumption of the cultural metaphor is the concept of context and facilitation. Both of these preclude, to a large extent, the possibility of a deterministic solution. If approaches and solutions are dependent upon the organizational context, the problem to be solved and the skills and abilities of the people managing the process, then an all encompassing methodology for all situations will not be possible, however attractive an idea it may appear.

Flood and Jackson (1991) have developed a classification of system methodologies grouped by their underlying metaphors and assumptions about problem contexts. While discussions on BPR reflect the full range of metaphors addressed in this model, the approaches are principally focused on the mechanistic and simple organistic processes. This is not necessarily a criticism of BPR but may reflect a lack of practical techniques to address the more complex problems contexts.

The increasing focus on the softer elements of the organization reflects a growing awareness that implementing and sustaining new processes is the critical element for continued success in BPR. This is one area that structured and mechanistic approaches cannot prescribe solutions to. This is a general criticism of many management science methodologies which focus on developing a blueprint but not on implementing the changes.

CONTEXT

Context refers to the conditions and situation under which a BPR initiative is being undertaken. Our research would suggest that before embarking on a re-engineering programme it is imperative to understand the context within which it is taking place. We would go even further and suggest that it is this lack of understanding which is one of the principal reasons for the limited success of BPR. Our studies highlight narrowness of process scope and the lack of any linkage to business strategy as two critical areas of context which organizations fail to address.

Addressing the former, many organizations re-engineer processes with such narrow scope that it is impossible for significant business benefits to be achieved. For example, the case of the Ford Motor Company redesigning its accounts payable process, perhaps the most widely quoted example of BPR, exhibits all the attributes of a process which was re-engineered but is unlikely to have had any major impact on Ford's bottom line. We would argue that many of the reported improvements in process performance are in fact relative to that process prior to BPR and not to the overall company performance.

Secondly, many of the re-engineering initiatives which we have examined have been devoid of any strategic direction. For example, Mutual Benefit

Life's re-engineering of its process to issue a life insurance policy, while a successful illustration of a redesigned process, did little to stop the company filing for Chapter 11 bankruptcy. In a similar vein, by re-engineering its credit division, IBM redesigned a process which was no longer core to the business with the move from mainframes to low cost PCs.

An analysis of context can be undertaken at both a macro and micro level. At a macro level, it is easy to discern the changes taking place in the environment and the consequential demands and challenges which such developments place on organizations. Globalization of markets, commodization of products and services, and intense competition all challenge the way that organizations traditionally compete. New information and communication technologies are changing the very nature of business itself and many industries are rapidly moving from the market-place to the marketspace (Rayport and Sviokla, 1994).

New competitive strategies are demanded in response to such challenges, such as flexibility, speed of response, quality, and innovation. Increasingly, companies want to achieve what used to be considered strategic contradictions: both low cost and high variety. However, in order to deliver these competitive strategies, innovative ways of organizing for work are required. At this micro level is the recognition that traditional ways of organizing and the fundamental assumptions that underlie the design of organizations are outdated. One of the messages of BPR is that breakthroughs in performance cannot be achieved by cutting fat or automating existing processes but by challenging old assumptions and shedding old rules that made businesses under-perform in the first place.

An organization's business strategy addresses the macro environmental concerns. It outlines how the firm will compete in the market-place and the competitive posture to be taken. This has traditionally been articulated in terms of products and markets: what products will be sold and to whom will they be sold. Clearly a firm's particular chosen competitive position and the products it sells are important, but only at any given point in time. In a rapidly changing competitive environment products and services quickly become obsolete and static competitive positions are rapidly overtaken. Such dynamics places additional demands on firms to be able to respond consistently to changing markets with new products/services and ever improving competitiveness.

Addressing this concern the emerging view of strategy focuses on the resource side rather than analysing organizations from the product side which has traditionally been the case (Wernerfeld, 1984). This perspective proposes that what sustains competitiveness is not a firm's endowments, but its capabilities (Prahalad and Hamel, 1990; Stalk *et al*, 1992). Capabilities are a company's proficiency in combining people, process and systems/technology which allow it to continually distinguish itself along the dimensions that are important to its customers. For example, in a high-tech industry, the ability to quickly develop new state-of-the-art products with features and performance that deliver value to customers creates an enduring advantage. In a commodity industry, it may be the ability to constantly reduce costs through innovative actions that creates lasting competitive advantage. Continued renewal is achieved by identifying, developing, and maintaining these critical capabilities.

Supporting this view, Hammer (1994) suggests that re-engineering offers 'an alternative perspective on formulating strategy, one based on operating process rather than on products and markets'. He argues that by significantly improving a firm's operating capabilities, BPR allows the implementation of new strategies and to envision new strategic options. This is true as long as these processes support new strategies; it falls down when they don't. Organizations often use BPR to improve what they are already doing; yet what they are doing is often not what they should be doing. For many companies, switching to a new business may be more sensible than simply doing the old one efficiently. What is the point, for example, in a record company re-engineering its manufacturing process if its competitors in the future are cable companies downloading music selections on cable? The strategic context of any re-engineering is therefore paramount.

In order to articulate a link between business strategy and the redesign of business processes, one of the authors has made a distinction between business re-engineering and business process re-engineering (Edwards and Peppard, 1994a). Illustrated in Table 9.4, *business re-engineering* involves the development of an organizational architecture and it entails identifying and linking the strategy of the business with the required organizational processes to ensure that this strategy is actually delivered. With this perspective, the organization engages in a fundamental re-thinking and redesign of the business and its underlying processes. This is very much a top-down view driven by senior management. *Business process re-engineering*, on the other hand, refers to the redesign of any organizational process. This can include anything from the total supply chain to a single process within an individual function or department. Much of the literature in relation to BPR addresses the latter with little attempt made to articulate the link with strategy.

Table 9.4   Business re-engineering v business process re-engineering

Business re-engineering	• aligning processes to the business strategy • high-level view of the organization and its underlying processes • identifying a small number of processes • defines the business architecture
Business process redesign/re-engineering	• redesign of individual processes for step improvement in performance • usually relates to high-level processes although principles apply to all processes

Source: adapted from Edwards and Peppard, 1994a.

To further develop this link with business strategy organizations can be seen as having a portfolio of processes, a view which is echoed by Ghoshal and Bartlett (1995). Peppard and Edwards (1994b) have developed a framework which categorizes processes based on the contribution which they make to delivering the business strategy. This framework recognizes that firms must be competitive given their existing product and customer base, but also the firms should look to 'creating the future' and articulate future competencies. Illustrated in Figure 9.3, processes are classified as being either competitive, infrastructure, core or underpinning.

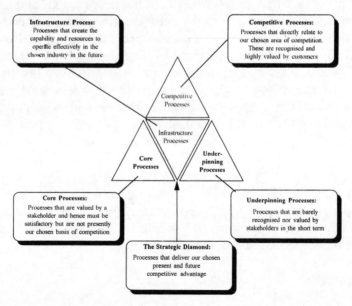

Figure 9.3   Classifying business processes: the process triangle
Source: Edwards and Peppard, 1994b.

Competitive processes are those processes which are used to deliver today's products and services. A company's performance in relation to these processes is what differentiates it from its competitors in today's market-place. While a company might seek to create the future it should not forget that to survive into the future it must be competitive given today's products. The future starts with today and competitive processes support the current strategic thrust.

The future is also important, and an organization must also identify those capabilities which they need to be competitive in the future. Processes are then constructed which support the creation of these capabilities. Capabilities may enhance the performance of existing competitive processes, but significantly create future competitiveness through the creation of new competitive processes.

Competitive processes support today's product and market-based strategy by encapsulating current capabilities. Infrastructure processes create the capability for tomorrow's competitive processes and hence support tomorrow's competency-based strategy. Together, these two critical types of processes are termed the *strategic diamond*.

Core processes are those processes that are valued by stakeholders and hence must operate satisfactorily but are not presently the chosen basis of competition. They are necessary for the organization to avoid disadvantage; in short they are the minimum entry requirements into the market or may be necessary due to legislation.

Underpinning processes are processes that are undertaken but are not recognized nor valued by stakeholders, at least in the short term. Such processes exist in all organizations and are collections of closely related activities that are grouped together for efficiency and recognized as a process. In reality, such processes directly support, or contribute to, other categories of processes. For example, in the performance of competitive, infrastructure and core processes, some administrative support is probably necessary. The recruitment of this staff may therefore be an aspect of a number of processes. For efficiency reasons, management may decide to combine this element and manage them as a single process.

THE PROCESS OF RE-ENGINEERING

Both paradigms and metaphors are mental processes whereas the methodology is the way in which a real situation is dealt with. Significantly, the three are connected as a methodology is an extension of a set of core beliefs and is metaphorical in that it will focus on particular aspects of the problem situation. Science, for example, focuses on quantifiable and objective information and the scientific method is concerned with collecting and validating this. Qualitative and subjective knowledge are not explored and are in fact seen to be aspects of 'poor science'.

In management science we look to methodologies to do two things:

- to structure and manage problems
- to capture and transfer learning from other problems and contexts, thereby improving our chances of future success.

Referring to the first point, a methodology provides a framework for structuring the way we make sense of the world and allows us to do one or more of the following three things:

- structure problems
- analyse problems
- tackle problems.

The structuring of problems is important because we make decisions about what we are interested in exploring before we engage in the task. In classical systems analysis we take the view that the key elements are the functions the organization performs, the data used to execute those functions and the structural relationships between them. A psychoanalyst exploring the same organization would be much more interested in individual thought processes. These are very different focuses based on different assumptions about the world. They do not necessarily conflict because they are looking at different attributes of the same situation. An organization has functions and data as well as human psychology and both have an effect on the behaviour and management of the organization but to comprehend these within a single methodology or model is very difficult – hence the need to establish partial or metaphorical views of the organization. Each view is useful for highlighting certain aspects of the organization yet is limited by those features it does not address.

Having decided what our area of interest is we can then proceed to analyse the situation. Based on our beliefs of what is important we can do this in a number of ways. Simplistically we can focus on qualitative or quantitative techniques. The former might focus on human relationships and perceptions believing that they are the guiding force behind action; the latter might seek to objectively measure environmental conditions believing that they drive action. We may choose to approach the situation with a predefined model or hypotheses and collect data in order to solve a particular problem. This is a 'hard' view of the world and underlies many of the methodologies that we have available in the social sciences. Alternatively we may decide that we do not know enough about the problem and need to take a much more exploratory approach. This is a fundamental assumption about the soft systems methodology and re-quires that we neither prejudge our findings nor use a methodology that constrains our understanding of the richness of the picture we are attempting to build. Systems analysis, for example, is a hard methodology where we are not interested in anything other than functions or data; in selecting our model we have, by consequence, decided what is important. Quantitative methods are more developed and more explicit than qualitative ones. This is partly because qualitative work is by definition less prescriptive but also, as argued earlier, that the harder aspects of social science have dominated research methodologies for most of this century.

The final stage is taking action where we look to manage problems within the real world. Either based on conclusions from our analysis or from those we are given we will define objectives and targets for those objectives that are consistent with our requirements. Project management is frequently used as a common approach to implementation and other stages, but it only provides a structure, it does not define an approach for managing the changes. Other techniques such as organizational development and process consultancy focus more on the process of how organizations and the people with them go through the process of change. Although the management of the process of change, particularly the human and cultural aspects, is frequently quoted as one of the critical success factors for organizational change, it is not always obvious that these approaches are effectively integrated into mainstream organizational change. Focus is often given more to the structural elements of the organization, such as functional hierarchies and reporting lines, rather than the dynamic and behavioural aspects.

It is at the implementation stage that we test the ultimate validity of our conclusions, particularly in management science. A plan however, like any other methodology or method, is a tool to making a decision or taking action. A plan that fails does not necessarily mean that we made the wrong conclusions or selected the wrong methodology. Equally, a perfectly conceived plan, if such a thing could be defined, does not guarantee success. It is the human judgement and interaction and the management of the human processes that ultimately mediate any potential success. Managing change itself is a task fraught with difficulty, and is increasingly seen as the corner stone of BPR (Champy, 1995; Earl and Khan, 1994).

This is fundamental to our choice of methodologies. We could, for example, believe that the methodology is prescriptive and if followed successfully will provide the correct answer. Alternatively, we could believe that the methodology provides a framework for action that we have to cater to our own context and problem. The physical installation of a computer system, for example, will be the same in every situation because the technology operates in a consistent and predictable manner, regardless of the context of its use. The actual usage of the system may well be determined by the prevalent culture or politics. These are primarily contextual factors that the methodology can focus on but not prescribe solutions to. It is *how* the system is used and not what it *is* that defines the operation of the process and its ultimate outcome.

This is also central to the debate over hard and soft systems – considered generally to represent two different paradigms. One of Checkland's (1981) assertions is that models are partial views of reality and we are in effect 'filling in the detail' in order to aid in making a decision. The models are therefore not reality but are seen as mental abstractions that do not exist in reality. This is a conceptual point but an important one. If we believe the former then we must seek the requisite level of detail to complete the model. This is a common view of the harder paradigms. If we believe the latter then our process maps, for example, are merely lines and symbols on a piece of paper that need to convey or allow us to infer enough information for us to make useful decisions.

What this softer view implies is that the criteria for success are in the skills of the practitioner and the knowledge of the problem and the context of the problem that the practitioner has or can facilitate. From this perspective it is important to understand that a tool is no measure of success and a prescriptive methodology will not guarantee that success either. For example, a skilled artist could no doubt produce a better picture with the end of a burnt stick than an apprentice could with the finest brushes or oils.

We have applied these ideas to a study of a wide range of methodologies, methods and tools. Some of these are directly targeted at the BPR market, others are taken from existing management science and change management philosophies covered in previous sections of this chapter. Invariably it appears that the majority of BPR specific methodologies are endorsed by management consultancies. The focus of the academic and management literature is more on the content, and not the process, of BPR. There are some writings on the methodological aspects such as Davenport (1993); Hammer and Champy (1993); Johansson *et al.* (1993). We have also looked at a wide range of computerised tools that are designed or have the capability to structure, analyse and enact changes to business processes. We have developed an approach based on this work.

This approach, illustrated in Figure 9.4, has been tested in a number of companies currently engaged in BPR initiatives, against the methodologies offered by a range of consultancies and methodological approaches proposed by writers on BPR. The approach, described in detail in Peppard and Rowland (1995), is focused around five stages:

- create the environment
- analyse, diagnose and redesign business processes
- restructure the organization
- pilot and roll-out
- realize vision

These five phases can be exploded to a lower level of detail, outlined in Figure 9.5. This identifies the potential stages that a BPR project may go through.

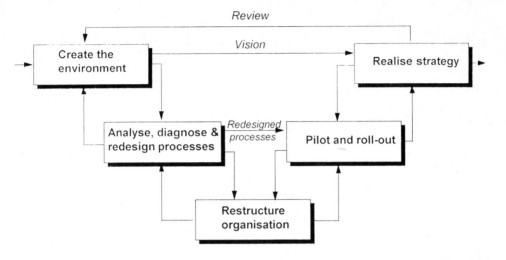

Figure 9.4 An overall approach to BPR

Although shown as a linear progression, it is not suggested that each step is followed in sequence or necessarily has to be performed. Rather, each stage represents a potentially significant event in a BPR exercise, each of which requires that a number of questions are addressed. There are certain implications of this however. For example, embarking on detailed process analysis before the strategic context and problem scope have been set is not recommended. The value of the framework is as a reference model that enables the BPR practitioner to position their initiative against the identified stages and identify key milestones they may need to address. The emphasis on different stages will undoubtedly vary from one organization to another with factors such as time, culture, scope of the initiative, etc, undoubtedly influencing the approach taken.

In Figure 9.5 we also map existing tools and techniques against the stages. An important observation from the framework is that different approaches lend themselves to different stages of the initiative and that BPR is more than the modelling, mapping and redesign of organizational processes. To be successful may demand the exercise of a wide range of skills and disciplines – an important point when choosing a facilitator or champion, either internally or externally. This will demand different mind sets and personal styles to manage.

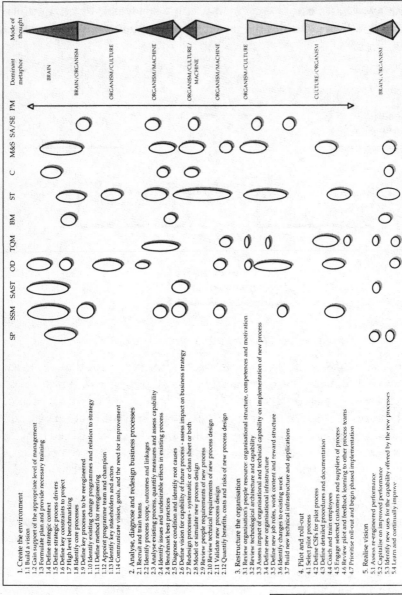

Figure 9.5   Key stages of the BPR process mapped against tools and techniques

The softer approaches are more relevant in the earlier stages where the problem is less well defined and during implementation where human processes are central. More quantified techniques become applicable as we move into the analytical stages. Despite this general trend it is important to realize that the distinction between soft and hard techniques is not always clear. For example, 'hard' modelling techniques can be used to help define and document individual perceptions during the problem structuring phase. This applies to both the analysts and the people who will be subject to the changes. Equally, managing and motivating the redesign team is very important.

What the approach highlights is the necessity to structure and define the problem before analysis can begin. In management terms this entails providing a strategic context for the project and using that context to focus on what the aims and objectives are and, crucially, what the focus of the project will be.

Although the strategy must consider the roles, relationships and processes across the entire company, attempting to re-engineer the entire organization at once is unlikely to succeed. There must be a narrowed focus, possibly as part of a phased programme, to increase the chances of success. Articulating this will then define the necessary approach to re-engineer the processes in question. It is also possible that BPR may not be the answer to the problem. Issues to do with unclear strategy and business direction, ineffective management, poorly targeted and trained employees are issues that a BPR initiative may highlight but are not areas that BPR is designed to resolve. A project based improvement programme, essentially what BPR is, cannot replace a lack of business appreciation and poor management. Equally without these, the improvements fostered by BPR cannot succeed or be sustained.

During the process analysis, diagnosis and redesign stages phases there are essentially three key stages:

- understanding the current process and its capability to support the business drivers and strategy
- diagnosing the nature and root causes of the problems that limit this capability. These root causes need to be addressed in the new process design as they will undoubtedly reflect fundamental weaknesses in the organizational structure and processes
- redesigning the processes to improve these problems and to support the new business direction.

The balance between the present-push and future-pull approach is an interesting debate. To a large extent, the result will depend upon the context of the problem and the problem itself. Regardless, unless it really is a greenfield site, an understanding of both current and desired states must be developed in order to migrate between the two.

Understanding and settling on the right level of detail is also key. For example, too much analytical rigour in the early stages of a BPR project can kill off momentum and creativity; too little rigour in the design stages can lead to poorly thought out plans damaging credibility, causing rework and wasting time. Equally, the amount and level of detail required to sell the concepts of re-engineering to senior management are not the same as those required to define and manage operational changes, particularly in people's work content and behaviour. Both must be managed effectively to be successful. Again the balance between the two is heavily contextual.

Creativity, often seen to be the essence of the redesign phase, is an intuitive process and a potential leap of faith. This is an area that classical management science does not address. Creating new ideas and ways of doing things requires us to diverge our thinking or, to quote a common cliché, to think 'out of our box'. The further the leap, the harder it is conceptualize and the greater the risk involved. Equally, validating this vision becomes increasingly difficult but may offer an increasingly significant competitive advantage to the organization. Interestingly, most of the BPR literature addresses creativity as a task internal to the project team. If the new ideas are to be accepted by the organization, however, the senior managers and stakeholders may need to be equally creative in their acceptance. Classical management science techniques aim to converge on a solution to a problem. Both thought processes are necessary but must be balanced to achieve the appropriate levels of creativity and develop rigorous and effective solutions.

A final point on change management and BPR. Many discussions on BPR refer to or imply the need for radical change and cite this as a key difference between BPR and TQM. This is misplaced. The objective of BPR is to create step improvements in performance, by frequently challenging the current mode of operation. While a new process design may be radical, high levels of change cause turmoil and generate risk. Incremental change is more easily managed and less risky and, we believe, a more appropriate change model for BPR. Davenport and Stoddard (1994) recently reported that rarely is 'clean slate' change found.

CONCLUSIONS

Our conclusion is that BPR is a philosophy, not a methodology. It offers no prescriptions for the way organizations should work day-to-day but rather is concerned with how organizations can improve performance. These improvements have to be related to a clear business strategy. There is a clear process focus that allows us to harness existing tools and techniques for improving business performance. We have observed that BPR may not necessarily be a new way of thinking or doing but an amalgamation of previous theories and practices of organizations, systems and management thinking, utilizing them with a distinct focus. That is not to discredit the concept as it offers a number of opportunities:

- it provides a holistic approach to combining a range of tools and methods that can be matched to the organizational context and problem
- it allows us to take a new perspective of old approaches which failed to deliver the expected benefits
- there is a clear focus on outcomes and not on a predetermined structure
- it highlights that design of an organization should be tied to its strategic context.

It is clear that there is no one tool or methodology which will address the entire process of BPR. It is more relevant to think of a framework within which different tools can be used, depending on both the content and context of the problem. The message is that the discerning practitioner must select carefully: understand your context and your problem before selecting an approach and choosing tools and techniques.

REFERENCES

Ackere, A van, Larsen, E R and Morecroft, J D W (1993) 'Systems Thinking and Business Process Redesign', *European Management Journal*, 11, 4, 412–23.

Ascari, A, Rock, M and Dutta, S (1994) 'Reengineering and Organisational Change: Lessons From a Comparative Analysis of Case Studies', *Working Paper, 94/28TM/OB/SM*, INSEAD, Fontainebleau, Paris.

Bales, R F (1950) *Interaction Process Analysis*, Addison-Wesley, Reading, Mass.

Bartlett, C A and Ghoshal, S (1990) 'Matrix Management: not a Structure, a Frame of Mind', *Harvard Business Review*, July–August, 138–45.

Belmonte, R W and Murray, R J, 'Getting Ready for Strategic Change: Surviving Business Process Redesign', *Information Systems Management*, Summer, 23–9.

Bertalanfy, L von (1956) 'General Systems Theory', *General Systems*, I, 1–10.

Burrell, G and Morgan, G (1979) *Sociological Paradigms and Organisational Analysis*, Heinemann, London.

Carter, L, Haythorn, W, Meirowitz, B and Lanzetta, J (1951) 'A Note on a New Technique of Interaction Recording', *Journal of Abnormal Social Psychology*, 46, 258–60.

Champy, J (1995) *Re-engineering Management: The Mandate for New Leadership*, HarperCollins.

Chapple, E D (1940) 'Measuring Human Relations: an Introduction to the Study of Iinteraction of Individuals', *General Psychological Monogram*, 22, 3–147.

Checkland, P B (1981) *Systems Thinking: Systems Practice*, John Wiley, Chichester.

CSC Index (1994) *The State of Re-engineering*, CSC Index, London.

Davenport, T H (1993) *Process Innovation: Reengineering Work Through Information Technology*, Harvard Business School Press, Boston, Mass.

Davenport, T H and Stoddard, D B (1994) 'Re-engineering: Business Change of Mythic Proportions', *MIS Quarterly*, June, pp 121–7.

Davenport, T H and Short, J E (1990) 'The New Industrial Engineering: Information Technology and Business Process Redesign', *Sloan Management Review*, Summer, 11–27.

Dixon, J R, Arnold, P, Heineke, J, Kim, J S and Mulligan, P (1994) 'Business Process Reengineering: Improving in New Strategic Directions', *California Management Review*, Summer, 93–108.

Duck, J D (1993) 'Managing Change: the Art of Balancing', *Harvard Business Review*, November–December, 109–18.

Earl, M and Khan, B (1994) 'How New is Business Process Redesign?', *European Management Journal*, 12, 1, 20–30.

Edwards, C and Peppard, J (1994a) 'Business Process Redesign: Hype, Hope or Hypocrisy?', *Journal of Information Technology*, 9, 251–66.

Edwards, C and Peppard, J (1994b) 'Forging a Link Between Business Strategy and business Re-engineering', *European Management Journal*, 12, (4), 407–16.

Flood, R L and Jackson, M C (1991) *Creative Problem Solving*, Wiley, Chichester.

Forrester, J W (1968) *Principles of Systems*, Wright Allen.

Ghoshal, S and Bartlett, C A, 'Changing the Role of Top Management: Beyond Structure to Processes', *Harvard Business Review*, January–February, 86–96.

Hall, G, Rosenthal, J and Wade, J (1993) 'How to Make Reengineering *Really* Work', *Harvard Business Review*, November–December, 119–31.

Hamel, G and Prahalad, C K (1994) *Competing For The Future*, Harvard Business School Press, Boston, Mass.

Hammer, M (1990) 'Reengineering Work: Don't Aautomate – Obliterate', *Harvard Business Review*, July–August, 104–12.

Hammer, M (1994) 'Hammer Defends Re-engineering', *The Economist*, 5 November, 96.

Hammer, M And Stanton, S (1994) 'No Need for Excuses', *Financial Times*, October 5, 14.

Hammer, M and Champy, J (1993) *Reengineering The Corporation: A Manifesto for Business Revolution*, Nicholas Brealey Publishing, London.

Horsted, J and Doherty, N (1994) 'Poles Apart? – Integrating Business Process Redesign and Human Resource Management', *Business Change & Re-engineering*, 1, 4, 49–56.

Jarvenpaa, S and Stoddard, D B (1993) *Business Process Reengineering: Tactics for Managing Radical Change*, Working Paper, Harvard Business School, Boston, MA.

Johansson, H J, McHugh, P, Pendlebury, A J, and Wheeler, B (1993) *Business Process Reengineering: Breakpoint Strategies For Market Dominance*, Wiley, Chichester.

Katz, D and Kahn, R (1966) *The Social Psychology of Organisations*, Wiley, New York.

Kiernan, M (1993) 'The New Strategic Architecture:Learning to Compete in the Twenty-first Century', *Academy of Management Executive*, 7, (1), 7–21

Lawler, E E (1994) 'From Job-based to Competency-based Organisations', *Journal of Organisational Behaviour*, 15, 3–15.

Leavitt, H J (1965) 'Applying Organisational Change in Industry: Structural, Technological and Humanistic Approaches', in J G (ed) March, *Handbook of Organisations*, Rand McNally, Chicago, Ill.

Lewin, K (1951) *Field Theory in Social Science*, Collected Papers of Kurt Lewin, ed D Cartwright, Harper and Row, New York.

Mayo, E (1971) 'Hawthorne and the Western Electric Company', in D S Pugh, (ed), *Organisation Theory*, Penguin, Middlesex.

Morgan, G (1986) *Images of Organisations*, Sage, Newbury Park, California.

Ouchi, W (1981) *Theory Z*, Addison-Wesley, Reading, Mass.

Peppard, J and Rowland, P (1995) *The Essence of Business Process Re-engineering*, Prentice Hall International, Hemel Hempstead.

Pettigrew, A M (1987) 'Context and Action in the Transformation of the Firm', *Journal of Management Studies*, November, 649–70.

Prahalad, C K and Hamel, G (1990) 'The Core Competence of the Corporation', *Harvard Business Review*, May–June, 79–91.

Prahalad, C K and Hamel, G (1994) 'Strategy as a Field of Study: Why Search for a New Paradigm?', *Strategic Management Journal*, 15, 5–16.

Preece, I and Peppard, J (1993) *Business Process Redesign: Literature Review*, Information Systems Research Centre, Cranfield School of Management.

Rayport, J F and Sviokla, J J (1994) 'Managing in the Marketspace', *Harvard Business Review*, November–December, 1994, pp 141–50.

Schein, E H (1988) *Process Consultation Volume 1: Its Role in Organisation Development*, Addison Wesley, Reading, Mass.

Schonberger, R J (1994) 'Human Resource Management Lessons from a Decade of Total Quality Management and Reengineering', *California Management Review*, Summer, 109–23.

Scott Morton, M S (ed) (1991) *The Corporation of the 1990s: Information Technology and Organisational Transformation*, Oxford University Press, New York.

Senge, P M (1990) *The Fifth Discipline: The Art and Practice of the Learning Organisation*, Doubleday/Currency, New York.

Shah, J, Peppard, J and Preece, I (1994) *Business Process Redesign: Literature Review II*, Information Systems Research Centre, Cranfield School of Management.

Stalk, G, Evans, P and Shulman, L E, 'Competing on Capabilities: The New Rules of Corporate Strategy', *Harvard Business Review*, March–April, 57–69.

Trist, E and Bamforth, K (1951) 'Some Social and Psychological Consequences of the Long Wall Method of Coal Getting', *Human Relations*, 4, 3–38.

Venkatraman, N, 'IT Induced Business Re-configuration' in M S Scott Morton, (ed), *The Corporation of the 1990s: Information Technology and Organisational Transformation*, Oxford University Press, New York, 122–58.

Wernerfelt, B (1984) 'A Resource-based View of the Firm', *Strategic Management Journal*, 5,(2), 171–80.

10

TQM AND BPR COMPARED

Chris Morgan, Nene College

INTRODUCTION

A major new management theory or philosophy appears on average every five to ten years. Why practising executives are prepared to try these new theories while often abandoning established successful practices is a mystery. Some would claim that a new theory can re-energize executive thinking and inspire them to new and better goals. Some might claim that the 'bandwagon effect' is in operation and that the change is adopted to maintain a competitive edge. Others change because their organization is in need of revitalizing. Whether it is need, greed, fear or simply boredom that drives executives, it would seem prudent to evaluate new ideas in a logical and consistent manner.

This chapter seeks to explore the relationships and differences between Total Quality Management (TQM) and Business Process Re-engineering (BPR). TQM is still being actively adopted by many organizations. However, it can be regarded as a mature philosophy having been around in one form or another for some time. BPR, on the other hand, is relatively new and is growing in popularity. So, will BPR replace TQM? Is it a case of 'the king is dead – long live the king', or are we approaching the state in which management theories and philosophies are beginning to converge? By understanding the BPR–TQM relationship it might be possible to gain a greater insight into the wider issues that face managers today and in the future.

TQM VS BPR

When trying to evaluate the differences between TQM and BPR it is important to decide whether or not they are theories or philosophies. The OED defines a theory as a '... system of ideas explaining something', and a philosophy as a '... system of principles ...'. Not a great deal of help, it might be argued, but on balance labelling TQM and BPR philosophies would seem to be more appropriate as they both claim to establish a framework for effective management action.

The next problem is to establish what is to be compared with what. Here it is necessary to make the assumption that a management philosophy is universally applicable – a tenuous assumption to be sure as very few organizations appear to have much in common. It is true that organizations may have similar products, use similar resources and comply to certain statutory requirements, but beyond this comparisons become difficult. Even a cursory exploration of Johnson and Scholes' (1993) 'cultural web' leads to the conclusion that the range of interrelated variables that make an organization's paradigm is very large indeed. However, the cultural web at least predicates the possibility of eventual change in all organizations. If this change is directed by a management philosophy, so much the better. On the basis of this assumption it is necessary to establish a framework of comparison.

Currently there is no universally accepted comparative framework for management philosophies, no taxonomy. Because of this the author would suggest that a reasonable comparative framework based on three factors – impact on management and management systems, impact on operational organization and impact on work people – be used. These three factors may then be subdivided to provide a reasonably balanced comparative view. The analysis in Table 10.1 has been derived from a broad reading of current literature (Hammer and Champy (1993), Johansson (1993), Morris and Brandon (1993), Harrington (1991), Crosby (1979), Dean and Evans (1994), Ernst & Young (1992), Fiegenbaum (1991), Ishikawa (1985), Morgan and Murgatroyd (1994), Oakland (1994), Price (1992)), and from the author's own experience of implementing these philosophies.

While these comparisons are not exhaustive, what is immediately apparent is how limited the areas of agreement actually are. This is surprising as both philosophies claim to improve organizational performance. Clearly no weighting has been ascribed to these comparative features and to some extent the authors interpretation must be taken into account. In spite of these factors it is clear that the differences outweigh the similarities. This can only be explained by emphasis. TQM is essentially a normative theory that seeks to change people's attitudes, and through this organizational effectiveness. BPR is a structuralist theory that seeks to change processes and through this organizational efficiency. TQM is a 'soft' philosophy with its roots in Human Resource Management. BPR is a 'hard' philosophy with its roots in Scientific Management. Both philosophies claim to have a clear focus on satisfying customer needs, but can such apparently different theories actually deliver the goods?

Table 10.1 Comparative framework of management philosophies

	TQM	BPR
Impact on management and management systems:		
• Responsibility for implementation	Top management	Top management
• Nature of initial implementation	Top down	Top down
• Main control measure	Cost of quality	Cost of process
• Change in management structure	Marginal change	Radical change
• Impact on management careers	No special impact	Restricted promotion
• Agent of change	Quality team	BPR team
• Change in management systems	Marginal change	Radical change
Impact on operational organisation:		
• Scope of change	Organization	Organization or department
• Element of change	Individual	Process
• Change process	Quality awareness	BPR projects
• Enabling medium	People	Technology
• Focus for change	People	Process
• Team structures	Marginal change	Radical change
• Market sensitivity	Improve response	Improve response
• Information focus	Organization	Process
• Information access	Functional	Universal
• Impact on jobs	Marginal change	Multifunction workers
Impact on work people:		
• Focus for responsibility	Individual	Process
• Scope of work	Marginal change	Multifunction
• Change in flexibility	Marginal change	Considerable
• Focus for initiatives	TQM team	BPR team
• Pay structures	Marginal change	Restructuring needed
• Impact on promotion	Marginal change	Fewer opportunities
• Training requirements	Quality training	Skill training
• Education requirements	Marginal	Vital (for flexibility)

In truth, the answer to this question can only be *we do not know*. If either philosophy provided a totally correct framework to all organisational problems, failures would not occur. There are, however, several well-documented cases of TQM failures which are often due to management problems rather than philosophical problems. The evidence for BPR failures is more limited – probably due to the newness of the philosophy.

Another reason may be that at the time of writing no organisation has completely re-engineered their business. Cane (1993), quoting the OTR consultancy, suggests that 'nobody has re-engineered their whole business: it is too risky .... no company dares risk removing the pillars that support its business, rearranging and putting them back into place – the worry is that the business would collapse before the reassembly was complete.' Conversely the claims for success of the two theories are often overstated and the success transitory. A sanguine observer might draw the attention of TQM and BPR acolytes to Mayo (1933) and the effects of the Hawthorne experiments!

TQM AND BPR

Clearly the previous analysis only highlighted the differences between TQM and BPR. Is there a case to be argued that commonality of intent (satisfying the customer) should provide some kind of synergy? Should TQM and BPR be regarded as two parts of a wider spectrum that includes other philosophies and approaches to management such as Just-In-Time (JIT), Kaizen or Chaos Theory? Certainly if it were possible to combine TQM and BPR then some powerful answers to organizational problems could be found. If it were possible to improve quality performance, people performance and process performance simultaneously this would be ideal. But would it be practical?

The answer to this question is not immediately obvious, *simply because no one has tried it*. However, if we examine the relationship between JIT and TQM a lot of evidence exists to show that in the manufacturing sector at least, they do work well together. In fact JIT actually needs an effective quality system to work at all. Is it possible to argue that JIT is in fact a kind of BPR?

JIT is certainly radical in its approach to reorganizing manufacturing and servicing facilities. The claims for performance improvement closely parallel those of BPR. The foci for JIT systems are quality and process efficiency and improvements come from automation and the extensive use of computers to achieve integration. The approach to change is holistic. The impact on management structures is to delayer in order to improve communications, and the impact on operatives is to broaden job spans and encourage ownership of problems and solutions. Surely, then, JIT and BPR are close in concept *de facto* if not *de jure*. Is it therefore reasonable to argue that if JIT and TQM can exist together then BPR and TQM can exist together?

The pragmatic approach to BPR advocated by Morris and Brandon (1993) suggests that BPR and TQM can work together. They argue that at the application level (the BPR team), there is no real conflict of interest.

There is still a need to ensure that re-engineered processes meet quality criteria as well as process criteria. While this assertion does not seem unreasonable, it does not explain how some of the wider issues of disagreement (previously identified) can be resolved. Perhaps the Morris and Brandon suggestion should be modified to say that *quality* needs to be a part of any BPR system. Pragmatically it may be that TQM and BPR *at full implementation* could possibly be made to work together, but the evidence suggests that they would make uncomfortable bed fellows.

CONCLUSION

What becomes evident from any reasonable analysis (which discounts marketing hyperbole) is that BPR like many other management philosophies has something to offer management. There is still much to be clarified about BPR. However, as Cane (1993) suggests, it may soon be possible to 'to distinguish the elements of lasting value through a smokescreen of misinformation and mystery'. It is unlikely that BPR will offer anything substantially better than TQM; more likely it will become another tool bag for management or consultants to use, more suitable for some circumstances than others.

This leads on to two other considerations. The first is associated with how we measure and evaluate new management theories; the second is the issue of convergence.

The confusion which has surrounded BPR clearly emphasizes how poor our approach is to evaluating many management theories and philosophies, in spite of several decades of academic study. We still rely to a greater extent upon hearsay evidence and small samples of companies to judge the correctness or otherwise of philosophies (or even to discover new ones). We still use the *ceteris paribus* argument when issues get too complicated to evaluate with mathematics – if the mathematics actually exists! After all this time should we have not at least have developed a rigorous approach to analysis which can quickly test new theories or philosophies in order to prevent expensive mistakes. Perhaps some kind of modelling technique can replace the current rather erratic sampling system which leaves more questions unanswered than answered.

Without an effective system of analysis it is impossible to judge what we see. The issue of convergence of management theories emphasizes this point. At the current time we cannot tell whether TQM, BPR, JIT, Kaizen and other management theories and techniques are truly independent phenomena, or a part of a wider spectrum. We cannot be sure that 'hard' and 'soft' management systems are better or worse, or simply more or less appropriate. We cannot truly evaluate the cultural effects of our observations and yet are quite prepared to lift ideas from one culture and transplant them in another – expecting them to work. Perhaps the issue of the relationship between TQM and BPR could be the starting point for better and more rigorous investigations. If we cannot make this move then we may as well revert to the wisdom of Sun Tzu, for organizations have many similarities with armies – surely we have outgrown these ideas!

REFERENCES

Cane, A (1993) 'Technology: Back to Square One – Or Two', *Sunday Times*, 20 April.

Cooley, M (1987) *Architect or Bee?*, Hogarth Press, London.

Crosby, P B (1979) *Quality is Free*, McGraw-Hill, New York.

Dean, J W and Evans, J R (1994) *Total Quality: Management, Organization and Strategy*, West, New York.

Ernst & Young (1992) *Total Quality: A Managers Guide for the 1990s*, Kogan Page, London.

Fiegenbaum, A V (1991) *Total Quality Control*, 3rd edn, McGraw-Hill, New York.

Hammer, M and Champy, J, (1993) *Re-engineering the Corporation: A Manifesto for Business Revolution*, Nicholas Brealey Publishing, London.

Harrington, J (1991) *The Breakthrough Strategy for Total Quality, Productivity, and Competitiveness*, McGraw-Hill, New York.

Ishikawa, K (trans D. Lu) (1985) *What is Total Quality Control – the Japanese Way*, Prentice-Hall, Englewood Cliffs, N J.

Johansson, H J, McHugh, P, Pendlebury, J A and Wheeler, W A (1993) *Business Process Re-engineering: Breakpoint Strategies for Market Dominance*, Wiley, Chichester.

Johnson, G and Scholes, K (1993) *Exploring Corporate Strategy*, Prentice-Hall, Hemel Hempstead.

Mayo, E (1933) *The Human Problems of an Industrial Civilization*, Macmillan, New York.

Morgan, C and Murgatroyd, S (1994) *Total Quality Management in the Public Sector*, Open University Press, Milton Keynes.

Morris, D and Brandon, J (1993) *Re-engineering Your Business*, McGraw-Hill, New York.

Oakland, J (1994) *Total Quality Management: The Route to Improving Performance, 2nd edn*, Butterworth-Heinemann, London.

Price, F (1992) *Right Every Time*, Gower, Aldershot.

Scott Morton, M (ed) (1991) *The Corporation of the 1990s: Information Technology and Organisational Transformation*, Oxford University Press, Oxford.

Stacey, R D (1991) *The Chaos Frontier: Creative Strategic Control for Business*, Butterworth-Heinemann, Oxford.

Storey, J (1994) *New Wave Manufacturing Strategies*, Paul Chapman, London.

Thom, R (1974) *Modèles Mathematiques de la Morphogénèse*, Union Générale d'Editions, Paris.

11

CREATIVE CHAOS OR CONSTRUCTIVE CHANGE: BUSINESS PROCESS RE-ENGINEERING VERSUS SOCIO-TECHNICAL DESIGN?

Enid Mumford, Manchester Business School

CHANGE – IS THERE ANY ESCAPE?

All the management books tell us that today change is a fact of life. Managers must change if they want to survive. The business environment is increasing in turbulence and becoming ever more demanding, competitive and international and only the dynamic and evolving company will remain viable. There is no longer any place for the stable slow-moving firm which relies on the existence of secure, unchanging markets for products which never alter.

This scenario has a great deal of truth in it but it is also a dangerous one if the managerial response is a belief that change will solve problems simply because it causes things to be done differently. Change has its own characteristics and risks. It can become a 'fashion industry' with the latest management 'buzzwords' acting as a stimulus to copycat behaviour. Managers feel pressured to introduce 'integrated systems', 'management by objectives', 'total quality', 'process re-engineering' and anything else the management gurus recommend and their competitors are trying. If managers are encountering serious problems then they may try a revolutionary approach and make major alterations to their activities and organization.

In the right situations, and used to address appropriate problems, all of these strategies may bring considerable benefit. Introduced as magic spells to solve ill-defined problems they are likely to bring with them more difficulties than they solve and the cure may prove more fatal than the disease. New processes always bring new challenges. These challenges will be new to the company and managers will have no experience in handling them. This can lead to organizational confusion and chaos.

Change can also be introduced as a form of 'shake-up' for a firm that is seen as slow-moving and complacent. Newly appointed senior managers are prone to introduce this kind of change. They believe that they must justify their appointment, make their mark, gain control. This kind of change often instils fear but it does not always achieve worthwhile results. Change will now be 'change for change's sake' and not a response to careful diagnosis, identification and evaluation of options. It may have high costs as morale drops and staff become anxious and insecure.

A more acceptable and safer form of change is change as a response to a careful monitoring of external events. The firm recognizes that its markets are altering and that it runs the risk of falling profits and a loss of market share. This careful monitoring of a company's environment is often recommended as today's approved approach for the 'thinking' manager. He or she must strive to achieve the learning organization. This is the company that consistently, systematically and continually examines its activities and its business environment and checks that the fit between these is good. It also assesses what is likely to change in its activities and environment in the short and long term and works out a range of alternative strategies for likely future contingencies. The appropriate strategy can then be implemented as the new situation appears on the company horizon.

This kind of response to change is at odds with the popular 'change or perish' for it may mean that a firm changes very little for quite long periods of time but that it always has the necessary ideas and strategies in place for when change is necessary. However, this conservative approach may indicate, not that the company is on a suicide course, but that it is both intellectually mature and organizationally healthy. Like good doctors its managers carry out constant checks on the company state of health, understand this and how it is likely to change over time. They also understand those factors in the environment that can most affect its health, and they have a range of treatments thought out, tested and available to prevent major problems occurring or to cure them if they do.

The managers of this kind of company require very special resources if they are to carry out this expert diagnosis and preventive treatment. They require employees who do not fear change, but understand, welcome and can handle it. And they require these employees, as individuals and groups, to be good diagnosticians and physicians in their own areas and jobs, to have the skills and knowledge to change as their situation changes and to be willing to learn and take responsibility. To achieve this management must create a supportive change culture, a participative philosophy, and an absence of victims. More than anything they must create and establish a set of shared values, they must willingly accept the viewpoints and interests of others, and they must ensure there are no unresolved, serious and deep-seated conflicts between groups and individuals. These are objectives which enlightened managers of the twenty-first century should strive towards even though, like the promised land, they are not easily attainable.

LEARNING HOW TO CHANGE

How do managers learn to do these very difficult things? Burgoyne (1992) believes that there are three levels of learning in most organizations. First, there is very simple learning. The firm learns how to introduce and manage processes, often production processes. It turns these processes into sets of procedures and keeps them going as a required method of working. Learning at this level assumes that the environment is stable and is not concerned with change. The second level of learning is when an organization can adapt to its environment. It recognizes when markets are changing or have changed and alters itself to meet these new demands. Often this alteration takes the form of improved performance. The objective behind this adaptation is survival.

The third level of learning is more complex and sophisticated. Managers now try and exert an influence on their environments so that they can exist more comfortably and avoid major crises. They try and improve the performance of their suppliers and please their customers through better quality goods and service so that their environment is less turbulent and there is less need for dramatic internal change. This makes them more stable and less concerned with constant reorganization. Controlling the environment in this way requires clear values, a high level of knowledge and the ability to persuade and help others to change their ways. It requires a willingness to agree things collectively as change should represent the views of all and this, in turn, requires open communication. It also requires an ability to identify the problems in external situations which can be influenced, reduced and possibly removed. And the aim is always to enrich the outside world and not to exploit it.

Bateson (1973) tells us that there is also a fourth level of learning. This is learning how to learn.

How can a firm start moving towards the mature learning states three and four that the more thoughtful of today's management gurus recommend? Where does it start, what direction does it take, how does it proceed? Perhaps the most critical factor is leadership from the top. A leadership which says firmly 'this is the culture of this company. This is how we are all to perform, behave, relate and, most important of all, learn' in order to be a *successful* and *caring* company. By 'successful' is meant surviving in a tough and volatile market environment through providing high quality products and services and helping those the firm interacts with to do the same. It also means introducing appropriate, steady and well-conceived change and avoiding the traumatic change that comes from major and unplanned for crises.

This, in turn requires excellent intelligence and communication so that managers understand their business environment and the direction in which it is moving at any moment in time. They must also understand their own particular skills, competencies and limitations and strive to improve these. It also means running an ethical business with high standards of required and expected behaviour.

By 'caring' is meant providing job satisfaction, a high-quality work environment and the opportunity for personal development for all employees at all levels in the company. It also means caring for customers, suppliers and others who provide the firm with services. It means understanding how they wish to relate to the firm and the kind of support and help that they want managers to provide. It also means caring for the immediate environment – the community in which the firm resides – by trying to enhance its quality and refraining from damaging it through pollution or damage of any kind. And it also means considering the wider world environment so that the firm's immediate environment is not protected at the expense of the environments of other countries, by exporting waste to the Third World, for example, or damaging the resources of poorer countries through other forms of exploitation.

All of these things require a leader with strong ethical principles, a broad vision and considerable intelligence at the top of the company. We are looking for a John Harvey Jones or a Pehr Gyllenhammar. We may even find some of these qualities in managers from other countries. The Japanese have brought to European firms a set of management practices that encourage high standards, efficiency and an ability to manage change successfully.

LEVERS FOR CHANGE

Successful action requires four things: the ability to change the way things are done, the ability to achieve objectives, the ability to reorganize and integrate activities once the change has taken place and the ability to keep the new system operating until it is time for the next change (Parsons and Shils, 1951). These four activities have been described as innovation, commitment, organizational efficiency and performance (Hart and Quinn, 1993). Change of this kind requires a vision of the future, the ability to persuade others to cooperate by communicating this vision, the successful creation and implementation of a new system and the ability to manage and sustain this.

Action also requires intelligence, an awareness of when the fit between what is taking place and what is required is starting to fail. Necessary change may not be introduced if there is poor information about what is happening in the environment. Inappropriate change may occur if there is misinterpretation of events outside. McCabe and Dutton (1993) have suggested that uncertainty may sometimes be in the eye of the beholder. Managers who see their firms as ineffective may see the environment as more uncertain than it is. Similarly, managers who are overconfident about the success of their companies may not perceive danger signals until disaster is approaching fast.

Today, innovation is seen as one of the keys to successful survival. This is more than adaptation or environmental control, it is the creation of new ways of doing things – new products, services, structures, processes, methods and skills. Innovation can take place at all levels in all functions, but it requires creativity, the capacity for original thought and the ability to turn thought and ideas into something of substance. Just as the values of the top become the values of those lower down in the well-integrated company, so creativity at the top will stimulate creativity lower down and creativity, in turn, becomes innovation and an aid to survival.

Successful change, particularly if it is large scale or dramatic, requires shared values and mutual understanding. Commitment to change requires that employees at every level must know and understand the vision of the future that is being striven for. They must appreciate and approve what is involved and how they can personally contribute. Commitment to change is greatly assisted by accurate communication and free and open discussion. There must be opportunities for those who will be affected to raise issues, ask questions and participate in the debate on future action. They must also be able to express their ideas, attitudes, feelings, concerns and doubts. In this way barriers to change which arise from limited or distorted communication will be removed and reduced.

Participation or the involvement of all those who will be affected by change in its planning, design and implementation has been recommended by many writers for many years (Mumford, 1983). In the United States, Lawler (1986) has been advocating an approach called 'high involvement management' as the key to successful change and effective performance in the modern company. High involvement management is the extension of decision-making power, business information, rewards for performance and technical and social skills to the lowest level of the organization. Ledford and Mohrman (1993) suggest that the company with highly skilled staff dedicated to its values and interests will gain from the participation of all in decision-taking. Hopefully companies and managers are moving towards this but in most situations it is still an ideal rather than a reality.

Change can be facilitated by appropriate methods and tools which assist the identification and analysis of problems, the effective choice and use of technology and the redesign of work. Hirschheim and Klein (1994) have suggested that methodologies can reinforce an ethical design orientation by assisting individual and collective self-determination, critical self-reflection and freedom from unnecessary or undesirable social constraints. But, whatever route is taken to successful change it must be remembered that there is never 'one best way'. There must always be opportunities for choice and debate on what is a desirable and beneficial future and how best to achieve this. In Western organizations the ideal choice situation will increasingly be a group one, although individual interests must be understood and catered for.

SOCIO-TECHNICAL DESIGN AND BUSINESS PROCESS RE-ENGINEERING: TWO PHILOSOPHIES THAT MAY ASSIST SUCCESSFUL CHANGE

There are many prescriptions for successful change and some have been with us for a very long time. In this chapter it is proposed to concentrate on two that are proving popular today. These are the socio-technical approach and business process re-engineering. These will be examined critically, compared with each other and their strengths and limitations discussed.

> The more complex, fast-changing, interdependent world growing up in the wake of the second industrial revolution is rapidly rendering obsolete and maladaptive many of the values, organizational structures and work practices brought about by the first. In fact, something like their opposite seems to be required. This is nowhere more apparent than in the efforts of some of the most sophisticated firms in the advanced science-based industries to decentralize their operations, to debureaucratize their organizational form and to secure the involvement and commitment of their personnel at all levels by developing forms of participatory democracy.

This is not a quote from Michael Hammer in 1995 but a statement from Eric Trist when he gave a paper to the Edinburgh Conference on Science and Technology in 1971. Socio-technical systems theory and design was the product of Eric Trist and a group of social scientists who came together at the end of the Second World War and formed the Tavistock Institute of Human Relations in London (Mumford, 1987). The Tavistock, or the Tavvy as it is generally known, was established in 1946 by this group, many of whom had collaborated in wartime projects and most of whom had been members of the Tavistock Clinic before the war. The Tavistock Clinic was, and is, a therapeutic establishment staffed by psychologists concerned with mental health and individual development. This was the initial focus and interest of members of the Tavistock Institute, although they were interested in applying their ideas to workers in industry. The founding group were later joined by people from other disciplines: psychologists, sociologists and anthropologists.

Eric Trist became aware of the influence of technology on people when he was working in the jute industry in Scotland, in the late 1930s. He was a member of a small interdisciplinary team studying unemployment when the spinning section of the jute industry was being rationalized. He found that this change in technology caused unemployment, deskilling and alienation. The technical and social systems were acting on each other in a negative way.

Right from the beginning, influenced by Eric Trist's knowledge and experience, the Tavistock pioneers recognized the need for a new model of organizations, one that would replace the traditional rational, bureaucratic one. Eric told the 1971 Edinburgh Conference:

> The problem was not of simply 'adjusting' people to technology nor technology to people but of organizing the interface so that the best match could be obtained between them. Only the socio-technical whole could effectively be 'optimized'. This encompassed the enterprise as a whole – in relation to its environment – as well as its primary work groups and intervening subsystems. It was necessary to change the basic model in which organization theory had been conceived ...Workers are no longer embedded in the technology, contributing their energy or even their manipulative skill to it, but they are outside it, handling information from it and themselves becoming sources of information critical for its management. This change of position and role makes them, in fact, managers different in degree but not in kind from those who traditionally have carried this title. For the task of management is the regulation of systems and the function of managerial intervention is to establish control over the boundary conditions. Such is the type of activity in which workers now primarily engage, as fact finders, interpreters, diagnosticians, judges adjusters and change agents: whatever else they do is secondary. (Trist and Murray, 1993)

The Tavistock Institute made its first major contribution to socio-technical theory, and applied these principles, in 1949 when it began a number of field projects in the British coal industry. The coal industry had recently changed its technology and, following the example of mass production industry, had mechanized its production system.

As a result of the stress created by this new system, morale amongst the miners was low and there were many psychosomatic disorders. The newly created Coal Board asked the Tavistock group if they would carry out studies to find the cause of the problems.

As the research progressed the team began to recognize that the new technical system had created an inferior and damaging form of social organization. They began to formulate one of the most important principles of socio-technical design. This is that if a technical system is created at the expense of a social system the results obtained will be sub-optimal. They decided that when work is being designed the goal must always be the joint optimization of the social and technical systems.

This early research together with many projects in Scandinavia and one in India, led to many of the work design principles which are proving useful and relevant today. These principles were developed as a result of practical experiments but were reinforced by the Tavistock's interest in scientific theory. Their ideas were greatly influenced by an Austrian biologist, Bertalanffy, who wrote an article on biological open systems in nature, and by ideas drawn from cybernetics and psychology.

By the 1960s the team had developed and published their ideas on (1) the concept of a socio-technical system; (2) their definition of an organization as an open system; (3) the principle of organizational choice – the need to optimize and bring together social and technical systems; (4) a recognition of the importance of self-managing groups, and (5) better understanding of the problems of work alienation.

In the 1970s they recognized five salient issues that needed to be tackled. These were:

1. The pervasive influence of alienation caused by industry defining men and women as spare parts in dead-end, locked-in jobs or as 'operating units' to be adjusted and used for the needs of society.
2. This anti-human industrial culture spreading to the service sector and the professions with negative consequences for clients as well as workers.
3. Advanced technology taking over routine activities and causing fear of unemployment since men and women are still seen as competing with, rather than complementary to, machines.
4. The accelerating change in technology was also raising questions of how to develop flexible people and organizations, and how to absorb change as a continuing part of working life.
5. Particular attention also needed to be given to how the disadvantaged and the powerless could progress into the mainstream of society: simply providing entry was not enough. (Davis and Cherns, 1975)

Socio-technical design, as it developed, came to have a clear ethical principle associated with it. This was to increase the ability of the individual to participate in decision-taking and through this to exercise a degree of control over the immediate work environment. Managers were advised to tell work groups what to do, but not how to do it. The latter would come from the knowledge, experience and skill of each work group. Ways of working might differ as each group decided on the approach that would enable it to provide an optimal result with a particular focus on high quality.

In order to facilitate group performance the Tavistock group developed a set of guidelines and principles to assist themselves and other consultants or managers who were concerned with improving the design of work situations. (Cherns, 1976). These, in a simplified form, were as follows.

Step 1. Initial Scanning.

The consultant should first get an understanding of the pre-change situation by making a description of the existing production system and its environment. He or she should determine where the most serious problems were located and where the emphasis of the analysis should be placed.

The description of the existing system should cover the following: the physical layout of the production system, the way work was organized, the main inputs and outputs, the changes in the product that occurred as it progressed through the system, the principle problems or 'variances', and the production and social objectives that were to be achieved.

Step 2. Identification of Unit Operations

Next, the consultant should identify the main stages of the production process: sets of activities which helped move the product into its finished state yet which were relatively self-contained. Usually there would be some kind of discontinuity between each stage – for example, the introduction of a new set of procedures, a new material or an elapse of time.

Step 3. Identification of Variances

The consultant should now look in more detail at the problems or variances, a variance being defined as a weak link in the system where it became difficult to achieve required or desired norms or standards. A variance was considered 'key' if it affected the quantity or quality of production, or operating or social costs. Variances should be carefully documented.

Step 4. Analysis of the Social System

The social system should next be examined and documented. This would cover the work relationships associated with the system and include

- A brief review of the organizational structure
- A table of variances noting the following:
  - where the variance occurred
  - where it showed up and was seen
  - where it was corrected

- who did this
- what they did to correct it
- what information they needed to correct it
- A note of other activities unconnected with the control of variances
- A description of the relationships required between workers for the optimal production of the product
- A note on the extent of work flexibility – the knowledge each worker had of the jobs of others
- A description of pay relationships – the nature of the pay system, differentials, bonuses, etc
- A description of the workers' psychological needs.

Step 5. How the Workers Saw their Roles

The consultant should examine the extent to which the workers thought the work structure and their roles met their psychological needs.

Step 6. The Maintenance and Supply Systems

An assessment should be made of how the system of machine maintenance in operation impacted on, and affected, the production system. The same should be done for the system that supplied materials and services to the department.

Step 7. The Corporate Environment

Information should be obtained on how development plans might affect the future operation of the department.

Step 8. Proposals for Change

Finally the consultant should gather together all this information and, after discussions with the different interest groups in the department, should arrive at an action programme. Proposals for action must contribute both to the improvement of the production system and to the improvement of the social system. The latter requires actions directed at improving job satisfaction and the quality of the work environment.

In many situations the Tavistock concept of self-managing groups was found to be the solution that best achieved both production and social objectives. Although the degree of self-management permitted depended on the views of management, a degree of self-management was found to increase motivation and assist the better control of production problems, quality improvement and the achievement of production targets.

SOCIO-TECHNICAL DESIGN IN PRACTICE

Today, business process re-engineering is being hailed as an entirely new approach to efficiency improvement. However, it is difficult to see how it differs from socio-technical design. In fact, the first major socio-technical design experiment might now be seen as a classic example of process re-engineering although it had as its principal goal the improvement of working conditions rather than higher production. This project was carried out in 1949 in a colliery in the North East of England. Here a new method of mining called 'long wall' was causing psychosomatic disorders amongst the miners (Trist and Bamforth, 1951).

The development of this system was influenced by the assembly line methods of production which were now becoming common in British factories. Mechanization now removed the old hand-got approach of working in small, tightly knit, self-regulating groups and substituted an impersonal system in which forty or fifty men would be strung out along a coal face, each responsible for a single task and with little opportunity for social contact (Scott *et al.*, 1963).

The new system required a cycle of work in which different operations were carried out on each shift. If one shift failed to complete its task, men on subsequent shifts would experience serious difficulties. The hand-got approach had been carried out in small teams in which each man undertook all the necessary tasks associated with hewing the coal and loading it into tubs. These teams were often composed of members of the same family and each individual accepted responsibility for the welfare of his mates. In contrast the new system created a high stress situation in which there was little opportunity for close social contact and which bred interpersonal and intergroup conflict.

The author of this chapter was also involved in a three-year study of coal mining financed by the National Coal Board. The focus of this was on industrial relations problems rather than work redesign although it soon became clear that these greatly influenced each other. As part of this study she spent a year working underground and became closely involved with the long wall method of mining. She describes below how she believes the Tavvy team would have set about socio-technical design at her colliery. This was called Maypole and located in the North-west coalfield. It was known as an unlucky pit as in 1913 there had been a major underground explosion and all the miners had been killed.

As any business process engineer would do today, the Tavistock team would begin by analysing in detail the long wall work system starting with an *initial scanning* to identify the cause of problems and moving onto a more detailed analysis which focused on the main phases of the production process which were named 'unit operations'. They would find that in long wall mining a seam of coal, which could be between eighteen inches and seven or eight feet in thickness and might extend horizontally for about a mile, was worked in a series of panels.

The first phase of the production cycle took place on the night shift where a coal-cutting machine was driven along the bottom of the coal face and a thin horizontal band of coal removed. This provided a space for loose coal to fall into when it was broken up with explosives on the next shift. The machine was controlled by a high status miner called a 'cutter'. At the same time a group of young miners called 'packers' were also on the night shift making packs of stone at intervals along the face so that when they removed the pit props from the worked space the unsupported roof fell in a safe and controlled manner. Sometimes the face was also packed with dirt because subsidence could easily occur at ground level and buildings suffer damage to their walls and foundations.

The second phase of the cycle took place on the day shift. This was the main production shift and was usually referred to as the 'winding' or 'coaling' shift. The first activity on this shift was for a small number of men called 'drillers' to drill the face, creating holes four foot six inches in depth. A grade two deputy called a 'shotfirer' next inserted explosives into these holes and fired these. This operation broke up the coal and left a mass of loose coal on the face. The main production workers, called 'fillers', shovelled the coal onto a moving conveyor belt which ran the whole length of the face and carried the coal to the main haulage system. As they did this they inserted pit props and bars at intervals to hold up the roof once the coal was removed. Each filler was responsible for a section of the face about nine yards in length. This was his 'stint' and he worked there every day, moving forward four feet per day as the face advanced.

The third phase of the cycle took place on the afternoon shift. Men called 'conveyor movers' now arrived. These took apart the conveyor belt that carried the coal along the face and reassembled it four feet further forward next to the new section of the face.

Lastly, as the face advanced the haulage roads had to be extended to keep up with it and a team of 'rippers' did this on the afternoon shift. They had the skilled job of driving a new roadway through, blasting the rock and erecting steel girders to hold up the new roof.

The other principal underground operation was running the haulage and ensuring that the coal got from the coal face to haulage roads where it was loaded into tubs. These tubs were pulled to the pit bottom, placed in the cage that transported men and coal to the surface, and sent up to the surface workers who sorted and graded the coal.

The face work cycle of operations was stressful and alienating even when it worked smoothly. There was little opportunity for social contact or teamworking underground with the exception of the rippers who worked as small integrated groups. Unfortunately underground conditions in many collieries were far from stable. There could be falls of roof, underground water, seams of rock instead of coal and, on occasion, methane gas. This meant that the work cycles would get out of phase. The fillers would be unable to complete the filling operation on their shift and so would leave coal on the face at the end of the shift. The conveyor movers would then arrive and find that they had to clear coal before they could start moving the belts. The same could happen to the packers who might have to finish the conveyor moving operation before they could start packing the face. Often the correct cycle could only be returned to normal at the weekend.

The Tavistock team would now do an *analysis of variances* and note all these problems. They would recognize that the major problems occurred at the boundaries between each cycle activity and the next when one occupational group replaced another. Key variances were factors due to physical conditions underground such as water, gas or rock replacing coal in the seam. These variances could not be eliminated but they could be more effectively controlled. Operational variances were affected by key variances and showed up as the inability of each face work group to finish its work by the end of the shift. This meant that the men on the next shift had to complete the previous shift's work, even though they were paid less, before they could start their own work.

The Tavistock *analysis of the social system* would examine these problems in detail and identify how they affected working relationships between the miners. They would find that they created a great deal of stress and conflict. Strikes that took place were often not against management action but against the behaviour of men on another shift. Some miners also increased conflict by taking retaliatory action. For example, the conveyor movers might become so annoyed at finding coal still on the face that, when they assembled the conveyor belts in their new position, they deliberately left some of the bolts undone. This meant that when the fillers shovelled coal onto the belts on the morning shift the belts fell apart.

When the researchers asked the miners what they thought of their *roles and relationships* they would find a great deal of bitterness. Those who were not in the top status and best paid groups of cutters, fillers and rippers were very bitter about the system and disliked its unfairness and the conflict it caused. Social relationships were worsened by the fact that men on different shifts had no contact with each other. Because of the shift system they did not meet socially and they passed each other in the dark when walking to and from the face at the beginning and end of each shift.

The final stages of the Tavistock analysis would be an examination of the *maintenance and supply systems* and an estimate of how change might affect the *corporate environment*. Maintenance and supply could cause management problems as time was lost if breakdowns occurred and supplies were slow in reaching the coal face, but these were not as serious as the working problems on the face. Colliery management hoped for a solution that would reduce the number of strikes and the miners, absenteeism both of which were causing the colliery to lose money.

What *proposals for change* could the Tavistock group now make that would leave the technology in place yet solve the organizational and human problems? The challenge was to create a new system of work that would ease these problems, reduce the stress felt by the miners and, if possible, provide more satisfying and interesting jobs for the face workers. In doing this the researchers would recognize that there were pressures and constraints. Pressures came from the new National Coal Board which was anxious to increase coal production and demonstrate the efficiency benefits of the long wall method. Constraints came from the area mining engineers who would not allow the technical logic of the long wall method to be tampered with.

How could this problem be solved? It was not going to be easy. In the original Tavvy project the solution came not so much from inspired thinking as by a visit by a member of the Tavistock team who had previously been a coal miner to his old Yorkshire pit. This was a drift mine where miners could get underground by walking and where faces were short. Here he found that although the long wall technology was in place the men were working in small teams as they had done with the hand-got method. Could this method of teamworking possibly be transferred to the long faces of the problem North-West colliery?

The Tavistock solution was to restructure the social organization underground by creating a number of multiskilled, semi-autonomous face work teams, each containing nine men. Each team had responsibility for all the tasks involved in managing a section of the coal face. This new system greatly altered the men's responsibilities and methods of working. Instead of doing one task only on one shift only – shovelling coal, moving the conveyor belts or packing the worked face – the men now learned all of these tasks, became multiskilled and organized themselves as a team. If there were likely to be problems on the day shift when the coal was shot fired and shovelled onto the conveyor belts, then four men instead of three would agree to do the work. The same flexibility occurred on the other shifts.

Also, instead of each activity being paid a different rate of pay so that the men shovelling got more than those who moved the belts and both groups got more than those who packed the face, management agreed that all the men in one team were paid the same rate. They could earn more if they increased productivity by taking responsibility for a larger section of the coal face. This reorganization applied only to the face workers. Rippers, haulage and the specialist cutter operators had never experienced major problems with the cyclical method of work and were not interested in change.

Although this new work system was only tried on one or two faces, the result was increased production, increased pay and higher morale in the experimental groups. Unfortunately, the experiments did not last or spread. The trade union, which had not been consulted about the new system, objected to some miners being paid more than others and to the altering of existing pay differentials. Colliery management was reluctant to enter into conflict with the unions, the experiment was stopped and the miners went back to the old routinized method of working. The Tavistock group transferred their research to Scandinavia were there was better cooperation between management and unions and a more sympathetic response to new ideas of work organization.

These early experiments led to the development of a number of work design principles which still have high validity today. These include the following.

- *The principle of minimum critical specification*. Tell employees what to do but not how to do it.
- *The principle of variance control*. Problems must be corrected as close to their point of origin as possible and preferably by the group that caused them.
- *The principle of multiskilling*. Give individuals a range of tasks, including some routine and some challenging.
- *The principle of boundary management*. Identify boundaries between groups and functions by looking for discontinuities of time, place and product development, or changes in the group responsible for action. Ensure these boundaries are well managed and that the people on them have the information necessary to pass the product smoothly to its next transformation stage.
- *The principle of information flow*. Information systems should be designed so that information goes directly to the place where action is to be taken or to the source that originated it.
- *The principle of design and human values*. An important objective of organizational design should be to provide a high quality of working life for employees, for example the need to be able to learn on the job; the need for an area of decision-making; the need to relate work to social life; the need to feel the job leads to a desirable future.

- *The principle of incompletion.* The need to recognize that design is an ongoing and iterative process.

The socio-technical approach has continued until the present time and efforts are now being made to apply it to white-collar groups and to management. Unfortunately, the tremendous contribution of the Tavistock pioneers is now starting to be forgotten. It is not unusual to read in management texts that multiskilled teams are a Japanese invention or that a process approach to work reorganization is new and American. The great strength of the Tavistock approach is that it combines good practice with good theory and it always has the dual objective of using technology and people as effectively as possible.

BUSINESS PROCESS RE-ENGINEERING – HOW DIFFERENT IS IT?

The management gurus and journals tell us that an important new technique has arrived – one that will revolutionize business success and must be adopted by modern companies if they are to survive. This technique is called business process re-engineering and it is described in a book written by Hammer and Champy (1993) called *Re-engineering the Corporation*. Peter Drucker has endorsed the approach on the cover saying 're-engineering is new and it has to be done'. But is it new and what are the problems of doing it or not doing it? How does it differ from socio-technical design which originated in the late 1940s and is still going strong in many parts of the world? What about Total Quality Management, how does this fit in? Is the automobile industry's lean production a version of re-engineering or is this something very different? These are interesting questions and we will try and answer them.

First, what is re-engineering? Its supporters argue that the old ways of doing business are obsolete and no longer bring business success. Today's business world is complex and rapidly changing with customers that are increasingly demanding – wanting more variety, better quality and service and prompt delivery dates. This means that the old ways of organizing business with functional groups, vertical hierarchies and clearly defined tasks must be abandoned and replaced by a focus on 'process'. By process is meant what happens as things travel through a factory, department or office passing through and over organizational boundaries on the route from first input to final output. First input may be a customer order while the final output is the handing over of the product or service to the customer. Re-engineering views companies as a series of horizontal processes, through which information moves at speed, instead of as a series of vertical building blocks with barriers between each unit and layer.

The proponents of re-engineering often argue for a revolutionary approach. This is typified by an article by Michael Hammer in the *Harvard Business Review* (1990) headed 'Re-engineering Work: Don't Automate, Obliterate'. The argument here is that the need for major change is so great that existing structures and methods should be removed altogether and new systems based on an analysis of work processes substituted.

These new systems will be enhanced by the inclusion of appropriate information technology which also crosses all the old boundaries. Many writers in computer journals suggest that the introduction of new information technology will provide the stimulus for this kind of major change. The result is seen to be dramatic improvements in performance and customer satisfaction. Quality will be improved, time cycles and costs reduced. One British insurance company claims to have used business process re-engineering to introduce multiskilled, multifunctional teams that handle all the processing activities associated with a particular group of customers. But this is the application of a socio-technical approach similar to many that have appeared in the last fifty years. There is nothing new here (Mumford, 1983).

An interesting question is how this fits with Deming's Total Quality Management, an old methodology but another of the latest prescriptions for success in the modern business world. This focuses on pleasing the customer and may require considerable change for an improved relationship to take place. Is TQM a part of business process re-engineering or a stimulus for it? Or is it closer to socio-technical design? Adherents of re-engineering suggest that it is less effective. Hammer and Champy (1993) argue that while TQM applied slowly and incrementally can provide performance improvements of 5 to 10 per cent, the revolutionary re-engineering with its sweeping changes can increase performance by 30 to 40 per cent.

All this sounds splendid but is it new, will it work and how painful is it likely to be?

Some writers produce words of caution on this last point. An article by Stewart (1993) in *Fortune* tells us in macho terms:

> Business process re-engineering is the hottest trend in management. Done well it delivers extraordinary gains in speed, productivity and profitability. But it is strong medicine and almost always accompanied by pain.

It seems that, like most revolutions, re-engineering is difficult to bring to a successful conclusion and often has unexpected results. Few managers seem able to realize this new vision without encountering serious problems while Michael Hammer, its principal exponent, tells us that 70 per cent of all re-engineering efforts fail. There may be many reasons for this.

Old attitudes may be difficult to change, senior managers may be unenthusiastic and even feel threatened or, even more likely, the problems of running an unknown horizontal flow system may prove more difficult and expensive than those of running a well understood but inefficient vertical one. The successful firm of the future could be the one that gets on with some quiet, regular and conservative improvement while watching its rivals tearing themselves apart with revolutionary re-engineering projects.

Here again there is the problem of how to carry out and make acceptable this kind of revolutionary change. In many situations the results have not been benign in human terms and the word re-engineering has come to be viewed as synonymous with redundancy. When considering re-engineering the first question managers must ask is 'Can we afford to take the risk? Will major change be hazardous or helpful?' The answer will depend on a number of factors – the kinds of problems the company is experiencing, the nature of the pressures from the environment, the ability of the company to handle a major restructuring, the extent to which a good result could be obtained from a more cautious and conservative solution. This analysis should lead to a clear and agreed corporate strategy of which the re-engineering of some area may form a part.

It must always be recognized that re-engineering, as well as producing a major shock, is a trip into the unknown. New, untried systems bring new, unfamiliar problems and the costs of these may prove greater than the advantages. Re-engineering is not a decision to take lightly or to take because rival firms are embarking on this strategy.

Re-engineering has been described by unbelievers and doubters as 'the latest in a long line of management fads that must be survived'. What starts out as 'creative chaos' can easily end as 'total destruction'. From an economic point of view this upheaval may prove disappointing. Radical innovations are discontinuous events which often combine the redesign of product, process and organization. However, despite the size of the change the economic impact on the company may be small and localized. There may be few financial rewards unless a number of innovations are linked together so that new products and services can be provided.

It must also be recognized that revolutionary change of this kind requires major changes of attitude and behaviour in the individuals and groups associated with them. The new system's demands may be very different from the well tried, understood and tolerated requirements of the old system. If this change of attitudes does not take place, or is accepted reluctantly, then even the best piece of re-engineering may fail because of a lack of motivation and enthusiasm. Alternatively, early enthusiasm may turn to frustration once the system is in place and its defects become apparent.

Perhaps we are all being taken in by the attraction of new strong and emotive words which make an untested product easy to sell. Instead of prescriptive terms like total quality and re-engineering it may be better to use descriptive terms such as 'flexibility' and 'integration'. Socio-technical is another good descriptive term, describing the need to optimize the use of technology and the skills and potential of the human being.

BUSINESS PROCESS RE-ENGINEERING AND LEAN PRODUCTION

While socio-technical design has a very clear set of values and a precise methodology, few articles on re-engineering provide guidance on how to do it. They rely on vague generalizations such as 'get the strategy straight first', 'lead from the top', 'design from outside in', 'combine top-down and bottom-up initiatives'. All probably sound advice but short on the detail of 'this is what you do if you want to re-engineer'. However, there is one example of re-engineering that has been with us for a few years and can provide guidance on how it was done, why it was done and the consequences of the change. This is the introduction of lean production into the Japanese automobile industry.

An international study by a research group at MIT found that the Japanese were much more successful than other countries in creating an efficient and profitable car industry. (Womack, Jones and Roos, 1990). The research conclusions were that this was not just because the Japanese used the latest technology but because they associated this advanced technology with new organizational structures which the MIT group named 'lean production'. The researchers suggested that this form of work organization was so powerful and profitable that other countries and industries should copy it. It was tomorrow's replacement for mass production.

Another, longer-term study was carried out by a Swedish researcher, Christian Berggren (1992). He compared Japanese lean production with the socio-technical experiments carried out by Volvo in the 1960s and 1980s and compared the advantages and disadvantages of each system.

Lean production requires a process re-engineering approach which examines each part of a production activity in order to establish where idle time can be eliminated and the production process speeded up. A major component of lean production is 'Just-in-Time' control. Idle time is now squeezed out of each work station through the elimination of waste and of buffer stocks. This enables staff numbers to be reduced. At the same time quality is ensured through establishing a high commitment to this in the workforce together with statistical quality control techniques. Just-in-Time techniques are carried through to suppliers who are expected to replenish stocks on demand. Other aspects of lean production are delegation, problem-solving, teamwork, quick set-up times, etc. When compared with traditional car manufacture lean production is claimed to use one half of everything – effort, space, investment, time and inventory. It results in fewer defects and greater productivity.

Lean production requires the effective use and integration of technology and work organization. Both of these must be flexible, acceptable to staff and reinforce each other. It also requires a culture committed to quality and competitive advantage and a willingness and ability to train, educate and motivate staff. In theory this should work well and in practice it has greatly increased the productivity of Japanese automobile manufacturers, wherever they are located in the world. But it is a very tight system and this has been criticized by American, and more recently Japanese, trade unions for subjecting employees to an intensified work effort and considerable stress. It also can increase the length of their working day. Whereas on conventional lines buffer stocks used to provide additional time if there were problems, workers are now asked to work extra time on the line if problems occur. They do not receive extra pay for this.

Many writers argue that this tight form of work organization is more acceptable to Japanese workers than to those of other countries for a variety of reasons. First Japanese workers are prepared to accept tightly controlled jobs if they have security of employment and good managers. They are less concerned with autonomy and decision-taking than, for example, Scandinavian workers. They are also strongly identified with the companies they work for and prepared to give them loyalty and long hours of work. Berggren, in his comparison of the Scandinavian and Japanese car industries, identifies considerable cultural differences between the two groups. He claims that although the Japanese work in teams these are not teams which take decisions and solve problems, they are teams which strive to attain the standards set by management. In this sense they are more of a 'clan' than a team. They are there to follow the system, not to question it. He also suggests that quality circles are used by Japanese management to get their ideas accepted, rather than to stimulate discussion of employees' ideas.

The MIT researchers saw lean production as the system to follow mass production while they viewed the Scandinavian experiments with self-managing groups in the 1960s as expensive and inefficient. Berggren does not agree and cites later Volvo socio-technical projects with trucks and buses as very successful. He believes that the lean production system needs humanizing if it is to be acceptable. At present its tightness places workers under too much stress. Whereas the Scandinavian socio-technical approach introduced buffer stocks as a means for providing a time space between self-managing groups, lean production removes them. This can lead workers to take risks to prevent the line stopping. If a stoppage does happen this can be very expensive as the whole system comes to a halt.

The Scandinavian approach of independent groups assembling entire cars in separate docks means that a breakdown affects only one group.

Although the socio-technical approach largely ceased in Volvo in the 1970s because of Sweden's economic problems, it came back again in the 1980s, especially in plants making trucks and buses where production runs were small. Volvo tried many variations of lines and docks and many different degrees of self-management. In Berggren's view the ones most liked by the workers were those where they had maximum discretion for teamwork which involved decision-taking and problem-solving and which offered opportunities for learning and personal development.

Cultural factors exerted considerable influence on the organization of work in each country. In Japan, Toyota and other automobile manufacturers had little difficulty in attracting labour, self-management was not highly valued by the workforce, while security was very important. In Scandinavia, in contrast, the motor industry had great difficulty in obtaining labour with most Swedes refusing to accept the routine and pressurized work of the assembly line.

Both Berggren and Wickens (1993), a personnel director with the UK Nissan plant, suggest that a combination of lean production and the socio-technical approach may be the ideal solution. The Japanese system is carefully organized, efficient and has high quality standards but it places employees under a great deal of pressure and offers little opportunity for learning and problem-solving. The Scandinavian approach is less pressurized and more humanistic, requiring a greater range of skills and with much greater emphasis on problem-solving by the team. But standards and efficiency can be less than optimal. An amalgamation of the two could provide an excellent production system.

Automobile engineering is an example of manufacturing work where it is difficult to escape the influence of technology. An assembly line approach, which even Volvo uses in its mass production car plants, will always restrict what can be done to humanize work and multitasking may replace multiskilling. The dock approach, where teams assemble an entire car, has proved viable in bus and truck plants where production runs are small but less viable where speed and volume are important factors.

SOCIO-TECHNICAL DESIGN AND BUSINESS PROCESS RE-ENGINEERING – SIMILARITIES AND DIFFERENCES

How then do the socio-technical approach and business process re-engineering differ? Probably very little in the initial analysis of system needs and problems, although socio-technical design appears to have a more tightly specified method for doing this than process re-engineering. Business process re-engineering is probably stronger in its incorporation of technology, particularly information technology, into systems design. Although socio-technical design has as a primary objective the optimal use of both technology and people, historically it was never able to exert much influence on the design of technology. Even today when many American firms claim they are associating multiskilling and teamwork with flexible manufacturing, the technical system is a given and not available for redesign. This may also be true of business process re-engineering if it concerns itself with manufacturing technology. Its current focus on information technology means that considerable flexibility is available when technical decisions are taken.

The main difference between socio-technical design and business process re-engineering seems to be one of emphasis, theory and values. The emphasis of the socio-technical approach has always been as much on quality of working life and job satisfaction as on efficiency. In the early Tavistock experiments the considerable increases in efficiency and quality were an unexpected and surprising bonus.

The emphasis of business process re-engineering is firmly on efficiency and although Michael Hammer recommends that it should include team work, multiskilling and group problem-solving, as in the lean production example, it does not always do this in any fundamental way. On the contrary the streamlining and tightening of the production process can reduce staff and make work more stressful for those that remain.

A second difference is the macho push of business process re-engineering to throw existing systems out and start again. Socio-technical design may in fact result in one kind of system being replaced by another, as in the coal mining example, but it would do this more slowly. A systematic diagnosis of needs would be carefully carried out with users playing a major role. Great emphasis would be placed on designing work to provide learning, challenge and personal development as well as efficiency and effectiveness. And participation and consultation would ensure that the system was not implemented until it was generally approved and accepted. As research has shown that employee acceptance is a critical factor in successful change, it will be interesting to see how business process re-engineering fares where this does not happen.

A third, and most important, difference is the apparent absence of a clear theory associated with business process re-engineering. Socio-technical design has always been dedicated to developing good theory as well as good practice with the two supporting each other. A new theory would lead to a practical test of its viability. A new practice would lead to the development of new theory.

Gareth Morgan (1993) has described how socio-technical theory fits very well with the notion of a holographic organization. The four principles of the theory are shown in Figure 11.1.

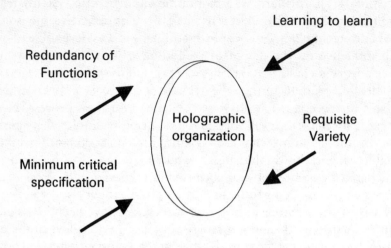

Figure 11.1 The holographic organization

Redundancy of functions means that instead of cutting down functions to a minimum by removing buffer stocks and introducing Just-in-Time procedures, there is a conscious effort to introduce redundancy, or slack, into the system. The theory here is that any system that is trying to self-organize, to be creative and to respond easily to change must have an element of redundancy in its design. Without this, everything is tight and prescribed and the system has little capacity for taking appropriate action when unforeseen events occur.

Morgan argues that systems based on redundant functions are holographic because capacities for the effective functioning of the whole are built into each part. The system is specialized and generalized at one and the same time. He also suggests that the amount of redundancy that needs to be provided can be arrived at through considering Ross Ashby's law of requisite variety (Ashby, 1956). This states that 'only variety can control variety'. Therefore if a system is operating in a complex, unstable environment, it must itself contain the requisite variety to cope with this environment.

Morgan suggests that the principles of redundant functions and requisite variety create systems with a capacity for self-organization. The principles of *learning* and *minimum critical specification* enhance this capacity for self-organization.

Learning to learn is Bateson's fourth level of learning described at the begining of this chapter. It leads logically to the socio-technical belief in teamwork and multiskilling. *Minimum critical specification* recognizes the ability and need of the human being to be creative as well as efficient in the workplace. Employees should therefore be given guidance and goals on what they are expected to achieve. But they should have the freedom to decide a large part of how they are going to get these results. This leaves the workteam with responsibility and discretion.

In Morgan's view the interaction of these four variables provides a means for designing organizations with each part of the system striving to embrace the qualities of the whole and to self-organize as a continuing process. The Tavistock group believed, and still believes, that self-regulating teams of this kind are increasingly important in an environment of increasing complexity, uncertainty and interdependency. These cannot be managed in the top-down hierarchies found in bureaucratic forms of organization. Bureaucracy acts as variety reducer and there is not enough internal variety to manage the external variety.

It can be argued that without some clear theoretical underpinnings business process re-engineering could produce 'chaotic systems' which do not appear to conform with any rules. Chaos has been defined as structures which are highly iterative, recursive or dynamic and change over time. They also show highly discontinuous behaviour such as sudden shifts in organizational policy, downsizing, product discontinuations, etc. They are systems that dynamically transform themselves from one moment to the next. It is very difficult, if not impossible, to control systems of this kind (Gregersen and Saller, 1993).

Socio-technical design therefore seems more cautious, stable and humanistic than business process re-engineering in its present form. It also appears to provide more guidance on how to do the essential analysis of needs and subsequent design of the work situation through its combination of good theory and appropriate action. Business process re-engineering appears dramatic, fast, risky, discontinuous and even 'chaotic'. It is accepted that when firms are in serious trouble a fast response may sometimes be essential and survival requires that costs must be cut in any way possible. Business process re-engineering would then come into its own.

REFERENCES

Ashby, W R (1956) *An introduction to Cybernetics,* Chapman & Hall, London.

Bateson, G (1973) *Steps to an Ecology of Mind,* Paladin.

Berggren, C (1992) *The Volvo Experience: Alternatives to Lean Production,* Macmillan.

Burgoyne, J (1992) 'Creating a Learning Organization', *RSA Journal,* April, 321–330.

Cherns, A (1976) 'The Principles of Socio-Technical Design', *Human Relations,* 29, 783–904

Davis, L and Cherns, A (1975) *TheQuality of Working Life. Vol.1,* Free Press.

Hammer, M. (1990) 'Re-engineering Work: Don't Automate, Obliterate', *Harvard Business Review*, 90, 104–112.

Hammer, M and Champy, J (1993) *Re-engineering the Corporation: a Manifesto for Business Revolution*, Nicholas Brealey Publishing, London.

Hart, S and Quinn, R (1993) 'Roles Executives Play: Behavioural Complexity and Firm Performance', *Human Relations*, 46, 543–574.

Hirschheim, R and Klein, H (1994) 'Realizing Emancipatory Principles in Information Systems Development: The Case for Ethics, in *MIS Quarterly*, March 18, 83-102.

Lawler, E (1986) *High Iinvolvement Management*, Jossey-Bass, San Francisco, Calif.

Ledford, G and Mohran, S (1993) 'Self-Design for High Involvement: A Large Scale Organizational Change', *Human Relations*, 46, 143–174.

McCabe, D and Dutton, J (1993) 'Making Sense of the Environment: The Role of Perceived Effectiveness', *Human Relations*, 46, 623–644

Morgan, G (1993) 'Organizational Choice and the New Technology', in Trist, E and Murray, H (eds), *The Social Engagement of Social Science: vol. 2: The Socio-Technical Perspective*, University of Pennsylvania Press.

Mumford, E (1983a) *Designing Human Systems*, Manchester Business School.

Mumford, E (1983b) *Designing Participatively*, Manchester Business School.

Mumford, E (1987) 'Socio-Technical Design: Evolving Theory and Practice', in Bjerknes, Ehn and Kyng (eds), *Computers and Democracy*, Avebury.

Mumford, E and Beekman J-G (1994) *Tools for Change: A Socio-Technical Approach to Business Process Re-engineering*, CSG Publications.

Parsons, T and Shils, E (1951) *Towards a General Theory of Action*, Harvard University Press.

Scott, W, Mumford, E, McGivering, I and Kirby, J (1963) *Coal and Conflict*, Liverpool University Press.

Stewart, T A (1993) 'Re-engineering, the Hot New Management Tool', *Fortune*, 128, 32–37.

Trist, E (1993) A Socio-Technical Critique of Scientific Management', in Trist, E and Murray, H (eds), *The Social Engagement of Social Science: vol 2: The Socio-Technical Perspective*, University of Pennsylvania Press.

Trist, E and Bamforth, K (1951) 'Some Social and Psychological Consequences of the Long Wall Method of Coal Getting', *Human Relations*, 4, 3–38.

Wickens, P (1993) 'Steering the Middle Road in Car Production', *Personnel Management*, June, 34–38

Womack, J, Jones, D and Roos, D (1990) *The Machine that Changed theWorld*, Rawson.

12

IMPROVING THE CHANCES OF SUCCESS FOR BPR INITIATIVES BY LEARNING FROM THE SUCCESS AND FAILURES OF OPERATIONS MANAGEMENT PHILOSOPHIES

Colin Armistead, University of Bournemouth and Philip Rowland, Cranfield School of Management

It has become clear that Business Process Re-engineering (BPR) draws on the knowledge and skills from many of the traditional management disciplines. The adoption of the process paradigm for managing enterprises creates new challenges of reconciling the relative roles of functions and processes within an organization. While these issues have yet to be resolved there are other aspects of BPR concerned with activities to improve performance which have many similarities with existing concepts and techniques in the domain of Operations Management. There is a danger that the learning in areas of Quality Management, Just-in-Time and Simultaneous Engineering may be disregarded or hidden from those engaged in BPR programmes. The purpose of this chapter is to indicate where such knowledge lies and identify some of the lessons learned from these improvement methods so that they may be applied to BPR.

INTRODUCTION

The development of the concept and practice of Business Process Redesign from 'The Management in the 1990's' research programme at MIT (Scott-Morton, 1991) and Hammer's well known initial article on Re-engineering in *Harvard Business Review* (1990) was at first sight highly biased towards the exploitation of IT. While this theme has been continued by some authors (Davenport and Short 1990; Davenport, 1993), it was clear that many of the examples given of BPR had a very strong operations management and services management content.

Some authors on BPR do of course already acknowledge antecedents in manufacturing, logistics and supply chain concepts (Johansson *et al.*, 1993; Earl and Khan, 1994). The purpose of this chapter is not to claim BPR as an operations management approach but to examine the concepts and techniques of the field which might have application for BPR. Hence the learning which has been gained from other improvement philosophies may be valuably transferred to BPR programmes.

Our starting point for this examination is in a description of BPR along the lines:

> An organization may be considered as a collection of processes characterized as strategic, operational and enabling. BPR is an approach to achieving radical improvements in performance by using resources in ways which maximize value added activities and minimize activities which only add cost – either at the level of the individual process or at the level of the whole organization.

Implicit in this definition of BPR is the consideration of organizational structure. If an organization is viewed as a collection of processes, how do the processes impact on a functional view of the organization? The debate about the relative importance of processes over functions where processes cross traditional functional boundaries is likely to be a feature of the implementation of BPR (Womack and Jones, 1994).

As a prescription or framework for how to undertake BPR we have combined the principles of re-engineering proposed by Hammer (1990) and the characteristics of a re–engineered process (Hammer and Champy, 1993) into a list of eight 'rules' for the improvement of processes.

The Rules of BPR

1. Organize around outcomes not tasks.
2. Have those who use the output of the process perform the process.
3. Treat geographically dispersed resources as though they were centralized creating hybrid centralized/decentralized organizations.
4. Link parallel activities in a natural order instead of integrating their results.
5. Perform work where it makes most sense, particularly, decision-making, information processing, checks and controls, making them part of the process.
6. Capture information once and at the source, minimizing reconciliation.

7. Combine several jobs into one possibly creating a case manager or case team as a single point of contact.
8. Create multiple versions of processes when appropriate.

We will use this list to examine and consider which techniques and concepts originating in the operations management domain provide insights into the implementation of the rules for BPR.

WHAT RINGS TRUE FROM OPERATIONS MANAGEMENT?

Operations Management is concerned with the management of processes, people, technology and other resources in the production of goods and services. Any textbook on Operations Management includes chapters dealing with the main areas of the design of products, the design of operations, planning and control of capacity, materials, quality and resource productivity. The content included in these main areas may be essentially descriptive and qualitative or may include a quantitative approach to solving operational problems.

There exists in the Operations Management domain two main areas which have resonance with the concept and prescription of BPR: first the use of the process paradigm, and second the concepts and techniques for designing, managing and improving operational processes.

A Process Paradigm

The systems approach to Operations Management (Buffa, 1969; Wild, 1980) is founded on the paradigm of a transformation process. Transformation processes are held to be associated with a limited number of transformations. Wild characterizes these as manufacturing, transport, supply and service. Armistead (1990) suggest improving, moving, caretaking transformations applying to materials, people or information. So Operations Management presents a taxonomy of processes in terms of characterizing the transformation and identifying the transformed entity and any resources used in the transformation process.

The transformation process paradigm brings with it aspects of measurement for control purposes, the concepts of different transformation processes being linked together and the concept of a main transformation being built on subprocesses and individual operations or tasks.

While the process paradigm is a powerful way of understanding the flows of materials, information and people, Operations Management specialists would acknowledge the problems which can occur in defining the boundaries of a process, or disaggregating several of the simple types of transformation processes occurring within the confines of one set of physical resources.

The process paradigm in Operations Management focuses on operational processes rather than strategic or enabling processes. A major problem often highlighted within these operational processes is the linkage of the marketing and sales departments, responsible for 'winning' the customer, to the operations department responsible for delivery to the customer.

Developments in Operations Management

There have been three important developments of the Operations Management field which have a bearing on BPR. First has been the concept of *operations strategy* (Skinner, 1969; Hill, 1985; Heskett, 1986; Voss, 1987; Armistead, 1990) for providing a link between the competitive strategy of an enterprise and its operational capability. The overriding concept in operations strategy is one of fit between the competitive intent and operational capability on the premise that no one operational configuration of resources can do everything, ie produce the highest quality product or service in a customized form in the shortest time, on time every time and at the lowest cost.

The second development has been the widening of the Operations Management field from its manufacturing and production origins to include and focus on the production of services and the effect of a customer as part of the operations (Sasser *et al*, 1978; Heskett, 1986; Voss 1987; Armistead, 1990).

The third influence has been the development of specific operations concepts as a result of the actions of practitioners in enterprises rather than the work of academics. The biggest change has come in the last 15–20 years from the work in Japanese companies manufacturing cars, electrical and electronic products and their followers in the US and Europe (Shingo, 1991; Schonberger, 1987). These developments have brought to the fore concepts and practices of Total Quality Management (Crosby, 1980; Deming, 1986; Oakland, 1989), Just-in-Time (Voss 1988; Harrison, 1992), Supply Chain Management and Lean Production (Womack and Jones, 1991; Laming, 1993), and Simultaneous Engineering (Voss, et al, 1991; Siegel, 1991).

THE APPLICATION OF OPERATIONS MANAGEMENT EXPERIENCE TO BPR

Without necessarily developing in detail all aspects of each area of operations management we have tried to abstract the key feature which seem to us to have a bearing on the development of a BPR programme under the eight 'rules' of BPR developed earlier. The results are the following.

Organize around Outcomes not Tasks

The messages from operations strategy in either a manufacturing or service domain is the importance of establishing the *operations task*. The operations task defines what the operational processes need to do well to meet customer requirements efficiently. Here the concept of order winning, order qualifying and order losing criteria (Hill, 1985) for features of a product service offering is key to establishing the nature of the delivery process.

Have Those Who Use the Output of the Process Perform the Process

The concept of internal customers as well as external customers has been central for TQM (Schonberger, 1987). This concept brings with it the idea of partnership between different entities along a chain of activities in any process or along a supply chain. In practice the dangers of focusing only on the next step in the chain rather than the customer at the end of the chain have been realized. A BPR approach offers some resolution to the problem by challenging the idea that any departmental, and thus internal customer, boundaries are legitimate. BPR makes processes supreme.

Treat Geographically Dispersed Resources as though they were Centralised Creating Hybrid Centralized/decentralized Organizations

The operational linking of geographically dispersed operations is key within service operations which are facilitated by the use of telecommunications, for example telephone response centres situated geographically to give 24-hour global service. Similarly Just-in-Time supply may make physical inventories visible across a network with the capability to transfer material from one or a small number of locations without the need to hold stock locally.

Link Parallel Activities in a Natural Order instead of Integrating their Results

Simultaneous Engineering and Design for Assembly has enabled organizations to speed up new product development and improve quality by linking the development of new products to the development of the processes by which they will be manufactured.

Perform Work Where It Makes Most Sense, Particularly Decision–making, Information Processing, Checks and Controls, Making Them Part of the Process

Quality Assurance within the context of TQM has tended to drive a move from final inspection of products to inspection at source by operators. Such quality control has in some cases been driven hard by the application of statistical process control to reduce the variability within the operational processes. Such moves can require considerable training in the understanding and application of SPC techniques. The Just-in-Time principle of *Jidoka* places further emphasis on control with the people actually doing the work allowing them to halt production to fix a problem as it arises.

Capture Information Once and at the Source, Minimizing Reconciliation

Developments in integrating supply chains, utilizing electronic interchange, have allowed organizations to track the movement of materials through each stage in the chain without the need to rekey data at each point. This minimizes the need for reconciliation by ensuring each party is working on the same information.

Combine Several Jobs into One possibly Creating a Case Manager or Case Team as a Single Point of Contact

The move to create manufacturing cells responsible for a significant part of the production process requiring multiskilling of the cell operators is now being widely mirrored in service operations through BPR. Cells reduce lead time, movement of materials, worker motion and build commitment amongst members of the cell.

Create Multiple Versions of Processes When Appropriate

The Lucas Engineering classification of *runners, repeaters* and *strangers* is widely taught in Operations Management as a way of understanding the process requirements of products and services. Matching the appropriate process approach to product complexity and volume has long been a mainstream task in manufacturing systems design.

A further Operations Management technique from the TQM/JIT philosophies which is increasingly applied to BPR programmes is that of micro-response analysis (Schonberger and Knod, 1991; Schonberger, 1987). This technique takes a ratio approach to understand the performance of process in three main ways: lead time to work content (or throughput efficiency), process speed to use rate and pieces to work station, operator or office worker. The ideal for all ratios is 1:1 yet in many cases ratios are significantly greater than this. The last of the three ratios is particularly challenging when applied in office environments as the notion of only one piece of paper being worked on with none sitting in the in-tray challenges the fundamental assumptions of how an office should work. Yet this challenge is necessary if poor throughput efficiency is to be understood and improved.

LESSONS FOR BPR

The examination of the aspects of Operations Management within the framework of the BPR rules focuses attention in key areas of TQM, JIT and SE. It is here that there has been research to investigate reasons for success and failure (Schaffer, 1993; Katz 1993; Kendrick, 1993; Easton, 1993; Billesbach, 1991; Voss, Russell and Twigg, 1991; Siegel, 1991). Such lessons would seem to be relevant to BPR.

1. The role of the CEO is important in setting the direction for TQM and in establishing the reasons and extent of JIT. Commitment from the top is all important and responsibility cannot be delegated. CEOs should treat improvement programmes as any other strategic priority.
2. The application of TQM and JIT must be in the context of the business environment of each organization. The use of benchmarking, however, to establish best practice for specific processes can be useful in breaking paradigms and providing clues for a better way of working.
3. Training at the right time and for the right level. Training should take place once support is established. It should not be conducted as a mass exercise ahead of any action but rather rolled-out to support implementation. Don't miss out middle management in training and implementation. These people may feel most threatened and need the training most in order to adjust to new roles.
4. Listen to customers, suppliers and employees seeking facts to build understanding. Actions must be focused on those aspects which are a priority for customers. Suppliers and employees, where they will influence the outcome, as well as customers as appropriate, must be included in any programme. Facts should be sought throughout the research to support assertions and communicate the actual situation without a blame mentality being adopted.
5. Don't focus on technical tools too early or too much; people, leadership skills and creativity are more important. Sophisticated process mapping tools can shift attention from redesign to understanding existing processes and can deter non-technical staff from participation, stifling innovation and commitment.
6. Involve suppliers in the programme where they influence the outcome. Organizations are only as good as their supply chains and a

partnership approach to supplier and customer relations within the supply chain can yield significant benefits for all parties.

7. Don't try to do too much at once. Celebrate successes to bolster confidence and momentum recognizing that it may take years to gain enough experience before the new orientation starts to work well. As with anything there is a learning curve to improvement methodologies.

8. TQM and JIT involve challenging messages which must be disseminated. This communication process can be facilitated by the use of games and simulations to explain and demonstrate the message (Graham, *et al.*, 1991). Indeed there are already indications of the same approach being adopted for BPR (Wiesbord, 1989).

9. Use the right measures to demonstrate success. An over-reliance on short-term financial measures without understanding key operational indicators may paint a false picture of the operation's performance and the improvements made (Kaplan, 1984; Kaplan and Norton, 1992).

CASE EXAMPLES

While we have been able to identify contributions to the implementation of BPR from the operations management area we are aware that companies are approaching BPR from different backgrounds which has a bearing on the approach which is taken. We have three examples to illustrate this point.

The Royal Mail has been implementing a TQM programme as a way of changing the way the business thinks and conducts its affairs. Recently it has incorporated a process paradigm for the business as a whole without declaring this move under the label of BPR, preferring Business Process Improvement. The approach is to develop the skills acquired within the quality programme to facilitate the move to managing key processes and re-engineering as required. The Royal Mail is experimenting with JIT working in some offices and is building confidence in process management, although it is too early for quantified results to be identified.

The TSB has adopted BPR on the back of a quality programme but has taken an approach which directly transfers much of the learning from a manufacturing environment. A systematic redesign approach, based on detailed process mapping, has been used to understand waste throughout the process and eliminate it, similar in many ways to a JIT waste elimination programme. The BPR programme to date has yielded a significant reduction in the time to formally respond to a mortgage application with average response time down from 30 days to seven and still reducing. Workload on the part of the customer, as well as staff, in completing the application has also been reduced.

Reuters re-engineered their customer-facing processes after a period of significant organizational growth. A cell approach was adopted to operate a new process design with account teams responsible for the delivery of products to a range of customers. Problems of coordination, cooperation and communication have been largely overcome by locating staff together, paying particular attention to desk layouts just as manufacturing cell design places great emphasis on the positioning of workstations. Lead time to provide products is now days to weeks rather than weeks to months, delivery reliability is now over 95 per cent, and billing accuracy has been raised to about 98 per cent, leading to more prompt customer payment.

WHERE OPERATIONS MANAGEMENT CANNOT HELP IN BPR

We have tried to indicate where aspects of Operations Management knowledge can help BPR programmes. However, we can also see some aspects of BPR where it does not provide answers. There seem to us three areas which are vital to the success of BPR.

First, if BPR is adopted it will lead organizations to adopt a process paradigm. While this is useful from a systems point of view it does nothing to indicate to managers how they should manage an organization in this form. It raises the question of what it means to manage processes at different levels or managing operational, strategic and enabling processes and the interaction between the different types.

Second, if the process paradigm is used, how can measurement and control systems be realigned to support this mode of operation? It is our assertion, based on what companies tell us as well as literature on the subject, that the debate about how to construct an appropriate performance measurement system has never been satisfactorily re-solved (Kaplan, 1984, 1988; Eccles, 1991, Kaplan and Norton, 1992, 1993; Neely, 1993). Indeed this question goes beyond the operations management domain to include finance and accounting, human re-sources and strategy.

Third, there would seem to be an emerging conflict in method between information systems developers and operations staff. The explosion of computer tools to support BPR (Miers, 1994) demonstrates the demand which exists for sophisticated process mapping tools. Yet these types of tools are difficult for non-technical specialists to use. As detailed in our lessons from previous philosophies, emphasis on the use of these tools may prove damaging to BPR initiatives. This dilemma, again, cannot be resolved in the domains of IS or operations in isolation. As with MRP, only by working on all aspects of process, people and technology can success be achieved.

CONCLUSIONS

The Operations Management discipline can provide a number of valuable insights into how pitfalls likely to befall BPR programmes might be avoided. JIT, in our opinion, offers some prescription on how to construct processes while TQM and Simultaneous Engineering offer more on how to go about the change. Like these other philosophies BPR can only succeed with the commitment of top management and a cross-disciplinary approach. Because many of BPR's principles seem to be a transfer of manufacturing principles to the office and service environment, it would be worth more organizations considering the inclusion of skilled manufacturing people in their BPR teams.

REFERENCES

Armistead, C G (1990) 'Service Operations Management and Strategy: Framework for Matching the Service Operations Task and the Service Delivery System', *International Journal of Service Industry Management*, 1,(2).

Billesbach, T J (1991) 'A Study of the Implementation of Just-In-Time in the United States', *Production and Inventory Management Journal*, 32, (3), 1–4

Buffa, E S (1969) *Modern Production Management*, Wiley, New York.

Crosby, R (1979), *Quality is Free*, McGraw-Hill, New York.

Davenport, T H (1993) *Process Innovation: Re-engineering Work Through Information Technology*, Harvard Business School Press, Boston, Mass.

Davenport, T H and Short, J (1990) 'The New Industrial Engineering: Information Technology and Business Process Redesign', *Sloan Management Review*, Summer, 11–27.

Deming, W E (1986) *Out of the Crisis*, Cambridge University Press, Cambridge.

Earl, M and Khan B (1994) 'How New is Business Process Redesign?', *European Management Journal*, 12, (1), 20–30.

Easton, G S (1993) 'The 1993 state of US Total Quality Management: A Baldrige Examiner's Perspective', *California Management Review*, 35(3) Spring, 32–54.

Eccles, R G (1991) 'The Performance Measurement Manifesto', *Harvard Business Review*, January–February, 131–137.

Economist (1992) 323 (7755), 18 April, 67–68.

Graham, A K, Morecroft, J D W, Senge, P M and Sterman, J D (1991) 'Model-Supported Case Studies for Management Education', *European Journal of Operations Research*, 59, 151–166

Hammer, M (1990), 'Re-engineering Work: Don't Automate, Obliterate', *Harvard Business Review*, July–August, 104–112.

Hammer, M and Champy, J (1993), *Re-engineering the Corporation: A Manifesto for Business Revolution*, Free Press, New York

Harrison, A (1992) *Just in Time Manufacturing in Perspective*, Prentice-Hall, Hemel Hempstead.

Heskett, J L (1986) *Managing in the Service Economy*, Harvard Business School Press, Boston, Mass.

Heskett, J L, Sasser, W E and Hart C W L (1990) *Service Breakthroughs: Changing the Rules of the Game*, Free Press, New York.

Hill T J (1985) *Manufacturing Strategy: The Strategic Management of the Manufacturing Function*, Macmillan, London.

Johansson, H J, McHugh, P, Pendlebury, A J and Wheeler, W A (1993) *Business Process Reengineering–Breakpoint Strategies for Market Dominance*, Wiley, Chichester.

Jones, D T (1992), 'Beyond the Toyota Production System', in Voss, C (ed) *The Era of Lean Production in Manufacturing Strategy: Process and Content*, Chapman & Hall, London

Kaplan, R S (1984) 'Yesterday's Accounting Undermines Production', *Harvard Business Review*, 62, 95–101.

Kaplan, R S (1988) 'One Cost System Isn't Enough', *Harvard Business Review*, January–February, 61–66.

Kaplan, R S and Norton, D P (1992) 'The Balanced Scorecard – Measures that Drive Performance', *Harvard Business Review*, January–February, 71–79.

Kaplan, R S and Norton, D P (1993) 'Putting the Balanced Scorecard to Work', *Harvard Business Review*, September–October, 134–142.

Katz, A S (1993) 'Eight TQM Pitfalls', *Journal for Quality and Participation*, 16(4), July/August, 24–27.

Kendrick, J J (1993) 'Study Looks at TQM: Is It Forging Ahead or Falling Behind?', *Quality*, 32(5), 13.

Lamming, R (1993) Beyond Partnership: Strategies for Innovation and Lean Supply

Miers, D (1994) *Process Product Watch* (vols 1–4) Enix Ltd, Richmond, Surrey.

Neely, A, 1993, 'Performance Measurement System Design – Theory and Practice', Cambridge Manufacturing Report Group Internal Report, Cambridge University.

Oakland, J S (1989) *Total Quality Management: The Route to Improving Performance*, Heinemann Professional Publishing, Oxford.

Sasser, W E, Olsen, R P, and Wycoff, D D (1978), *Management of Service Operations*, Allyn & Bacon, Boston, Mass.

Schaffer, D S (1993) 'Why Total Quality Programs Miss the Mark', *Journal for Quality and Participation*, 16(5), September, 18–27.

Schonberger, R J (1987) *World Class Manufacturing Casebook: Implementing JIT and TQC*, Free Press, New York.

Schonberger, R J and Knod, E M (1991) *Operations Management: Improving Customer Service*, 4th edn, Irwin, Homewood, Ill.

Scott-Morton, M S (1991) *The Corporation of the 1990s: Information Technology and Organisational Transformation*, Oxford University Press, Oxford.

Shingo, S (1989) *The Toyota Production System*, trans. by A Dillon, Productivity Press, Cambridge, Mass.

Siegel, B (1991) 'Organizing for a Successful C E Process', *Industrial Engineering*, 23(12), 15–19.

Simons, R (1991) 'Strategic Orientation and Top Management Attention to Control Systems', *Strategic Management Journal*, 12, 49–62.

Skinner, W (1969) 'Manufacturing – The Missing Link in Manufacturing Strategy', *Harvard Business Review*, September–October, 136–145.

Voss, C (ed.) (1987) *Just-In-Time Manufacture*, IFS Publications Ltd, Bedford.

Voss, C (1988) *Just-In-Time*, IFS Publications Ltd, UK.

Voss, C A, Russell, V and Twigg, D (1991) 'Implementation Issues in Simultaneous Engineering', *International Journal of Technology Management*, 6(3), 293–302.

Wiesbord, M R (1989) 'The Flying Starship Factory', *Industry Week*, 3 April.

Wild, R (1980) *Production and Operations Management*, Wiley, Chichester.

Womack, J P and Jones, T D (1991) *The Machine That Changed the World*, Harper Collins, London.

Womack, J P and Jones, D T (1994) 'From Lean Production to the Lean Enterprise', *Harvard Business Review*, March/April, 93-103.

13

SUPPLY CHAIN MANAGEMENT – A BPR PERSPECTIVE*

Fred Hewitt, Aston Business School

CONCEPTS OF PROCESS EFFICIENCY AND EFFECTIVENESS

In their seminal article in 1990 Davenport and Short offer a working definition of a business process as: 'a set of logically related tasks performed to achieve a defined business outcome'. In effect this definition casts a business process, like any other process, as a transformation function, which can be thought of as using energy to convert inputs to outputs. As a simple extension to this concept, process efficiency can be defined and measured as the reciprocal of the loss of energy used during the transformation (usually expressed as the time and/or cost of the operating process). Equally, process effectiveness can be defined and measured as the frequency with which process outputs conform to their output specifications. A first order model of any business process can, therefore, be represented by Figure 13.1.

In this view of the world, business enterprises are made up of interconnected business processes, each of which consumes resources, applies these to a specific area of enterprise activity, and produces outputs in the form of products or services passed either to other business processes or to external customers. The practice of Business Process Management (BPM) concerns the maximization of efficiency and effectiveness of the existing business processes. Business Process Redesign (BPR), on the other

*   The author acknowledges the contribution of many logisticians whose ideas and comments have contributed to this chapter, in particular the members of Xerox Corporation and other companies who have participated in Supply Chain Roundtables since 1989.

A shorter version of the chapter appears in *The International Journal of Logistics Management*, 5 (2), (1994).

hand, is a different but related activity. It concerns itself with redesign initiatives aimed at improving process efficiency and effectiveness capabilities. These initiatives usually take the form of radical process simplification.

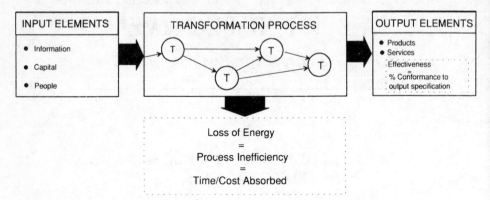

Figure 13.1   A first-order business process model

The generic model of Figure 13.1 can be tailored to a particular business process – the management of the supply chain – in order to further explore its validity and usefulness. The Supply Chain Process model can in turn be matched with leading-edge practitioner experience to derive some initial observations regarding BPR and BPM operating principles.

THE SUPPLY CHAIN AS A BUSINESS PROCESS

Although no universally acceptable template exists depicting the overall business process architecture of a typical business enterprise, most of the more advanced attempts to construct enterprise-wide schemas include a process known variously as 'order fulfilment', 'inventory management and logistics', 'production and delivery' or 'supply chain'*. Figure 13.2 depicts the essential elements of this process as a second-level model based upon the format of Figure 13.1

In a more traditional, functional view of an enterprise, the sub-elements of this process would include activities undertaken within most, if not all, of the operational divisions of the company, from procurement through distribution and manufacturing to sales and service. The process serves

---

*   Companies have identified between nine and 24 processes within their total schemas. The two most commonly identifiable processes were 'supply chain/order fulfilment' and 'product development/innovation'.

the purpose of linking suppliers into the enterprise and linking the enterprise to its customers. It therefore follows that the goal of any redesign initiative as regards this particular business process must be, in Christopher's (1992) words: '...to link the market place, distribution network, the manufacturing process and procurement activity in such a way that customers are serviced at higher levels and yet at lower costs'.

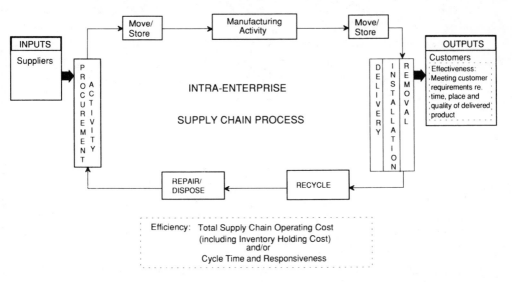

Figure 13.2   The supply chain as a business process

For this particular process, therefore, effectiveness is defined as the process's ability to deliver the right products to customers at the right place and at the right time. Efficiency is the reciprocal of total supply chain costs. These include the cost of holding the inventory used to overcome the inertia within the system. Total cycle time is sometimes regarded as a primary measure of efficiency (Stalk, 1988; Stalk and Hout, 1990). Alternatively, time may be viewed as a secondary factor, driving total supply chain costs. With the advent of activity-based costing, the difference between these two opinions is, in any case, becoming moot (Cooper and Kaplan, 1991; Dohlen, 1993). The main point is that efficiency of the process is relatively easy to measure, either in terms of cost or time or both, and measurements before and after re-engineering will therefore yield clear evidence of the magnitude of any resultant increase in efficiency.

The supply chain is of particular interest from a general business process analysis viewpoint for a number of reasons. Firstly, there is substantial well-documented historical evidence available to those who wish to study the emergence of process management thinking within this area. Secondly, this particular process is generally regarded as 'primary', 'core' or even 'strategic' within overall business enterprise process architectures, ie one that runs from suppliers to customers and the effectiveness of which has immediate impact on the successful operation of the enterprise as a whole. In this respect it differs from 'Human Resource Management' or 'Information Processing' and a number of other processes which, although vital to corporate success, are second-level processes supporting the core ones. Thirdly, a small but significant number of redesign initiatives have focused on this process and have claimed very substantial efficiency and effectiveness improvements. It should, therefore, be of use to those wishing to study the nature of BPM and BPR more generally to review the emergence of supply chain process management and the experience of supply chain process redesigners.

THE EMERGENCE OF SUPPLY CHAIN PROCESS MANAGEMENT

The US National Council of Physical Distribution Management, established in January 1963 and renamed as the Council of Logistics Management (CLM) in 1985, has maintained a comprehensive bibliography of significant works relating to logistics theory and practice throughout the last 30 years.* Since the 1970s it has also sponsored periodic comprehensive reviews of the logistics practices of several hundred companies in the USA, and more recently of a similar sample of European companies (Seger and Best, 1986; Bowersox *et al.*, 1989; O'Laughlin *et al.*, 1993; Byrne and Markham, 1991a). Taken together, the bibliography as a comprehensive history of academic thought in the subject area, and the company surveys giving insight into the evolving nature of leading-edge practice, present a clear picture of evolving and interacting theory and practice within this area of business activity over an extended period. What emerges is a long series of small steps leading to an increasingly cross-functional, increasingly process-oriented view of the activity. For analytic convenience, the CLM-sponsored reports have categorized these developments as falling into the stages of evolution illustrated in Table 13.1 (Seger and Best, 1986).

---

*   The *Bibliography on Physical Distribution*, first published in January 1967, has subsequently been extended by over 20 supplements entitled *Bibliography of Logistics Management*.

Table 13.1 Stages of logistics evolution

	Level of integration	Objective of optimization initiatives
Stage I	Fragmented technical disciplines	Local quick fixes
Stage II	Functional focus	Cost reduction
Stage III	Broad scope logistics	Network productivity improvement
Stage IV	Links with customers and suppliers	Integrated network planning

Source: A T Kearney

It is significant but unsurprising that the historical evidence shows that progressive coordination of existing functional activities, followed by rationalization of these activities, has been more common than radical moves to a totally revised process management approach. Currently, few of the companies surveyed in either Europe or the US have reached even the level of integration implied in Stages III or IV.

On the other hand, taking a BPR view of the reported findings, it is clear that a few enterprises are now going beyond cross-functional coordination to an explicitly process-oriented way of working, thereby truly justifying the term supply chain process management. In Europe a CLM sponsored study has noted:

> 'Those few case participants which have established long-range visions of logistics are adopting complex organizations, which align responsibilities throughout the organization neither by function nor by geography but rather by process...(O'Laughlin *et al.*, 1993)

This parallels the US evidence of a very small number of situations where '...a company transcends the functional and organizational boundaries and manages the operations of a business with a logistics process orientation' (Byrne and Markham, 1991 b).

This alternative view suggests an emerging new stage which is highly significant and possibly justifies a revision of the portrayal of logistics evolution from that shown in Table 13.1 to that shown in Table 13.2.

Table 13.2 An alternative view of the stages of logistics evolution

	Level of integration	Objective of optimization initiatives
Stage A	Fragmented technical disciplines	Local operational fixes
Stage B	Logistics functional integration	Logistics network cost minimization
Stage C	Cross-functional logistics integration	Logistics and asset rationalization
Stage D	Inter-company logistics coordination	Joint enterprise network rationalization
Stage E	Integrated intra-company and inter-company supply chain process management	Total business process efficiency and effectiveness maximization

A look in depth at those few companies already in 'Stage E' of development can reveal the true boundary between business process management and traditional management approaches, yielding a better understanding of both BPR and BPM in this particular process area.

INTRA-COMPANY SUPPLY CHAIN PROCESS REDESIGN EXPERIENCES

A number of major US corporations began supply chain redesign work in the late 1980s. In general they had already undertaken major TQM initiatives. They had also been involved in benchmarking since its inception in its modern form in 1979. It was natural, therefore, that these non-competitive companies should come together as their work progressed to share experiences. In the late 1980s this process-oriented experience sharing and benchmarking became regularized into a series of 'supply chain roundtables' initially hosted by Xerox and subsequently hosted on a rotating basis by all participants. The resultant process efficiency and effectiveness gains recorded by these companies are quite extraordinary.

Xerox formally began its supply chain re-engineering initiative in 1988. The company had already undertaken a major worldwide Total Quality Management (TQM) exercise which had gained its Japanese subsidiary (Fuji Xerox) the Deming Award in Japan in 1980 and subsequently led to the Malcolm Baldridge Award and the European Federation for Quality Management Award. In 1986, in association with this TQM work, the company formally initiated a total review of its business processes under the project title 'Xerox Business Architecture'. After formulating a total enterprise schema consisting of 14 business processes, three of these were selected for priority redesign, one of which was the 'Inventory Management and Logistics Process', later known as 'The Integrated Supply Chain'. This prioritization was based partly on the assessed impact which redesign could have on both customer satisfaction, the company's number one priority, and financial results. It also reflected the fact that, particularly in Europe, the company had already largely co-ordinated and consolidated its logistics activities, with major benefits to both customer satisfaction and return on assets. The further potential improvements identified in the Xerox Business Architecture exercise would, therefore, only come from 'true re-engineering'. In the terminology of Tables 13.1 and 13.2, much of Xerox's logistics activity had already reached Stages III and IV, only process management of the type envisaged in Stage E would yield substantial further improvement. In the event this diagnosis proved correct. The Xerox case is well documented, and since 1988 a further $750 million of inventory reductions and $200 million of annual operating expenses reflect massive efficiency gains on an already well tuned but conventional process, with a simultaneous effectiveness gain being reflected in 8 percentage points of Customer Satisfaction Index improvement (Bounds *et al.*, 1994).

Digital Equipment Corporation (DEC)'s experience parallels that of Xerox very closely. The company has retrospectively identified three stages through which its thinking and practice has evolved in relation to supply chain management. From 1957 to the late 1970s procurement, production, materials management and distribution were discrete functions. In the late 1970s DEC entered its 'Stage 2' with the launch of its programme of 'Logistics Functional Excellence' which coordinated the four functions, set common goals and concentrated upon network optimization. The results were impressive. Between 1985 and 1990 DEC experienced a 60 per cent reduction in work in progress (WIP) inventories, a 50 per cent reduction in manufacturing space and a 75 per cent reduction in customer installation problems. The exercise released over $1.5 billion of cash during the second half of the 1980s. DEC then entered the third phase with the formal announcement of its 'Enterprise Integration' initiative, and, like Xerox, chose the supply chain process as the first area for process redesign. The objective has been defined as:

> 'The integration of the company's functions and business processes resulting in the smooth flow of goods, services and information in support of customer needs'. (DEC internal non-confidential working papers)

DEC managers currently claim to be on target to achieve a further release of cash totalling at least $1 billion between 1990 and 1995 and a simultaneous effectiveness improvement measured in terms of a reduction of the customer dissatisfaction gap by between one-third and two-thirds.

AT&T's Network Computer Systems Division has identified 12 process re-engineering initiatives, one of which addresses 'the entire order fulfilment chain'. The objective of the redesign activity is to produce a process capable of guaranteeing 95 per cent on-time delivery of full systems on the first promise date at substantially reduced costs to AT&T. 'Order Fulfilment Process' is also the terminology used by Hewlett Packard in relation to its breakthrough strategy, begun in 1990, aimed at six sigma performance levels of on-time, defect-free delivery of HP products. Similar projects, under different names, have already produced significant benefits and are now at various stages of further development in Apple, Siemens, Unilever, 3M and Becton & Dickinson.

In order to learn from these pioneering experiences, workshop outputs and individual in-depth discussions with these leading-edge supply chain practitioners have been used to establish consensus on the ways in which the 'desired state' redesigned supply chain processes differ from the processes which they have replaced. A free-form, iterative discussion approach has been used in preference to a more restrictive, structured interview or questionnaire technique. Although some elements of the Delphi approach were used, anonymity was not required. In essence, therefore, the output presented below represents panel consensus from a set of over 30 successful supply chain redesign practitioners selected from 'Stage E' companies.

Figure 13.3 illustrates the three key dimensions of process redesign identified by these practitioners as being most critical to the success of their BPR efforts. In each case three important characteristics of the dimensions are noted. These express the differences between post-redesigned business processes and their prior states. Taken together, these characteristics represent a definitional statement of true process redesign. In the area of decision-making, also known as 'management processes', there is a strong outward-looking focus and a recognition that customer interfacing employees need to be given decision-making authority. In the area of 'information processes', integrated and readily accessible data is viewed as a corporate rather than departmental asset. The 'work process' area is characterized by widened job responsibilities, often accomplished through teamworking.

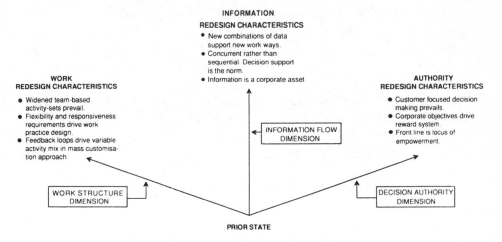

Figure 13.3 Dimensions and characteristics of redesigned supply chain processes

A further output which has emerged from these discussions is a very clear consensus concerning the nature of the redesign process itself. This is that true process redesign is only likely to be successful if it is recognized as a multidimensional activity, simultaneously and explicitly addressing the work activity dimension, the information flow dimension and the decision/authority dimension (see Figure 13.4).

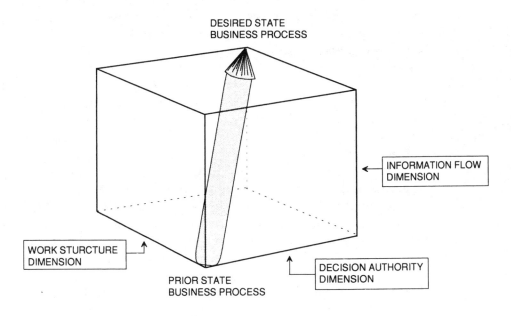

Figure 13.4 BPR as a multidimensional activity

This is not to say that major improvements cannot be made to the existing process through more conventional one or two-dimensional projects. In effect, the message is that if the initiative is to merit the term 'redesign' as opposed to 'improvement', (ie to result in a new business process capable of being operated in a completely new and holistic way), the redesign activity itself cannot be approached in a piecemeal fashion. The need for three-dimensional, simultaneous change reflects on the very nature of business process redesign, and distinguishes it from other forms of improvement programmes.

INTER-COMPANY SUPPLY CHAIN REDESIGN INITIATIVES

The initial focus of the discussions with leading-edge practitioners has been intra-company redesign of the supply chain process. During the discussions, however, it has become apparent that most leading-edge companies now view the supply chain on an inter-company basis. They are concerned not only with their own business processes, but also with those of their suppliers and their customers. In effect the supply chain can be seen as running from raw materials to final consumption as illustrated in Figure 13.5. It is the effectiveness of the total chain, in the eyes of the end consumer, that will determine the success or failure of the enterprises within the chain.

In this view the intra-company cross-functional process relationships of Figure 13.2 can be replaced by the inter-company process relationships of Figure 13.5. This leads to the hypothesis that the characteristics of successful intra-company process redesign outlined in Figure 13.3 might also be relevant to inter-company supply chain redesign initiatives. The best-practice workshops and interviews have therefore been widened to include companies involved in inter-enterprise supply chain redesign. Early indications from work with Procter & Gamble and with Bose Corporation (Stein, 1993), both of whom are leading practitioners of inter-company supply chain integration, are that the hypothesis may be valid. This also appears to be consistent with the results of the extensive work of Byrnes and Shapiro (1992) who have tracked US companies' experience in 'inter-company operating ties' (IOTs) since the late 1980s, interviewing over 100 executives in over 40 companies. As with the intra-company initiatives discussed above, they have concluded that the primary differentiator of the few, highly successful IOT initiatives is that the partners simultaneously revise their information flows, work practices and authority relationships. When this is done the process which emerges is radically more efficient and effective, with gains of 30 per cent or more in productivity for both partners. Not surprisingly, a growing number of companies are taking up this partnering approach, particularly in the retailer–wholesaler and retailer–manufacturer area under the banner of 'Quick Response' or 'Efficient Customer Response'(Christopher 1992). This is being facilitated by the US Voluntary Inter-industry Standards Group's initiatives on information interchange standards. Within the UK a related development is the Partnership Sourcing Initiative (MacBeth and Ferguson, 1994). Overall the combined efficiency and effectiveness gains of both intra-company and inter-company supply chain redesign are seen as having the potential to significantly improve total economic productivity and thus total economic well-being, providing that the lessons learned by the pioneers in this area can be rapidly and effectively disseminated.

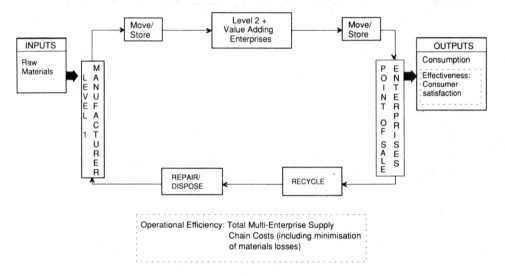

Figure 13.5   The multi-enterprise supply chain

CONCLUSIONS AND IMPLICATIONS FOR ACADEMICS AND PRACTITIONERS

The experiences of pioneering practitioners of supply chain redesign and process management tend to confirm that BPR and BPM, applied appropriately, can lead to breakthrough levels of intra-enterprise and inter-enterprise operational efficiency and effectiveness. Even within high-performance companies, massive productivity gains in logistics are being recorded when the supply chain is specifically redesigned to be operated in a holistic manner as a total 'process' or 'system'. This view of the supply chain as a 'process' differs from the conventional 'logistics networks' view primarily by simultaneously addressing all aspects of the operation of the supply chain, including work practices, information flows and authority/decision-making structures. In effect, the supply chain practitioners are confirming the theories of a number of earlier writers. These writers have noted that whereas the traditional, hierarchical model of management prevalent in most enterprises drives control and efficiency by segregating business activities into standardized subtasks, true process management is integrative by nature and drives even greater efficiency and effectiveness through flexibility and responsiveness (Davenport and Short, 1990; Bounds and Dobbins, 1993).

On the other hand, BPR initiatives in most companies and across most areas of activity are currently proceeding on a trial-and-error basis, with practice running ahead of theory. This is evidenced by the growing number of reported failures of these initiatives (*Fortune*, 1993; *Financial Times*, 1993). Such failures are not surprising given that the supply chain experiences confirm that BPR and BPM present managers with challenges which are very different from those with which they are familiar. In these circumstances, the key and urgent challenge facing academics is to establish a sound theory of BPM from which a robust set of principles and techniques can be derived. Although the output is unlikely ever to be totally prescriptive, it should be possible to reduce significantly the failures implicit in the current trial-and-error approach to BPR. Malone *et al.* (1993) have correctly indicated that disciplines which themselves are naturally integrative, such as coordination theory and inheritance theory, may prove pivotal in this endeavour. All aspects of management research can, however, have a role to play in this work. The only requirement will be that the researchers are willing to look beyond the boundaries of their traditional management science specialisms and adopt the same wide view of management adopted by the successful practitioners. For their part, practitioners will need to take on board the implications of the experiences of the supply chain pioneers. Business Process Redesign is not a one-time productivity improvement exercise. To be successful it requires a commitment to employ, on a permanent basis, a totally new set of management practices and principles for which they may be very poorly prepared. In effect they may have to be willing to relearn how to manage.

REFERENCES

Bounds, G *et al.* (1994) *Beyond Total Quality Management*, McGraw-Hill, New York.

Bounds, G and Dobbins, G. (1993) 'Changing the Managerial Agenda', *Journal of General Management*, 18 (3), Spring.

Bowersox, D J *et al.* (1989) *Leading-Edge Logistics*, Council of Logistics Management, Oakbrook.

Byrne, P M and Markham, W J (1991a) *Improving Quality and Productivity in Logistics,* Council of Logistics Management, Oakbrook.

Byrne, P M and Markham, W J (1991b) *Exploiting the Power of the Logistics Process,* A T Kearney, Chicago.

Byrnes, J L S and Shapiro, R D (1992) *Inter-Company Operating Ties (IOTs): Unlocking the Value of Channel Restructuring,* Harvard Business School Working Paper No 92–058.

Christopher, M G (1992) *Logistics and Supply Chain Management*, Pitman, London.

Cooper, R and Kaplan, R S (1991) 'Profit Priorities from Activity-Based Costing', *Harvard Business Review*, May–June.

Davenport, T H and Short, J E (1990) ' The New Industrial Engineering', *Sloan Management Review*, Summer.

Financial Times (1993) 'Time To Get Serious', 25 June.

Fortune (1993) 'Re-engineering the Company', 23 August.

MacBeth, D K and Ferguson, N (1994) *Partnership Sourcing: An Integrated Supply Chain Approach*, Pitman, London.

Malone, T W *et al.* (1993) *Tools for Inventing Organizations*, Sloan School Working Paper No. 3562-93, MIT.

O'Laughlin, K A et al. (1993) *Re-engineering European Logistics Systems,* Council of Logistics Management, Oakbrook.

Pohlen, T H (1993) *Application of ABC within Logistics*, Council of Logistics Management Annual Proceedings, Oakbrook.

Seger, R E and Best, W J (1986) *Intergrated Logistics Management*, A T Kearney, Chicago.

Stalk, G (1988) 'Time: The Next Strategic Advantage', *Harvard Busines Review,* July–August.

Stalk, G and Hout, T M (1990) *Competing Against Time*, Free Press, New York.

Stein, M (1993) 'The Ultimate Customer-Supplier Relationship', *National Productivity Review*, Autumn.

Part Four

IMPLEMENTING BPR-RELATED CHANGE

As we have already stressed, the objective of BPR is performance improvement through redesign of organizational processes *not* change *per se*. Change is but a consequence of any attempt to improve. Furthermore, if we are to believe the 'revolutionary' school of BPR and their guru Michael Hammer, then BPR is about making changes which are 'radical', 'violent' and 'transformational'. Others would argue for a more incremental approach of continuous improvement through small-scale changes. Either way, redesigning business processes will result in change – and lots of it. The chapters in this part address issues related to change and managing change, specifically when brought about by BPR initiatives.

The question of whether BPR is radical change or reactionary tinkering is addressed by Bob Wood, Richard Vidgen, Trevor Wood-Harper and Jeremy Rose in Chapter 14. However, they take a somewhat different perspective than that usually found. Using a framework developed by Gibson Burrell and Gareth Morgan they analyse what seem to be the core tenets of BPR, concluding that the current set of theoretical assumptions which underpin BPR are too restrictive in nature. They assert that the present 'mechanistic' conception of re-engineering both business processes and organizational culture within which such processes take place will not bring about the expected gains in business performance. They argue for the inclusion of ideas drawn from Soft Systems Methodology and Assumption Surfacing in order to provide a richer and more rigorous methodological basis for undertaking a BPR study. They outline a multiple perspective approach, which is illustrated with reference to a project the group is currently working on. The chapter concludes by proposing that a theoretical understanding of the contribution of multiple perspectives should be allied to a practical understanding achieved through carrying out BPR interventions. Such a mixture of theory and practice, they argue, should enhance both the methods for carrying out such interventions and add to an increasing body of knowledge about how and why people organize themselves as they do.

In Chapter 15, Mark Keen attempts to shed light on the process of BPR implementation. He examines BPR as a change management phenomenon and the perceived role of senior managers within it. In trying to place BPR within the context of change management, the chapter compares it with three models of achieving planned change as suggested by David Buchanan and David Boddy: project management, participative management, and the political perspective of change. The chapter then elaborates on the view that BPR is predominantely a linear and rational change management methodology, interpreting it within the concepts of 'bold strokes' and 'long marches' as developed by Rosabeth Moss Kanter.

In Chapter 16, Lance Revenaugh views BPR as an ongoing process rather than a one-time 'cure' contending that it is particularly important to be able to implement new redesigned processes with a minimum amount of difficulty (or failure). Past research has revealed that corporate culture is a key variable in implementing any major business change and that the strategic relevance of a proposed change affects implementation difficulty and success. In order to address the implementation challenge of BPR, the chapter uses the information technology strategic grid to consider the strategic relevance of processes and the corporate tribes cultural model to assess the potential impact of cultural types on BPR implementation. The combined impact of culture and strategic relevance is then integrated into a thought-provoking framework for research.

14

BUSINESS PROCESS REDESIGN: RADICAL CHANGE OR REACTIONARY TINKERING?

*J R G Wood, R T Vidgen, A T Wood-Harper,
University of Salford, and J Rose, Manchester
Metropolitan University*

INTRODUCTION

The subject of Business Process Re-engineering or Business Process Redesign has generated a considerable amount of interest in a relatively short period of time. Despite, or perhaps because of, the lack of any coherent body of knowledge upon which such re-engineering or redesign may be based many organizations and individuals lay claim to be undertaking fundamental reviews of the nature of their business. There seem to be almost as many approaches or methodologies for undertaking BPR as there are projects underway.

However, there would now appear to be a sufficient body of literature from which one may distil the core ideas of BPR as it stands at the moment. Using a well-established framework (Burrell and Morgan, 1979) to analyse these ideas would suggest that the current set of theoretical assumptions which underpin what might be termed 'first-generation' BPR (Cypress 1994), are too restrictive in nature. We assert that the present 'mechanistic' conception of re-engineering both business processes and the organizational culture within which such processes take place will not bring about the expected gains in business performance (Vidgen *et al.*, 1994).

The structure of this chapter is as follows. The next section will seek to establish the core ideas upon which the current conception of BPR is based and these are then analysed in section 3 through the use of paradigms of inquiry (Churchman, 1971). We then argue for the inclusion of ideas drawn from Soft Systems Methodology (SSM) and Assumption Surfacing in order to provide a richer and more rigorous methodological basis for undertaking a BPR study. The following section sets out in more detail a multiple perspective approach, which is then illustrated by examples drawn from a project that the group is currently involved in. Finally we draw some conclusions from our work and suggest some areas for further research in this field.

CENTRAL TENETS OF BPR

Business process redesign is '... the fundamental rethinking and radical redesign of business process to achieve improvements in critical, contemporary measures of performance such as cost, quality, service, and speed.' (Hammer and Champy, 1993).

The central notion of BPR, therefore, is of 'an initiative which combines process orientation with an edict for radical change' (Kawalek, 1993). This definition may be expanded to include the following necessary principles:

- Radical change and assumption challenging
- Process and goal orientation
- Organizational restructuring
- Exploiting enabling technologies, such as IT.

These underlying ideas may be extended further in order to explore their implications. For example, if change is to be radical then the basic assumptions underpinning the prevailing view of the organization must be challenged in order to avoid falling into the trap of reifying the way things are currently done. Change becomes the norm rather than being something to be avoided. It is the catalyst by which the organization can get ahead, and stay ahead, of the competition. BPR is concerned with innovation and not simply with 'patching up' defective areas.

The process orientation gives emphasis to the need for purposive, goal-oriented processes which are seen as part of a 'chain', where each individual process adds 'value' to the products it handles. Processes are thus viewed as purposive activities that achieve a goal, and which may transcend existing organizational boundaries and structures.

Organizational restructuring is thus brought about by considering such revisioned processes, and not through the consideration of existing structures. This view is coupled with a post-industrial and post-modern perspective which emphasizes a craft orientation characterized by a multiskilled workforce and flexible manufacturing. Possible changes, therefore, are not restricted to merely internal rearrangements – whole activities may be removed and outsourced, even to competitors

In much of the current BPR literature Information Technology (IT) is given a central, pivotal role in which it is typified as presenting previously unimaginable opportunities for change. There is a sense of innovatory solutions looking for problems, of serendipity overcoming planned strategies, and of the organization exploiting unexpected or emergent consequences.

The current position of BPR may thus be summarized as consisting of a mixture of practical experience and some limited conceptual thinking. Such experience as exists has largely arisen as a result of a mixture of creative experimentation and blind faith!

ANALYSIS OF THE ASSUMPTIONS UNDERPINNING BPR

A challenge to the current school of thinking on BPR is provided by recent research developments in the field of Information Systems. Increasingly IS research and practice is being influenced by an interpretivist as opposed to a functionalist paradigm (Burrell and Morgan, 1979, Hirschheim and Klein, 1989) whereas BPR remains firmly rooted in the mechanistic thinking of reductionist science (Vidgen *et al.*, 1994) *For example, there appears to be little concern in the BPR literature for the ambiguity inherent in the notion of 'customer' (Mitroff and Linstone, 1993).*

Burrell and Morgan classified assumptions both about the nature of ontological belief (that is, the nature of reality itself) and about the nature of epistemological belief (that is, how we come to knowledge about such a reality). They suggested that ontology could be seen as being either objective (that is a belief in the existence of an absolute social world independent of the observer) or subjective (that is a belief that reality is constructed from the views of the individuals acting within it) in nature. Assumptions about the nature of society itself are classified as either being concerned with regulation or with radical change. The former deals with the maintenance of order through consensus and other mechanisms, whereas the latter considers conflict, dissonance, and the exertion of control through the possession of power.

This classification yields the four paradigms labelled functionalism, interpretivism, radical structuralism, and radical humanism. We assert, therefore, that the assumptions made by the advocates of BPR place it within the functionalist paradigm, in that the nature of reality is taken to be objective and emphasis is placed upon increasing the efficiency of the system through the logical rearrangement of processes. As with many other so-called 'hard' approaches, BPR studies seem to assume that the problem of the change itself is well-defined and that human behaviour is largely deterministic, thus ignoring the cultural and political dimensions of any human intervention of this nature.

Following Morgan, we may also examine the current conception of BPR using the notion of metaphor (Morgan, 1986). We may use different metaphors to represent underlying sets of assumptions which in turn govern the mental models we use to try and understand organizational behaviour. The dominant metaphor underpinning BPR is that of the organization as *machine*. Even the use of the term re-engineering itself is based on this metaphor, and it emphasizes a view of organizational processes as being poorly optimized parts of a machine in need of complete overhaul.

The adoption of different organizational metaphors, however, can lead to very different stances being adopted as to the nature and priorities of a BPR study. For example:

- *Organism*: how subsystems interact with themselves and with the environment
- *Culture*: perspectives of stakeholders and consensus to change work practices
- *Coercive*: power and enforcing change.

We assert that it is necessary and desirable for BPR to move beyond its present position both with regard to its paradigm (functionalism) and its metaphor (machine).

SSM AND ASSUMPTION SURFACING

The achievement of radical change within organizations requires people to become aware of and make public the underlying assumptions that they have about the business (Mitroff and Linstone, 1993) These assumptions must then be challenged, confronted or opposed if they are to be replaced by a new vision of how the organization might be structured (Senge, 1990) It is likely, therefore, that the overthrow of deeply held beliefs about the nature of the organization will require much more than a mere shift of focus to the satisfaction of 'customer' requirements.

Soft Systems Methodology is a powerful approach to problem formulation and analysis, which is firmly rooted in the history of systems ideas and systems thinking (Checkland, 1981). There is also a strong body of reported experience in the use of the methodology (Checkland and Scholes, 1990).

We believe that SSM provides an appropriate framework within which a BPR initiative can take place. In particular, the use of conceptual models provides a means of representing purposeful human activity irrespective of whether such activity is tangible (eg manufacturing) or rather more abstract (eg service). Such models are also based on formal, system principles and as such provide a much more rigorous, as well as holistic, foundation upon which organizational processes may be revisioned.

Other concepts such as Root Definitions and Weltanschauung (worldview) enhance the modelling process by giving emphasis to the differing perspectives of the various parties involved in a BPR change, and by offering a coherent means of visualizing a number of different alternative futures for the organization (Galliers, 1993).

In addition to this stream of logic-based enquiry (Checkland and Scholes, 1990), SSM also offers guidance on the analysis of the political and cultural factors which impinge upon any intervention of this kind and which are often the major determinants of success or failure. Using Burrell and Morgan's framework we may consider SSM to be classified within the *interpretivist* paradigm since it emphasizes the subjective construction of organizational reality through the perceptions of the individuals involved.

SSM, however, provides little guidance, apart from the drawing of Rich Pictures, as to how the different actors within the problem situation may be identified. This is particularly crucial to any BPR study given the need to consider all those who may affect, or be affected by, such a change. We therefore propose to supplement SSM with Stakeholder Analysis and Assumption Surfacing (Mitroff and Linstone, 1993). This additional process involves the identification of stakeholders, the surfacing of assumptions, dialectical debate and a final synthesis.

Stakeholders are taken to be any individual, group, organization or institution that can affect, as well as be affected by, an individual's, group's, organization's, or institution's policy or policies. The identification of such people is of crucial importance in any BPR initiative given the goal of bringing about radical change in a pluralist environment, where multiple stakeholders may have a central compatibility of interest but may differ fundamentally over both ends and means, and may have divergent values and beliefs (Flood and Jackson, 1991).

Having identified the different stakeholders through a process of analysis, the next stage is to identify and then question the assumptions that are held about members of the stakeholder group. If BPR is truly concerned with the bringing about of radical change within organizations then such assumptions will not only need to be understood, they will very probably have to be overthrown. Also since the redesign of the organization may well be founded on such assumptions, it is very important that they are in some way validated. For example, it is often the case that even in customer-led change projects the basis for revisioning the organizational processes is a set of *beliefs* about what the customer requires in terms of service, cost, quality and so on.

We therefore believe that SSM is strengthened by the inclusion of Stakeholder Analysis and Assumption Surfacing in order to provide a fuller consideration of all the actors involved in a BPR initiative, and to give support to the identification of relevant and innovative Weltanschauungs.

A MULTIPLE PERSPECTIVE APPROACH TO BPR

We have established a research agenda for BPR within our own group which includes:

- The use of Soft Systems Methodology (Checkland, 1981; Checkland and Scholes, 1990) as a tool for revisioning business processes, together with Assumption Surfacing (Mason and Mitroff, 1981; Mitroff and Linstone, 1993) to support radical change
- An investigation of the organizational context within which BPR takes place with particular emphasis on how a multiple perspective approach (Avison and Wood-Harper, 1991) might be used to support radical change given the need for cultural feasibility.

Since no single perspective will be sufficient when addressing the kind of messy problem situations confronted in any BPR initiative we advocate the adoption of a multiple perspective approach based on organizational, personal and technical perspectives (Mitroff and Linstone, 1993). These differing perspectives correspond to the different forms of interest, technical, practical and emancipatory, identified by Habermas (Winograd and Flores, 1986). We therefore need to apply various methods which reflect these different knowledge interests, and to find a way of reconciling and balancing the conflicting requirements produced by the use of such methods.

In a BPR study SSM could be used to represent the organizational perspective through the modelling of purposeful human activity. The personal perspective may correspond to the idea of employee empowerment, and may be treated through the use of socio-technical systems theory. Finally, the technical perspective may be concerned with how IT (Information Technology) might be employed to enable new organizational forms and work processes.

A possible multiple perspective approach to BPR is shown in Figure 14.1. In the diagram, the left-hand side represents a process of understanding the context within which the BPR initiative is taking place through the adoption of multiple perspectives. This process consists of identifying and analysing stakeholders, together with the surfacing of their assumptions. The future analysis looks at how the BPR change might alter both the nature of stakeholders and the relationships between them.

The right-hand side of the diagram illustrates the different stages of the Multiview methodology embedded within a continuous learning cycle (Avison and Wood-Harper, 1990). Some of the stages correspond to the three perspectives referred to earlier: organizational (information analysis), personal (socio-technical analysis) and technical (technical design).

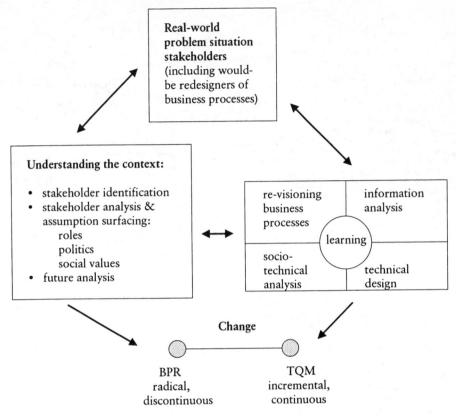

Figure 14.1 Multiple perspective approach to BPR

A significant advantage of this approach is that it offers a coherent framework within which BPR may be linked to the information system development necessary to underpin the organizational change brought about. In this way BPR can be both envisaged and enacted as a learning rather than an optimizing process, and it becomes systemic rather than systematic in nature.

THE METHODOLOGY IN USE

In order to illustrate both the need for a multiple perspective approach to BPR and the use of such an approach in practice we shall now describe some findings from a study currently being undertaken in conjunction with a major pharmaceuticals company. For reasons of confidentiality, and because the outcome of the study is not yet complete, the examples quoted here are not necessarily those which are under active consideration by the management of the company. We shall also draw upon a comparable example cited by Mitroff and Linstone in order to justify the methodology we are putting forward.

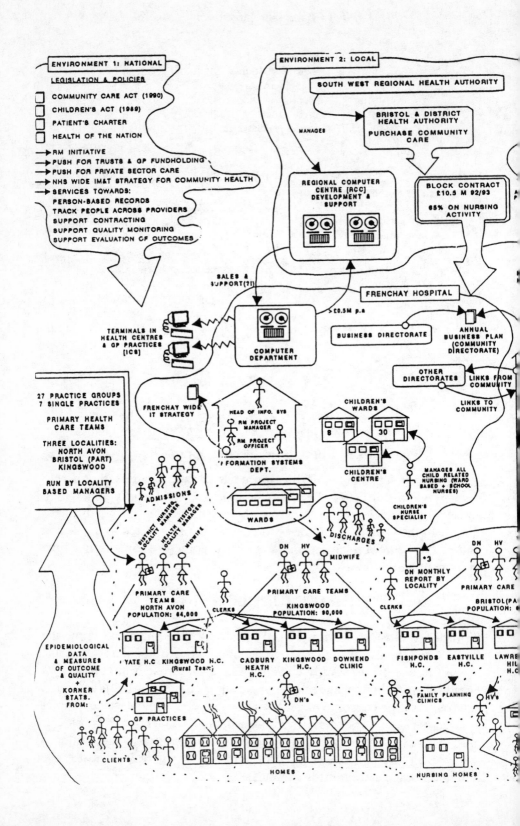

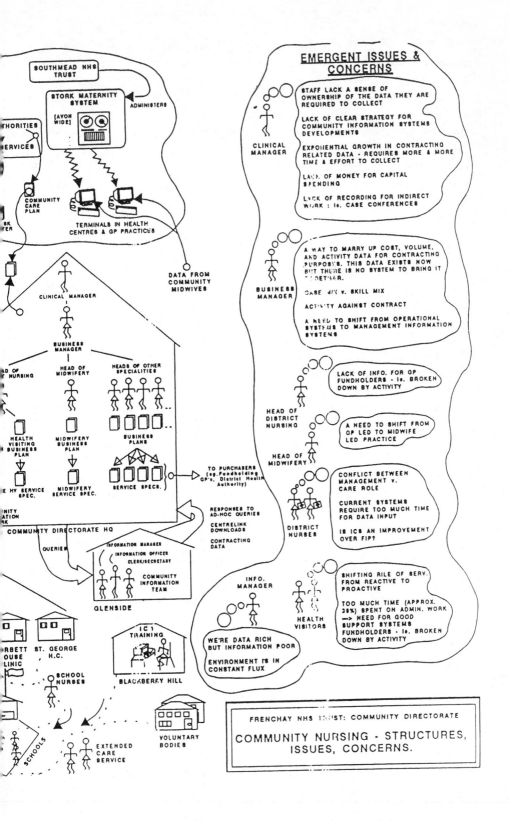

EMERGENT ISSUES & CONCERNS

SOUTHMEAD NHS TRUST

STORK MATERNITY SYSTEM
[AVON WIDE]
ADMINISTERS

THORITIES
ERVICES

COMMUNITY CARE PLAN

TERMINALS IN HEALTH CENTRES & GP PRACTICES

DATA FROM COMMUNITY MIDWIVES

CLINICAL MANAGER
- STAFF LACK A SENSE OF OWNERSHIP OF THE DATA THEY ARE REQUIRED TO COLLECT
- LACK OF CLEAR STRATEGY FOR COMMUNITY INFORMATION SYSTEMS DEVELOPMENTS
- EXPONENTIAL GROWTH IN CONTRACTING RELATED DATA - REQUIRES MORE & MORE TIME & EFFORT TO COLLECT
- LACK OF MONEY FOR CAPITAL SPENDING
- LACK OF RECORDING FOR INDIRECT WORK : Ie. CASE CONFERENCES

BUSINESS MANAGER
- A WAY TO MARRY UP COST, VOLUME, AND ACTIVITY DATA FOR CONTRACTING PURPOSES. THIS DATA EXISTS NOW BUT THERE IS NO SYSTEM TO BRING IT TOGETHER.
- CASE MIX v. SKILL MIX
- ACTIVITY AGAINST CONTRACT
- A NEED TO SHIFT FROM OPERATIONAL SYSTEMS TO MANAGEMENT INFORMATION SYSTEMS

CLINICAL MANAGER

BUSINESS MANAGER

D OF NURSING

HEAD OF MIDWIFERY

HEADS OF OTHER SPECIALITIES

HEALTH VISITING BUSINESS PLAN

MIDWIFERY BUSINESS PLAN

BUSINESS PLANS

HE HV SERVICE SPEC.

MIDWIFERY SERVICE SPEC.

SERVICE SPECS.

NITY ATION K

COMMUNITY DIRECTORATE HQ

QUERIES

TO PURCHASERS (eg. Fundholding GP's, District Health Authority)

RESPONSES TO AD-HOC QUERIES

CENTRELINK DOWNLOADS

CONTRACTING DATA

HEAD OF DISTRICT NURSING
- LACK OF INFO. FOR GP FUNDHOLDERS - Ie. BROKEN DOWN BY ACTIVITY

HEAD OF MIDWIFERY
- A NEED TO SHIFT FROM GP LED TO MIDWIFE LED PRACTICE

DISTRICT NURSES
- CONFLICT BETWEEN MANAGEMENT v. CARE ROLE
- CURRENT SYSTEMS REQUIRE TOO MUCH TIME FOR DATA INPUT
- IS ICS AN IMPROVEMENT OVER FIP?

INFORMATION MANAGER
INFORMATION OFFICER
CLERK/SECRETARY
COMMUNITY INFORMATION TEAM

GLENSIDE

INFO. MANAGER
- WE'RE DATA RICH BUT INFORMATION POOR
- ENVIRONMENT IS IN CONSTANT FLUX

HEALTH VISITORS
- SHIFTING RILE OF SERV. FROM REACTIVE TO PROACTIVE
- TOO MUCH TIME (APPROX. 38%) SPENT ON ADMIN. WORK → NEED FOR GOOD SUPPORT SYSTEMS FUNDHOLDERS - Ie. BROKEN DOWN BY ACTIVITY

ICT TRAINING

RBETT OUSE LINIC

ST. GEORGE H.C.

SCHOOL NURSES

BLACKBERRY HILL

SCHOOLS

EXTENDED CARE SERVICE

VOLUNTARY BODIES

FRENCHAY NHS TRUST: COMMUNITY DIRECTORATE

COMMUNITY NURSING - STRUCTURES, ISSUES, CONCERNS.

It is important to note that this particular study was not originally conceived of as being one involving BPR. The recognition of the real nature of the change being undertaken by the company has evolved through a series of other initiatives which were prompted by the general need to respond to the massive changes taking place within the 'customer', the National Health Service. Even now, people are reluctant to openly discuss the project as being concerned with re-engineering or redesigning the organization, even though that is clearly what is taking place. We shall return to this point at the end when we discuss the social and political analysis of the intervention.

The first stage in Multiview is concerned with understanding the context within which the BPR study is taking place. As Figure 14.1 shows, this understanding is attempted through the use of stakeholder identification, stakeholder analysis and assumption surfacing, and an analysis of possible future scenarios. The stakeholder analysis, in turn, focuses upon roles, social values and organizational politics.

As with any soft, messy problem situation we begin by summarizing the overall context of the intervention using the technique of *Rich Pictures* (Checkland, 1981). This is an intellectual construct used both to express the problematic context as it is seen by the various actors in the situation, and to enable those involved to start the project with a common understanding of the 'problem'. It is important to note, particularly for those people who are used to employing typical IT-based representations for analysis, that this technique does not prescribe any standard notation or rules. Rather it encourages the expression of ideas by individuals in whatever form they choose, so allowing us to begin to develop an understanding of their perspectives or Weltanschauungs. An example of just such a rich picture is given as Figure 14.2 (see pages 252-3). This illustrates part of a study undertaken into the provision of community health care in Frenchay, Bristol (Chatterjee, Parker and Wood, 1993) and as such represents only one element of the NHS 'customer' which interacts with the pharmaceutical company.

The attitude adopted in drawing such a rich picture is that reality is socially constructed, and not an objective given which is somehow out-there waiting to be collected. There is thus no right or wrong answer, only different degrees of meaningful-ness, in that we attempt to make sense of our observations by adopting an exploratory, learning attitude. The aim is to be creative in expressing views, not merely to follow some ritualistic form of documentation.

As well as using the rich picture to try and attain a general, and shared, understanding of the problem context, it also provides the means by which we can draw out and identify all the major stakeholders involved. We would argue that the notion of a stakeholder (Mitroff, 1983) is much richer, and hence more useful, than the traditional concept of the customer, not least in this particular situation because there is a good deal of confusion and uncertainty surrounding who the customer actually is. Figure 14.3 shows the use of a *stakeholder map*, in the form suggested by Mitroff and Linstone, to illustrate some of the key stakeholders interacting with the pharmaceutical company.

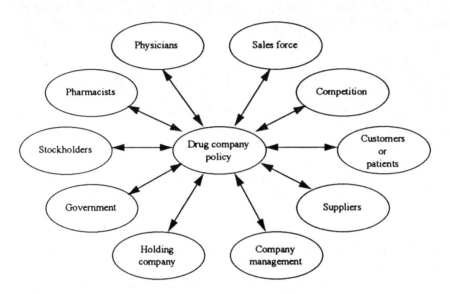

Figure 14.3 A stakeholder map of the drug company

The next step in the analysis is to try and draw out, or surface, the nature of the assumptions we have about the stakeholders and their views with respect to the problem context. In order to do this let us take the example of the threat posed to the pharmaceutical company by the increased propensity to prescribe generic as opposed to brand-named drugs This is as a result of a number of actions initiated by government aimed at driving down costs within the NHS. Put simply generics are, in general, cheaper than proprietary products and therefore in an atmosphere of cost-cutting are more likely to be favoured, particularly if prescribers have to be concerned for the management of their own finances.

Faced with the threat from generics, the pharmaceutical company might choose to respond in a number of ways (Mitroff and Linstone, 1993):

- Turn their proprietary products into 'generics' by *lowering* their prices
- Create a market difference for their products by *raising* the prices
- Reduce internal costs whilst keeping their prices the *same*.

Note that each strategy rests on a fundamentally different set of *assumptions* about the 'real' nature of the problem, and that these assumptions are the properties of *stakeholders*. The strategies, therefore, are based upon very different properties being ascribed to the stakeholders. For example, the strategy to increase prices assumes that doctors are concerned with the health and well-being of the patient irrespective of cost, *and* that physicians are more powerful than pharmacists. Lowering the price, however, implies that we believe that doctors are becoming increasingly price-sensitive, *and* that at some point the quality of treatment gives way to cost.

The point of this example is that these are *our* assumptions about the behaviour of others. How can the pharmaceutical company be sure that what they believe to be the assumptions held by doctors are in fact true?

In addition to this the role of doctors themselves is changing within the NHS. They are no longer the sole arbiters of prescribing decisions, and the influence of fund-holding has significantly affected their attitudes towards patient care in general and prescribing in particular.

We therefore require a more rigorous treatment of assumption surfacing in which we may generate possible models of future 'systems' which would satisfy the requirement for certain defined purposeful activities deemed to be meaningful in a given context. In other words, we may investigate what stakeholder assumptions would need to hold if certain organizational strategies were to succeed. We may then rate and test such assumptions through comparison with the problem situation itself. Finally we are able to challenge these assumptions in the hope of generating truly radical views of alternative organisational futures (Senge, 1993).

Identifying the elements of CATWOE allows us to construct both root definitions and conceptual models of the human purposeful activity described in the transformation (Checkland, 1981). For those unfamiliar with the mnemonic, the elements are as follows:

C	customers	the victims/beneficiaries of T
A	actors	those who undertake T
T	transformation	the conversion of input to output
W	Weltanschauung	the worldview that makes T meaningful
O	owners	those who can put a stop to T
E	environment	those elements outside the system

Identifying the elements of CATWOE allows us to construct both root definitions and conceptual models of the human purposeful activity described in the transformation. Since these models must be constructed in such a way as to be *systemically desirable* and *culturally feasible*, they provide two major advantages over many of the other techniques which have been advocated in the BPR literature as the basis for re-engineering or redesign (eg DFDs, IDEF, role activity diagrams or even the value-chain).

Firstly, they avoid the reductionist perspective inherent in the views of BPR advanced thus far. Since the contribution of any activity must be seen in terms of its value to the wider 'system' or whole of which it is an integral part, such an approach avoids the risk of eliminating important activities which are deemed, from an isolationist stance, not to add 'value'.

For example, given a primary task transformation (Checkland,1981) which is defined in terms of getting products out to customers it would be hard to justify the activity of providing health economic data to general practitioners. If, however, the transformation is redefined to describe a process of seeking to persuade doctors of the efficacy of a given drug so that they will prescribe it then the activity of providing such information becomes paramount.

Secondly, because we do not separate the act of modelling the revisioned processes from the process of achieving the change itself, that is the implementation of these processes, there should be less chance of meeting the kind of resistance to change that one would expect in such circumstances. The insistence on outcomes being *culturally feasible* means that the social and political factors which are likely to determine the success or failure of the BPR initiative must be considered as part of the analysis and not merely as some adjunct to it.

For example, it is already evident in the case of the pharmaceutical company that any change brought about by the current BPR initiative will have a major impact upon the role of the field salesforce. Their traditional way of working will have to alter although it is not exactly clear as yet in what way or ways this will take place. However, what is clear is that whatever the nature of the change it will have to be enacted by the individuals out in the field. The salesforce, therefore, are not only key stakeholders in the BPR initiative in that they more than anybody else have access to the views of prescribers on a regular basis, but are also the major 'victims' of the change itself. Thus it is vital that they play an active part in the BPR process if the results of the initiative are to be *culturally feasible.*

Having generated sets of assumptions from relevant root definitions and conceptual models it is now necessary to compare these with the problem situation as captured in the rich picture in order to check whether or not they exist, and if so how important they are. To do this we make use of a stakeholder assumption map, Figure 14.4 (Mitroff and Linstone, 1993), in which one axis measures the importance of the assumption, and the other the level of confidence we have about the assumption. It is important to realize that in complex problem situations there may well be disagreement over both the form of the assumption imputed to a particular stakeholder, as well as to the importance and rankings of particular assumptions. For example, there would be complete agreement that assumptions about the stakeholder 'patient' would be both very important *and* certain. The patient would be assumed to require the best possible medical attention, including access to the most effective drugs to treat whatever condition they may be suffering from. As we have seen already, however, although doctors may be generally held to be very important stakeholders, there may be a high level of uncertainty surrounding our understanding of the assumptions they might hold.

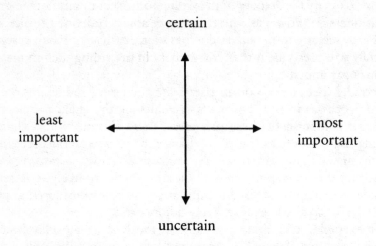

Figure 14.4 Challenging stakeholder assumptions

We must stress though that such uncertainty is itself an important part of the analysis as the actors within the organization surface their own assumptions about the situation requiring change. For example, during one meeting with senior managers of the pharmaceutical company a particular drug was under discussion and was labelled, after some discussion, as being predominantly a primary care product (ie mainly sold to GP's). In a later meeting with some of the line managers the same product was defined as being a 'special product' (ie sold mainly to hospitals). Each group had a very clear, although completely different, set of criteria for deciding which area the product was in. However, given that the field force is divided into two groups, one specializing in primary care and the other in special products, it is clear that such uncertainties will be of some significance in deciding between alternative strategies for organizational realignment.

Having made the assumptions explicit, the actors may now enter into dialectical debate in order to try and reconcile such differences in the nature of the assumptions and in the ratings. Such a debate will be followed by a process of synthesis in which changed or new innovative conceptual models may emerge. Additional evidence can be sought from both inside and outside the organization either to confirm or to deny the assumptions which have been identified through this process of analysis. It will almost certainly be the case, however, that the most important and uncertain assumptions will be precisely those which are most difficult to validate. Despite this truism we would contend that simply being aware of the assumptions upon which a BPR intervention is founded will increase the chances of the intervention being successful.

Finally we need to confront the very understanding upon which the various root definitions and conceptual models have thus far been based. It may well be that in the act of surfacing assumptions about others and about the problem situation, people will already have started to question some of the underlying beliefs that they hold both about the nature of the organization and about its reason for being. Experience tells us, however, that such beliefs are the most difficult for people to question precisely because they are the very means by which we interpret our experiences and thus make sense of the world around us (Senge, 1990). In the case of the pharmaceutical company, for example, to put forward conceptual models of purposeful activity which do not include the research and development of proprietary products, even though such models would satisfy the systemic transformation called for in the appropriate root definition, would be to invite expressions of amazement or even hostility. Yet if BPR is serious in its intent to radically rethink the structure *and* purpose of present-day organizations then this is precisely the kind of *thinking* which must go on, even if the eventual actions which are decided upon turn out to be evolutionary rather than revolutionary in practice.

SUMMARY AND CONCLUSIONS

Business Process Re-engineering came to the fore on the promise of achieving significant improvements in organizational performance through discontinuous change which would involve breaking away from the outdated ideas, rules and procedures that underlie so many business operations (Hammer, 1990). This kind of discontinuous thinking implies that models of existing business processes are rarely the basis for revisioning the organization. Instead we need to imagine new processes, solution spaces, and solution strategies (Cypress, 1994). Such processes and strategies will of necessity be:

- Cross-functional
- Inter-organizational
- Pan-industrial
- Pan-national.

BPR has to date concentrated on decomposing organizations into the sets of business processes which represent how value is created in a product from a customer's perspective (Porter, 1985). This has led to a relatively narrow focus on using IT to improve the efficiency of one or more of these business processes in such a way as to enhance customer satisfaction, increase sales and thus increase profits. At the same time, however, research studies have cast doubt on the extent to which such benefits have actually been achieved in practice (Hall, *et al*, 1993).

A significant factor in the failure of some BPR projects appears to be precisely this lack of breadth or depth in the area chosen for re-engineering.

There is already a call being made for BPR to move beyond this so-called first generation of applications and to focus attention on the wealth-generating behaviour of organizations which continuously increase measures such as market value added (Cypress, 1994). Alongside this are the appeals to empower workers, to create post-modern organizations and to employ IT in innovative and creative ways. Such a radical agenda for change will demand new ways of thinking about the nature and purpose of organized human activity, and it is in the spirit of such change that we offer our ideas and thoughts.

In this chapter we have argued that BPR is currently dominated by a functionalist paradigm and uses a prevailing metaphor of the organization as 'machine'. We recommend a multiple perspective approach which incorporates ideas drawn from the interpretive, systemic methods typified by Soft Systems Methodology. This will bring a degree of richness and rigour to the process of revisioning the organization that is currently lacking. Further areas of research that we are currently pursuing include:

- multiple perspectives and BPR in practice;
- SSM and stakeholder analysis: generating assumptions;
- necessary preconditions for radical and incremental change.

In summary we propose that a theoretical understanding of the contribution of multiple perspectives should be allied to a practical understanding achieved through carrying out BPR interventions.

Such a mixture of theory and practice should enhance both the methods for carrying out such interventions, and add to an increasing body of knowledge about how and why people organize themselves as they do.

REFERENCES

Avison, D E and Wood-Harper, A T (1990) *Multiview: An Exploration in Information Systems Development*, Blackwell, Oxford.

Avison, D E and Wood-Harper, A T (1991) 'Information Systems Development: An Exploration of ideas in Practice', *Computer Journal*, 34(2), 98–112.

Burrell, G and Morgan, G (1979) *Sociological Paradigms and Organizational Analysis*, Heinemann, London.

Checkland, P B (1981) *System Thinking, Systems Practice*, Wiley, Chichester.

Checkland, P B and Scholes, J (1990) *Soft Systems Methodology in Action*, Wiley, Chichester.

Churchman, C W (1971) *The Design of Inquiring Systems*, Basic Books, New York.

Cypress H L (1994) 'MS/OR Imperative Make Second Generation of Business Improvement Mode Work', *OR/MS Today*, February, 18–29.

Flood, R and Jackson, M C (1991) *Creative Problem Solving, Total Systems Intervention*, Wiley, Chichester.

Hall, G, Rosenthal, J and Wade, J (1993) 'How to Make Re-engineering Really Work', *Harvard Business Review*, November–December, 119–131.

Hammer M (1990) Re-engineering Work: Don't Automate, Obliterate', *Harvard Business Review*, July–August, 104-112.

Hammer M and Champy, J (1993) *Re-engineering the Corporation: A Manifesto for Business Revolution*, Harper Business, New York.

Hirschheim, R and Klein, H (1989) 'Four Paradigms of Information Systems Development', *Communications of the ACM*, 32(10), 1199–1216.

Kawalek, P (1993) 'Business Process Re-engineering – A Revolutionary Manifesto?', *Computer Bulletin*, December.

Mason, R and Mitroff, I (1981) *Challenging Strategic Planning Assumptions*, Wiley, New York.

Mitroff, I (1983) *Stakeholders of the Organizational Mind*, Jossey-Bass, San Francisco.

Mitroff I and Linstone, H (1993) *The Unbounded Mind, Breaking the Chains of Traditional Business Thinking*, OUP, New York.

Morgan, G (1986) *Images of Organization*, Sage, Newbury Park, Calif.

Porter M E (1985) *Competitive Advantage: Creating and Sustaining Suprior Performance*, Free Press, New York

Senge, P M (1990) *The Fifth Discipline*, Doublday, New York.

Vidgen, R T, Rose J, Wood, J R G and Wood-Harper A T (1994) 'Business Process Re-engineering: The Need for a Methodology to Revision the Organization', *Business Process Re-engineering: Information System Opportunities and Challenges*, IFIP TC8 International Working Conference, Queensland Gold Coast, Australia.

15

BPR: MANAGING THE CHANGE PROCESS – OR THE PROCESS OF CHANGE MANAGING BPR?

Mark Keen, Sheffield Business School

INTRODUCTION

The term, Business Process Re-engineering (BPR) and its various descendants and derivatives, is one which has gained increasing prominence in management thought and practice. An increasing number of companies are choosing to embark on BPR programmes – over 20 of the UK's top 100 companies (Woudhuysen, 1993), 88 per cent of large corporations (Bashein *et al.*, 1994) – and there is a burgeoning literature on the reasons for and requirements of successful implementation, and a plethora of consultancies offering to assist with the process. However, it is believed that up to 70 per cent of so-called re-engineering efforts fail (Hammer, cited in Moad, 1993) and only 20 per cent of endeavours to implement any major change initiatives, such as BPR, succeed (Belmonte and Murray, 1993).

This chapter arises from the author's ongoing research to more fully understand the process of BPR implementation, particularly given its high 'failure' rate. It contends that BPR, conceived of as a methodology for achieving dramatic revolutionary improvements in organizational performance, is at present not equipped to implement changes of this scale or nature.

The notion of BPR as a change initiative will be examined and compared to a set of approaches from change management. By attempting to contextualize it within a wider framework it is hoped to show that as a methodology BPR is at present one dimensional and unappreciative of the complex nature of radical organizational change. Espoused as an approach which urges organizations to be creative and to break free from the constraints of inappropriate improvement strategies of the past, BPR is currently a methodology for doing so centred firmly within 'classical' rational linear change theory.

The consequences of this will be highlighted by examining one variable – the need for senior management commitment – identified by BPR commentators as essential to an initiative's success, and then explored in terms of what this means for those currently trying to implement initiatives and for the long-term life expectancy of BPR as a distinct way of addressing some of the problems faced by organizations. It is hoped that this initial discussion will raise some questions and areas for more detailed research.

BPR AS A METHOD FOR ACHIEVING IMPROVEMENT

It is important to consider the fundamental elements of BPR if the concept and implementation process are to be examined. BPR guru Michael Hammer (1990, and with Champy, 1993) outlines the aims of BPR programmes, namely the achievement of dramatic improvements in organizational performance. Current structures based on the fragmentation of tasks are no longer effective in the modern, dynamic business environment. Increased liberalization, the globalization of markets and advancements in new technology have created uncertainty, undermining competitive stability and organizational security. What is required is radical change, or a 'new beginning', where organizations reassess what they are doing and how they are doing it. By focusing upon process rather than functional orientation, and forceably breaking away from the constricts of previous rules and ways of working, an organization is able to 'start over'.

Where previously in functionally based organizations jobs were based on tasks being simple, with complex processes knitting them together, now, in the re-engineered organization, it is the processes which will be simple. Bureaucracy, checks and controls will be minimized, with jobs becoming more difficult, substantive and rewarding as simple tasks are replaced by multidimensional work. Employees will be empowered as decision-making is delegated to those doing the actual work and managers change from being supervisors to 'coaches'.

At the core of any re-engineering effort is the notion of process. Davenport and Short (1990) define business processes as a set of logically related tasks performed to achieve a defined business outcome. Practitioners (Broddle, 1994) echo commentators (Hammer and Champy, 1993; Scherr, 1993) in stressing the need for those outcomes to be identified in terms of value to the customer.

Hammer and Champy (1993) and Davenport (1993), as pioneers of re-engineering, realize the methodology for actually 'doing BPR' is as yet an unpolished one; however, common core stages do seem to have appeared (eg Guha *et al.*, 1993; Talwar, 1993; Fried, 1991; Davenport and Short, 1990; Dale, 1991):

- The development by senior management, of a 'vision' for the future organization.
- The appointment of a re-engineering team. The team's role is twofold:
  - to analyse current organizational practices identifying the existing processes within the present structure (though these might not be currently linked in this way)
  - and to then redesign them to meet the requirements of the vision
- The re-engineered processes are then implemented to create the new organization.

Distinctions have been made concerning the scale of re-engineering efforts (eg Talwar, 1993; Davenport, 1993). These involve a differentiation between Process Re-engineering and Business Re-engineering, the former being the redesign of a particular process, the latter being organization-wide (Talwar, 1993). This may seem quite a difference in focus, but the distinction, the author believes, is not an attempt to affect the basic spirit of BPR, which is one of 'revolution' rather than 'evolution' (Earl and Khan, 1994). It involves a top-down, analytical and comprehensive approach rather than one of emergent change and continuous improvement. As Hall *et al.* (1993) stress, any re-engineering programme, to be considered successful, must significantly affect the performance of the organization as a whole. It is, anyway, perhaps difficult to think of a truly radical change which affects just a single proces.

Key roles have been identified, in particular the need for a 'champion' (or leader) figure, (Hammer and Champy, 1993; Hall *et al.*, 1993) to have responsibility for implementing the new processes. Strong leadership is required from an individual with a senior position within the organization, 'the person who makes re-engineering happen has to have a lot of clout, because a lot of people need to be clouted' (Hammer, cited in Moad, 1993: 24).

Business Process Re-engineering may be the business idea of the 1990s but, as previously mentioned, early findings suggest that initiatives are more likely to fail than succeed, and benefits fall short of those anticipated.

FRAMEWORKS FOR MANAGING CHANGE

In trying to place BPR within the context of change management it is useful to compare it with ideas and theories which address change on a number of different dimensions. For the purpose of this analysis three perspectives have been selected which address differing facets of the change process:

1. How to affect successful change
2. The degree or scope of the change being considered
3. Approaches to implementation.

These perspectives are not an attempt at an exhaustive coverage of change management thinking. They do, however, suggest pertinent areas which those who propound or attempt to implement BPR programmes need to consider if successful change is to be achieved.

The Boddy and Buchanan Framework

Boddy and Buchanan (1992) posit a framework of three models, that is useful in attempting to evaluate and examine BPR as an approach to affecting change, and look at the role senior management are expected to play in managing the process.

Project management is based on the concept of a project lifecycle and involves the clear statement and definition of objectives, responsibilities, deadlines and budgets. Successful change is due to a clarity in the dimensions of the initiative and effective monitoring and control to ensure that it remains on target. The implementation procedure is one of developing a strategy, confirming top-level support, using a project management approach and then effectively communicating the results. It is based on the effective implementation of a rational, linear, problem-solving model. The skill of the change agent or 'project manager' is in two spheres: the content or substance of the change and what it is attempting to achieve, and the maintenance of control through the effective definition of the activities required, monitoring progress and ensuring problems do not deviate the project away from its defined goal.

It is an approach which has been found to be most effective in a stable rather than uncertain environment (Fredrickson, 1984) and puts the involvement of those affected by the change as just one consideration in the overall implementation. This model is similar to that described as 'classical' strategic change (Whittington, 1993).

Participative management places much more emphasis on members within the organization who are affected by the change process. Terms such as involvement, ownership, communication, commitment and trust are part of an approach which stresses the need to overcome possible resistance towards a change programme. A feeling of inclusion and being a part of shaping and influencing the change initiative increases the chance that participants will be willing to accept and work with it. As a framework for managing change it needs a lot of involvement throughout the organization and requires a high level of management time and activity. It sees the change management task as multilayered and drawn out.

The nature of participative management and its emphasis on involvement may be inappropriate in certain situations. Where constraints are induced by a lack of time, expertise or resources, or shifting priorities and organizational politics, to fully include all those affected just might not be possible. Where management is powerful enough to force through effective change, increased participation could be an unnecessary delay and a waste of resources. If there is a fundamental disagreement, or inflexible opposition, then participation and any ensuing negotiating process may be used as a means to obstruct implementation. A participative approach is, however, seen as consistent with current societal values. It stresses notions of freedom, individualism and proactive human behaviour. By working through and highlighting benefits rather than imposing enforced change, members are more likely to accept it. For the change agent or senior manager, rather than emphasizing 'content' or 'control' skills, what is needed is an understanding of the process of change and the interpersonal and social skills to facilitate it.

As a model, as with project management, it lends itself easily to blueprint prescriptions with rules and guidelines for ensuring success (eg Watson, 1966; Kotter and Schlesinger, 1979).

A *political perspective* suggests that these models do not address the political and cultural aspects of change. Markus (1983), writing on the implementation of new systems, suggests that resistance based on individual personalities, preferences or values, or due to errors in planning and design, are easily identified and addressed. Her more sociological view suggests that organizational or politically focused resistance is more complex, more difficult to assess and more time consuming. It is also more common. Resistance to new patterns of work, changes in social relationships and ways of behaving, are manifestations of the lack of perceived fit between the results of a change initiative and its organizational context. Political resistance is due to the interaction between change and context and its effect on the distribution of power within the organization. A more holistic approach to effecting change suggests that potential barriers are often difficult to predict and are the result of the plurality of organizational life and the interests of organization members.

It is suggested that politics is likely to be most important when there is a disagreement over the nature of the problem, or if the goals and objectives of the organization are questioned. Uncertainty over whether the means for achieving change will prove effective, and any perceived threat to the power bases of individuals and sub-groups, are likely to cause disquiet about the appropriateness of implementing change. These conditions are felt to be most likely to occur when a change initiative cuts horizontally across several organizational units and involves a diverse range of people.

This framework, though dismissing the other models as being overly linear, rational and simplistic, and bearing little relationship to the actual unfolding of change, does accept that they have a part to play in implementation. Based on a belief that the dominant ideology within organizations is one of logical rationality it is important that any change effort, if it is to be accepted, maintains an appearance acceptable to this ideology. Using the concept of ritual, Buchanan and Boddy suggest that the presentation of a linear based change plan can play an important symbolic and legitimating function in gaining sufficient support for it.

A political perspective requires senior management to combine an effective 'public performance' of a rationally considered, logically phased and participative change programme, with effective 'backstage activity' in the recruitment and maintenance of support, and in seeking and blocking potential resistance.

Successful implementation of change requires senior management to be sensitive to the power and influence of key individuals or groups and to be aware of how existing patterns will be altered by a particular programme of change.

Boddy and Buchanan's Typology and BPR

Though the picture of BPR presented is necessarily simplistic, the author believes that in essence, BPR is predominantly a change management methodology based on the linear rational models of Boddy and Buchanan's 'project' and 'participant' management.

It is outlined as a number of discrete stages from planning and formulation through to implementation and evaluation. If objectives are not satisfactorily met it is not the model itself which is problematic but the performance of those who have implemented it. These two models of change suggest a framework which involves defining goals and the process of change clearly. Reasons for failure will be due to: the lack of clear objectives or definition of tasks; ineffective monitoring; the absence of adequate control; insufficient meaningful commitment or involvement; or the attempted autocratic imposition of change.

If the offending variable can be remedied, then, as implied by those who prescribe 'recipes for success', an effective project and participative management change framework can be developed.

The political perspective would suggest that this does not truly get to the complex nature of managing change within organizations. This is especially true considering BPR is attempting to completely overthrow functional hierachies and replace them with streamlined, redesigned processes. This change in structure is going to threaten existing power bases and accepted ways of behaviour. Organization change is more than altering the sequence and content of what people do and who they report to; it is about changing culture and interpersonal relationships. 'Revolutionary' change requires an even greater awareness of this dimension.

Writers such as Pelligrini and Bowman (1994) suggest project management methodologies which incorporate an awareness of culture. Their view is that radical change and therefore change in culture and structure shouldn't be attempted within the very form that they are aiming to change. By taking the change process, or project, out of the current structure effective change becomes more likely. Though this is an improvement on the model described by Boddy and Buchanan, the 'part' or 'piece' of the organization which has been taken out still has to be put back, which will have political and cultural consequences.

First- or Second-Order Change

A distinction made by some commentators concerns the degree or scope of change which organizations may experience or attempt to achieve. They differentiate between 'first-' and 'second'-order, or 'morphostatic' and 'morphogenic' change (eg Bate, 1994; Laughlin, 1991; Levy, 1986; Levy and Merry, 1986; Smith, 1982). First-order or morphostatic change is concerned with changes which take place within the existing organizational form or paradigm, or 'tinkering around the edges', whereas second-order or morphogenic change is more fundamental, attempting to transform the whole organization, altering the 'interpretive schemes' (Laughlin, 1991) and challenging the fundamental assumptions held by members concerning the way their organisation operates.

These two types of change are seen to require different approaches. First-order change is less problematic as it is at a more 'micro', tangible level and more predictable as the underlying frame of reference is fixed. The level of change is identifiable within known parameters and so is easier to plan and implement. Second-level change is of a more fluid, uncertain nature, concerning change of a much greater magnitude. Variables which can affect the process are difficult to identify, let alone predict, making planning or envisaging the result of the process difficult, if not impossible. Writers such as Bate (1994) and Whittle *et al.* (1991) cast doubt on the ability of organizations to predict morphogenic change, suggesting it entails change being seen as 'a journey rather than a destination' (Whittle *et al.*, 1991: 3), which has no best sequence: blurring, converging and diverging as it unfolds over time.

BPR with its philosophy of 'revolution' and radical change is clearly an attempt to provide organizations with a methodology for achieving second-order change. It attempts to map out the process, based on a vision of the future destination and then break down the organization into component parts before reconfiguring them. It is a model which if adhered to relies, to a certain degree, on predicting the future and then working backwards, splitting the change process into determinable and manageable tasks. It is an approach which is attempting to implement morphogenic change based initially on 'a snapshot of the future' – which at best is an informed guess (if not a leap of faith) – forming the basis of a sequential implementation process associated with change of a less problematic, morphostatic kind. Previous experiences suggest that attempts to simplify and impose a static approach to implement a dynamic process are unsuccessful.

This differentiation in the scope of change also highlights an inconsistency in attempts to categorize BPR initiatives. The notion that individual processes can be re-engineered in isolation, as implied by Talwar (1993) and Davenport (1993), has consequences for the fundamental philosophy of BPR as a methodology for implementing radical change. To attempt to re-engineer a single process presumes that one may be isolated as a contained set of tasks. If this is the case then any change achieved must be within the current organizational form and therefore not be revolutionary or overturn the existing form of the organization as a whole. It is a first-order change. It is unlikely, though, that a single discrete process which does not impinge on other processes can be identified. If this is the case then a knock-on effect has to occur with other unforseen changes being required if the redesigned individual process is to be implemented. If this line of argument is extended then the corollary is that if one process is redesigned then all of them have to be. If it is rejected then a single re-engineered process is just another incremental non-radical approach to implementing change, with little to differentiate it from other approaches. This undermines any notion that BPR is a unique way of addressing change.

Bold Strokes or Long Marches?

Moss Kanter *et al.* (1992) suggest a difference in the type of actions that are used in attempting to achieve change. These they define as 'bold strokes' and 'long marches'. Bold strokes are swiftly initiated, based on decisions from senior management. Leadership control is high and clear, visible results are expected quickly. Long marches, as might be expected, require more time. They usually involve different projects being started in various parts of the organization with little top management control. There aims are more long term and any initial impact is often unclear.

In their analysis, Moss Kanter *et al.* suggest that while bold strokes often make an immediate impact their long-term benefits are erratic and they are unlikely to greatly affect organizational culture. Long marches are more dependable as a means of creating sustainable change but they are fundamentally more difficult. They involve many or most organization members and require an unusual amount of commitment sustained over a long period of time. What they suggest is that both types of action need to be combined, bold strokes being used to galvanize an organization into starting a long march.

BPR as envisaged by Michael Hammer (Hammer, 1990; Hammer and Champy, 1993) is radical change. It is top-down and achieves major organization-wide improvements quickly. It is perhaps the archetypal bold stroke. Other commentators (Davenport, 1993; Talwar, 1993) have suggested re-engineering parts or single processes within an organization and Davenport describes varying degrees of scope within a framework of process improvement. Combining Hammer's radical vision with the longer march of process improvement has consequences for those managing the change and also for the concept of re-engineering itself.

For those managing the change fulfilling the behavioural requirements suggested becomes a complex process. They need to be able to switch from high to low levels of control and from being forceful and maybe autocratic to being facilitative and conciliatory. It needs to be achieved in such a way so that trust and commitment to the change programme is not undermined and resistance and obstruction created.

BPR began life as radical change. Kanter *et al.*'s analysis suggests that bold strokes do not produce sustainable change and other writers (Quinn, 1980; Mintzberg, 1987) question whether any form of single step or stroke change is possible. If this is the case and BPR has to adapt to include more incremental, time-consuming approaches, there is perhaps the likelihood that its distinct identity as a method for change might be lost or subsumed by other programmes such as Total Quality Management, which share its focus on process. The notion that BPR can achieve planned radical change – formulated, implemented and embedded in a short period – seems unlikely. A belief that it can suggests, once again, either a leap in faith, or a simplistic view of the dynamics of change.

THE NEED FOR COMMITMENT

It is the author's overriding belief that the analysis so far highlights a lack of understanding of change by those who write and purport to implement BPR programmes. An illustration of this delusion of simplicity, which underlies attempts to rationally impose BPR, is the emphasis and use of the term commitment.

Initial studies and analyses of BPR implementation have concluded that senior management commitment may be a – if not the most – significant contributing factor to the success of an initiative (Pearson and Skinner, 1993; Moad, 1993; Towers, 1993; Hall *et al.*, 1993). Indeed the faltering support or sponsorship of senior management is seen as a sign of lack of commitment and a major reason for the less than impressive results of BPR so far. Hall *et al.* (1993), in their research, noted that in four of the five successful companies they observed, new chief executives were brought in either before or during the project. They suggest that these individuals understood how to lead an organization through radical change by combining 'a tenacious pursuit of the performance objectives with a flair for building consensus at all organization levels' (p. 124).

Examples of the manifestation of this top-level commitment involved placing the most able and respected individuals on the redesign team, investing significantly in IT, providing new skills training, managing by decree if necessary, and allowing teams adequate time to finish the task. Insufficient commitment was demonstrated by a non-aggressive sponsoring of a re-engineering project and not involving sufficiently able individuals in the redesign process, so ensuring the team lacked respect within the organization.

They note that in most successful redesigns managers made few compromises, were generous with resources and encouraged open communication. What was identified as most important was the investment of their own time – in successful endeavours top executives spent between 20 and 60 per cent on the project.

As presented in the BPR literature, commitment is a concept which if understood and utilized can be used by management to increase the chances of successful implementation. This is perhaps rather a partial view of the properties of commitment. Change management suggests that at least as important a variable is the receptivity of organization members.

Duck (1993) suggests that most modern organizations contain 'change survivors' who are sceptical of proposed change as they have seen various programmes, though vigorously promoted, wither when faced with difficulties. The concepts of 'readiness for change' (Armenakis *et al.*, 1993; Zeira and Avedisian, 1993) and resistance to it (Bryant, 1979; Lewin, 1951) also attempt to understand an organization's willingness to accept the imposition of change, emphasising the ability of organisational members to block efforts regardless of management's commitment. Duck points out that a model which involves management getting organizational members to buy into a new corporate vision, which changes their behaviour leading to improved performance, which itself leads to employees recognizing the improvement and so confirming their commitment to the change, is an unrealistic one.

Commitment as an academic subject of study has focused on the nature of the relationship between individuals and organizations (Etzioni, 1961; Kanter, 1972). The conclusions of some theorists (Staw, 1977; Szilagyi and Wallace, 1980; Schwenk, 1986) would suggest that for a change initiative to be supported the benefits of proceeding would have to outweigh the costs. For some within the organization this might not be the case. The role of the change leader must be to understand how an impending BPR programme will be received and to adapt their behaviour according to the particular individuals involved. This might be problematic and in some cases involve behaviour which may be varied and inconsistent. If BPR is seen as a rational, sequential process then this inconsistent, seemingly irrational behaviour, as an actualization of commitment, may create a lack of trust. The idea that an individual, or set of individuals, are able to 'coach' and empower their subordinates on the one hand, and control and enforce successful implementation on the other, within the same change framework, appears to be incongruous. Commitment must be seen and communicated as an emergent dynamic requiring political flexibility rather than a consistent entity which can be used to impose successful change.

BPR – FUTURE DEVELOPMENTS

Gill and Whittle (1992) observe that in the last forty years large resources have been invested in various packaged change programmes. A consistent cycle has been identified beginning 'at birth' with a leader or guru writing a seminal work. 'Adolescence', followed by 'maturity', eventually leads to decline due to the benefits of the programme being outweighed by the costs. Practice is normally well in advance of research and there is a lack of concepts and theory with which to give it coherence and direction. Pettigrew (1994), echoing the views of Argyris (1992), suggests that BPR is just the latest of these management 'panaceas' to enjoy an inevitably limited period of attention and popularity.

Business Process Re-engineering may be shortlived but initiatives are currently widespread and will probably continue to be so, at least in the near future. From the perspectives of change management outlined earlier, this genre of programmatic change, in its current form, has little chance of success as it unlikely to create sufficient sustainable momentum to complete the change process. It is entirely possible that the espoused pure, 'guru' version of BPR is not practised in many organizations. The author's own research experience and the many slight variations in terminology perhaps back up that view. However, if BPR is to be more than just a 'fad' then some form of distinct identity, which, to at least some degree, is agreed upon, would seem to be necessary.

The general theme of this chapter is that planned change, in particular radical, second-order, bold stroke change, is difficult to acheive. It is a complex, multifaceted process which needs luck as much as foresight if it is to succeed. This difficulty is perhaps best approached through the use of more incremental methods. Rational, linear models designed to break down the complexity into manageable and predictable variables and so form the basis of an implementation are unlikely to take into account all dimensions of the change process. If BPR is to become a distinct approach which can manage radical change then it must embrace this uncertainty, unpredictability and chaotic nature and develop ways of addressing it.

For those currently implementing initiatives, however close they are to the outlines of theorists, it is perhaps best for BPR to be seen as a configurational lens, limited to suggesting a redesigned view of organizational processes and creating some momentum towards change for a less radical, incremental approach to then take over. If this becomes the norm and BPR is unable to develop as a unique response to the environmental pressures currently facing organizations, then it is likely to be overrun by other management disciplines and techniques until the next new idea comes along. What is clear is that managing change is a complex and difficult task which is more likely to control and alter the concept of BPR than vice versa. The role of senior management in that case should be to attempt to understand the very nature of the undertaking and not be constrained by prescriptive frameworks describing a formulaic set of required behaviours or competencies.

BIBLIOGRAPHY

Argyris, C (1992) *Overcoming Organizational Defenses – Facilitating Organizational Learning,* Allyn & Bacon, Boston.

Armenakis, A A, Harris, S G and Mossholder, K W (1993) 'Creating Readiness for Change', *Human Relations,* 46(7), 681–704.

Bashein, B J, Markus, M L and Riley, P (1994) 'Preconditions for BPR Success', *Information Systems Management,* 11(2), 7–13.

Bate, P (1994) *Strategies for Cultural Change,* Butterworth-Heineman, Oxford.

Belmonte, R W and Murray, R J (1993) 'Getting Ready for Strategic Change: Surviving Business Process Redesign', *Information Systems Management,* 10(3), Summer, 23–29.

Broddle, M (1994) *Business Re-engineering for Survival,* paper presented to Successful Application of Business Re-engineering, February, London.

Bryant, D (1979) 'The Psychology of Resistance to Change', *Management Services,* March, 9–10.

Buchanan, D and Boddy, D (1992) *The Expertise of the Change Agent,* Prentice-Hall International, UK.

Dale, M (1991) *Business Process Re-design: A Guideline to Best Practice,* Management Bridge Joint Venture, Impact, UK.

Davenport, T H (1993) *Process Innovation: Re-engineering Work through Information Technology,* Harvard Business School, Boston, Mass.

Davenport, T H and Short, E J (1990) 'The New Industrial Engineering: Information Technology and Business Process Redesign', *Sloan Management Review,* 31(4), 11–27.

Duck, J D (1993) 'Managing Change: The Art of Balancing', *Harvard Business Review,* November–December, 109–119.

Earl, M and Khan, B (1994) 'How New is Business Process Redesign', *European Management Journal,* 12(1), 20–30.

Forbrun, C J (1992) *Turning Points: Creating Strategic Change in Corporations,* McGraw-Hill, Boston, Mass.

Fredrickson, J W (1984) 'The Comprehensiveness of Strategic Decision Processes: Extension, Observations, Future Directions', *Academy of Management Journal,* 27(3), 445–466.

Fried, L (1991) 'A Blueprint for Change' *Computerworld,* 25(48), 94–95.

Gill, J and Whittle, S (1992) 'Management by Panacea: Accounting for Transience', *Journal of Management Studies,* 30(2), March, 281–295.

Guha, S, Kettinger, W J and Teng, J T C (1993) 'Business Process Re-engineering: Building a Comprehensive Methodology', *Information Systems Management,* 10(3), 13–22.

Hall, G, Rosenthal, J and Wade, J (1993) 'How to Make Re-engineering Really Work', *Harvard Business Review,* November–December, 119–131.

Hammer, M (1990) 'Re-engineering Work: Don't Automate – Obliterate', *Harvard Business Review,* July–August, 104–112.

Hammer, M and Champy, J (1993) *Re-engineering the Corporation – A Manifesto for Business Revolution,* Nicholas Brealey Publishing, London.

Kanter, R M (1972) *Commitment and Community,* Harvard University Press, Cambridge, Mass.

Kanter, R M, Stein, B A, and Dick, T D (1992) *The Challenge of Organizational Change: How Companies Experience It and Leaders Guide It,* Simon & Schuster, New York.

Kotter, J P and Schlesinger, L A (1979) 'Choosing Strategies for Change', *Harvard Business Review,* 57(2), 106–114.

Laughlin, P (1991) 'Environmental Disturbances and Organizational Transitions and Transformations: Some Alternative Models', *Organization Studies,* 12(2), 289–302.

Levy, A (1986) 'Second-Order Planned Change: Definition and Conceptualisation', *Organisational Dynamics,* 15(1), 5-23.

Levy, A and Merry, U (1986) *Organizational Transformation: Approaches, Strategies, Theories,* Praeger.

Lewin, K (1951) *Field Theory in Social Science,* Harper & Row, New York.

Markus, M L (1983) 'Power, Politics and MIS Implementation', *Communication of the ACM,* 26 (6), 430–444.

Mintzberg, H (1987) 'Crafting Strategy', *Harvard Business Review,* July–August, 66–77.

Moad, J (1993) 'Does Re-engineering Really Work', *Datamation,* 39(1), 22–28.

Pearson, J and Skinner, C (1993) *Business Process Re-Engineering in the UK Financial Services Industry,* Highams, University of Bristol.

Pelligrini, S and Bowman, C (1994) 'Implementing Strategy Through Projects', *Long Range Planning*, 27(4), 125–132.

Pettigrew, A M (1994) *Success and Failure in Corporate Transformation Initiatives*, paper presented at Business Re-engineering: Managing Radical Change, March, London.

Quinn, J B (1980) *Strategies for Change: Logical Incrementalism*, Irwin, Homewood, Ill.

Scherr, A L (1993) 'A New Approach to Business Processes', *IBM Systems Journal*, 32(1), 80–98.

Schwenk, C R (1986) 'Information, Cognitive Biases, and Commitment to a Course of Action', *Academy of Management Review*, 11(2) 298–310.

Smith, K K (1982) 'Philosophical Problems in Thinking about Organizational Change,' in Goodman, P S (ed), *Change in Organizations*, Jossey-Bass, San Francisco.

Staw, B M (1977) *Psychological Foundations of Organizational Behaviour*, Scott Foresman.

Szilagyi, P and Wallace, D (1980) *Organizational Behaviour and Performance*, Goodyear.

Talwar, R (1993) 'Business Re-engineering – A Strategy-Driven Approach', *Long Range Planning*, 26(6), 22–40.

Towers, S (1993) 'Business Process Re-engineering – Lessons for Success', *Management Services*, 37(8), 10–12.

Watson, G (1966) *Resistance to Change*, National Training Laboratories, Washington, DC.

Whittington, R (1993) *What is Strategy? and Does it Matter*, Routledge, London.

Whittle, S, Smith, S, Tranfield D and Foster, M (1991) *'Implementing Total Quality: Erecting Tents or Building Palaces?* Working Paper, Change Management Unit, Sheffield Business School, UK.

Woudhuysen, J (1993) 'Engineers of a Fresh Approach', *Marketing*, 3 June, p. 10.

Zeira, Y and Avedisan, J (1989) 'Organizational Planned Change, Assessing the Chances of Success', *Organizational Dynamics*, 18, Spring, 31–47.

16

CROSSING THE FINAL HURDLE IN BUSINESS PROCESS RE-ENGINEERING

D Lance Revenaugh, City Polytechnic of Hong Kong

INTRODUCTION

Implementation is the challenge that comes at the end of all new (and old) methods for improving organizations. Strategic planning, architecture development, change management, total quality management, new information systems technologies, and now Business Process Re-engineering are some of the concepts that are being advocated to radically improve organization performance. Advocates of each concept, however, struggle when questioned about successful implementation. As an example, in strategic planning, literature abounds on how to develop a plan, but there is comparatively little said about how to implement a strategic plan once it is developed.

Business process re-engineering (BPR) is a radical rethinking of an organization and its cross-functional, end-to-end processes (Hammer, 1993). BPR has taken corporate America by storm. In a recent survey of over 500 chief information officers (CIOs), the average CIO is involved in 4.4 re-engineering projects. That is up from an average of 1.6 the year before (Moad, 1993).

Despite the excitement over BPR, however, the rate of failure for re-engineered projects is over 50 per cent (Stewart, 1993; Belmonte and Murray, 1993). Michael Hammer himself estimates as much as a 70 per cent failure rate (Hammer and Champy, 1993). Why does a concept that is becoming so pervasive have such a large probability of failure?

BUSINESS PROCESS RE-ENGINEERING OVERVIEW

Whether Business Process Re-engineering (BPR) is called process innovation, business process redesign, business engineering or process engineering, companies are making dynamic and radical changes to the way they operate. With Michael Hammer's 1990 *Harvard Business Review* article, 'Re-engineering Work: Don't Automate, Obliterate', BPR began a frenzy among businesses to overhaul their existing business processes.

At the heart of BPR is two concepts: (a) organizations must view themselves in terms of *processes* instead of functions, divisions or products (Davenport, 1993), and (b) organizations must think *inductively* instead of *deductively* (Hammer and Champy, 1993).

Davenport (1993) defines a process as a 'structured, measured set of activities designed to produce a specified output for a particular customer or market'. Thinking about processes focuses on *how* work is done as much as on *what* is being produced ('The Role of IT', 1993). As such, processes are almost always cross-functional. Hammer adds that the cross-functional nature of process thinking requires a high-level manager to drive the re-engineering effort (Brousell, 1993). This manager must be at a level above all the functional managers.

RULE	DISRUPTIVE INFORMATION TECHNOLOGY
Information can appear in only one place at one time	Shared database
Only experts can perform complex work	Expert Systems
Businesses must choose between centralization and decentralization	Advanced telecommunications networks
Managers make all decisions	Decision-support tools (database access, modelling software)
Field personnel need offices where they can receive, store, retrieve & transmit information	Wireless data communication and portable computers
The best contact with a potential buyer is personal contact	Interactive communication
You have to find out where things are	Automatic identification and tracking technology
Plans get revised periodically	High-performance computing

Figure 16.1 Disruptive technologies

The second concept of BPR suggests that organizations must think inductively. Hammer and Champy (1993) state that instead of using deductive reasoning to look for new solutions to apparent problems, managers must learn the power of new information technologies and think of innovative ways they can be used to radically change how work is performed. This concept was the foundation of Hammer's (1990) 'Re-engineering Work: Don't Automate, Obliterate' article.

Hammer and Champy (1993) advocate that organizations must think inductively because they are consistently faced with disruptions to the current way of doing business. The proliferation of new information technologies is increasingly a major contributor to this disruption. Figure 16.1 describes some long-term business rules that are no longer rules because of disruptive information technology. For instance, one logical rule has been that *only* experts can perform complex work. New technology such as expert systems, however, has made that rule obsolete.

IMPLEMENTATION

Realizing the implementation failures of BPR, several authors have proposed general implementation frameworks (Hammer and Champy, 1993; Davenport, 1993; Belmonte and Murray, 1993; Stanton, Hammer and Power, 1993). Davenport (1993), for example, recommends the following five-step framework:

- Identify processes for innovation
- Identify change levers
- Develop process visions
- Understand existing processes
- Design and prototype the new process.

Davenport goes on to give a more detailed approach for the first step 'Identify processes for innovation'. Key activities for identifying these processes include:

- Enumerate major processes
- Determine process boundaries
- Assess strategic relevance of each process
- Render high-level judgements of the health of each process
- Qualify the culture and politics of each process.

Two of these activities, assessing strategic relevance and qualifying the culture, have been found to be particularly important in the implementation of major business changes of all types (Cash *et al.*, 1988; Raghunathan and Raghunathan, 1990; Allen, 1985; Deshpande and

Parasuraman, 1986; Kilmann, Saxton and Serpa, 1986; Peters and Waterman, 1982; Thompson and Strickland, 1987). The importance of these two concepts to the successful implementation of BPR will be discussed in the following sections.

STRATEGIC RELEVANCE/IMPORTANCE

In trying to assess the strategic relevance or importance of a process to the organization we can receive some help from strategic grid analysis. Many research projects in information systems have used the strategic grid for this purpose and it can be adapted to analyse business processes. First a description of strategic grid analysis in its information systems context is needed and so is presented here. This discussion will be followed by the strategic grid's application to BPR.

The strategic grid is a well-accepted strategic planning tool for evaluating the importance of a particular organizational element to the strategic direction of the firm. Cash *et al.* (1988) applied the strategic grid to information systems and labelled it the Information Technology (IT) Strategic Grid. The axes of the IT-strategic grid portray the current (shown as the y-axis) and future (x-axis) strategic importance of information systems activities to a firm. As shown in Figure 16.2, four quadrants are identified as 'Strategic', 'Turnaround', 'Factory' and 'Support'.

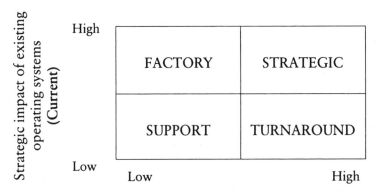

Figure 16.2 illustration: vertical axis labelled "Strategic impact of existing operating systems (Current)" with High at top, Low at bottom; horizontal axis labelled Low to High. Quadrants: FACTORY (top-left), STRATEGIC (top-right), SUPPORT (bottom-left), TURNAROUND (bottom-right).

Strategic impact of application
development portfolio
(Future)

Figure 16.2 Strategic grid model

Organizations classified in the *Strategic* cell are critically dependent on the smooth functioning of the IS activity for both their current and future IS needs. Strong IS planning is essential and should be closely integrated with corporate planning. The impact of IS on company performance is such that there should be significant top management attention and guidance in the IS planning process.

Firms in the *Turnaround* quadrant of the grid are not critically dependent on IS applications for their current operations, but applications under development are expected to play a vital role in the firms' future. Similar to organizations in the strategic quadrant, turnaround firms should have significant top management involvement in their IS planning process. Since turnaround firms are not used to this type of involvement, other changes should occur to enhance senior management's understanding and overview of IS.

Organizations in the *Factory* cell are critically dependent on existing IS support systems. However, applications under development are not crucial to the firm's ability to compete successfully. Strategic IS planning and linkage to long-term corporate plans are not nearly as critical in this environment. IS planning should continue to take place with guidance as to where the firm is going, but senior management involvement in the planning process is appropriately much less.

Support cell organizations are in the low-low quadrant of the grid which suggests that organizations in this cell would place the least amount of emphasis on IS and IS planning in terms of top management concern and involvement.

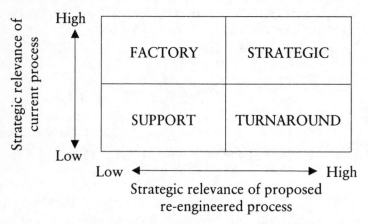

Figure 16.3 Strategic relevance grid

The four IS environments delineated by the strategic grid framework suggest that each environment does require a different IS management approach. IS is of great strategic importance in some organizations, while it has minimal importance in others. It is inappropriate to expect both types of organization to place the same amount of emphasis on IS strategic planning. The Cash *et al.* (1988) strategic grid is becoming an often cited framework for its assistance in determining the strategic importance of IS to firms and thereby its effect on IS planning and plan implementation

(Flaatten *et al.*, 1989; Raghunathan and Raghunathan, 1990).

The application of the strategic grid to BPR is straightforward. Figure 16.3 presents the transformed grid which has been labelled the strategic relevance grid (SRG). The first dimension of the SRG portrays the strategic relevance of the current process(es). The second dimension portrays the strategic relevance of the proposed re-engineered process. The labels for the four quadrants have been left the same as the labels for the strategic grid – strategic, turnaround, factory and support.

The strategic relevance of the re-engineered process is normally easy to determine as a great deal of study has already been applied in its development. Accurately describing which current process(es) that the proposed re-engineered process will replace or significantly alter, however, often requires additional and substantive analysis. A major point of BPR is not to simply improve the old process. Nevertheless, a reasonable determination of the current process(es) involved should be made and included in the SRG analysis.

Processes in the strategic quadrant receive the highest strategic importance on both the current process(es) and the proposed re-engineered process. Implementation of the re-engineered process is particularly critical and could be viewed as in the 'Survival' zone of Nolan, Norton's BPR Need/Readiness Analysis (Belmonte and Murray, 1993). Processes in this zone require maximum commitment and the re-engineering campaign should begin right away.

Processes in the turnaround quadrant are critical to improving business performance. Current processes are acceptable but not considered strategically relevant. The proposed re-engineered process is strategically relevant and is expected to produce better performance and/or competitive advantage. As such, the benefit of the proposed re-engineered process should be communicated clearly and the re-engineering campaign should begin soon.

Processes in the factory and support quadrants need to be re-evaluated for re-engineering. The nature of re-engineering suggests dramatic improvement in organizational performance. Even if the proposed re-engineered process itself is not strategically relevant, the results of the process–more efficiency, more effectiveness, less cost, etc – should be strategically important. Since support quadrant processes are not strategic and are not expected to be, it will be particularly hard to convince affected employees about the need for the proposed re-engineered process.

CORPORATE CULTURE

In addition to assessing the strategic relevance of a process to the firm, Davenport (1993) highlighted the importance of qualifying the culture and politics of business processes. In this context it is *organizational* culture (vs other types of assessment, eg national culture) that needs to be assessed. Many organizational culture analyses also include political considerations. Supporting Davenport's (1993), Hammer and Champy's (1993) and Davenport, Eccles and Prusak's (1992) emphasis on culture consideration is the fact that the study of culture is consistently becoming more prevalent as managers search for tools to help them handle the need for increased adaptability in their organizations as brought on by BPR. Corporate cultural assessment and understanding is clearly a key tool (Cash *et al.*, 1988; Kilmann, Saxton and Serpa, 1986; Saffold, 1988).

Many researchers assume that corporate culture is an important consideration for understanding and effectively managing organizations. They often fail, however, to validate their assumptions (Arogyaswamy and Byles, 1987; Reimann and Wiener, 1988; Saffold, 1988). These researchers simply posit that the importance of culture is self-evident as one analyses an organization. Thompson and Strickland (1987:237), for example, make this assumption as they state that the 'best way to understand corporate culture is by example'. They then go on to describe culture on a case description basis, discussing parallels with Peters and Waterman's *In Search of Excellence*. A significant omission is that no attempt is made to objectively measure culture.

Corporate Culture Defined

In order to measure corporate culture, however, we must first define it. As one studies culture it becomes clear that arriving at a common definition is not an easy task. Several definitions of culture have been offered. Kilmann, Saxton and Serpa (1986) describe culture as the shared philosophies, ideologies, values, assumptions, beliefs, expectations, attitudes and norms that knit a community together. In essence, it is 'the way things are done around here'. Meek (1988) adds that culture includes the myths, legends, rites and rituals of the organization. Reimann and Wiener (1988) view culture as the social or normative glue that holds the organization together. The corporate culture expresses the values and beliefs that members of the organization have come to share. Finally, Deshpande and Parasuraman (1986) define culture as the unwritten, often unconscious message that fills in the gaps between what is formally decreed and what actually takes place; it involves shared philosophies, ideologies, values, beliefs, expectations and norms.

These definitions reveal that culture is a complex concept that involves many factors. This has led some researchers to conclude that culture can only be studied in a piecemeal fashion. Many authors (eg Allen, 1985; Deshpande and Parasuraman, 1986; Kilmann, Saxton and Serpa, 1986; Peters and Waterman, 1982; Thompson and Strickland, 1987), however, assert that culture must also be analysed from a holistic, macro perspective. These researchers state that there are subcultures within organizations, but the subcultures are comparatively less significant than the overall corporate culture. This line of research then focuses on analysis of the overall corporate culture.

Corporate Culture Classification

One of the most comprehensive research results regarding culture classification is by Deal and Kennedy (1982). Their 'corporate tribes model of organizational culture' is one of the most popular and influential typologies for overall culture (Deshpande and Parasuraman, 1986). Their model suggests that corporate culture can be understood and managed by identifying four different 'tribes': Tough-Guy/Macho, Work Hard/Play Hard, Bet-Your-Company and Process. The degree of risk associated with company activities and the speed of feedback from the environment are the determining factors as to which quadrant best describes the overall culture of an organization. The corporate tribes model is shown in Figure 16.4.

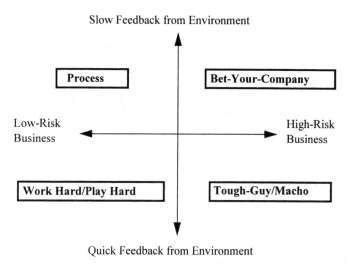

Figure 16.4 Corporate tribes culture model

Bet-Your-Company organizations operate in a high risk/slow feedback environment typified by the phrase 'play it safe'. Typical industries include oil, drugs, aerospace and public utilities. Large capital investments are usually required and the results from those investments are not usually known for a long time. A clear example would be NASA's development of the space shuttle.

Tough-Guy/Macho organizations have a high risk/quick feedback environment typified by the phrase 'Find a mountain and climb it'. Typical industries include advertising, entertainment and construction. Large capital outlays are usually required up front and the results (feedback) are usually known rather quickly. 'Go for it all' decisions would fit the Tough-Guy/Macho representation.

Work Hard/Play Hard firms operate in a low risk/quick feedback environment and can be described by the phrase 'Find a need and fill it'. Typical industries include retail and sales organizations. It is usually not very expensive to have a salesman make a particular sales call (low risk), but the feedback is rather immediate (quick feedback).

Process organizations operate in a low risk/slow feedback environment typified by the phrase 'be perfect'. Typical industries include banking, insurance and government departments. The process culture is exemplified by accounting departments and large, bureaucratic organizations where employees frequently focus on *how* they do something rather than on *what* they do (Deshpande and Parasuraman, 1986).

LINKING STRATEGIC RELEVANCE AND CORPORATE CULTURE.

As stated earlier, Deal and Kennedy (1982) have made one of the strongest efforts toward a general cultural classification with their corporate tribes model of organizational culture. This chapter combines the Deal and Kennedy (1982) corporate tribes model with the strategic relevance grid (SRG) to suggest a framework for identifying the level of effort needed to implement a re-engineered process (RP). The implementation plan for a re-engineered process is labelled RP plan (re-engineered process plan) in the ensuing analysis.

Table 16.1RP implementation implications *without* culture consideration

Strategic relevance grid position	RP implementation effort		RP implementation implications
Strategic	Considerable	(3)	The weaker the perceived
Turnaround	Difficult	(4)	need for the re-engineered
Factory	Difficult	(4)	process, the more difficult
Support	Importunate	(5)	the implementation effort (Davenport, 1993).

(RP = Re-engineered process)

Tables 16.1 to 16.3 present RP plan implications with and without culture consideration. When culture is considered and is considered as the first variable, it has been termed the 'culture re-engineering grid'. When culture is considered and the SRG position is considered as the first variable, it has been labelled the 're-engineered process implementation grid'.

Table 16.1 presents the RP plan *without* culture consideration. Davenport (1993) and Hammer and Champy (1993) advocate assessing the strategic importance of processes in order to decide which processes should be innovated. When it comes time to implement the innovated process (or RP) it makes sense that the stronger the perceived need for the RP, the 'easier' will be the implementation. Tables 16.1, 16.2 and 16.3 use six terms to describe RP implementation effort. The terms, shown in the middle column of Table 16.1, were developed to delineate the range of effort required for RP implementation, given an organization's position on the SRG. The terms represent a continuum of effort ranging from a fairly simple implementation to an extremely difficult implementation. The terms are defined as follows (ordinal numbers are also included):

1. Facile – able to be performed without great effort
2. Moderate – reasonable; between extremes in size, quality or degree
3. Difficult – hard to do; hard to deal with
4. Considerable–quite large in extent, amount or degree
5. Importunate – persistently demanding, especially in an annoying or unreasonable way
6. Herculean – demanding exceptional effort.

Table 16.1 is then expanded to suggest RP planning implications *with* culture consideration. The results are shown in Table 16.2 which is termed the culture re-engineering grid. The four categorizations of corporate culture (Deal and Kennedy, 1982) are in the first column. The second column lists the four categorizations of the SRG position for each culture. Proposed RP implementation effort and the RP plan implications for each pair are then developed and are presented in columns three and four.

A summarization of Table 16.2 according to culture is then analysed. If the RP plan implementation effort and the implications of the culture re-engineering grid are plausible, then several observations for each culture become apparent. Overall implications of Table 16.2 for each culture are presented below.

Table 16.2 Culture re-engineering grid: RP plan *with* culture consideration

Culture	Strategic Relevance Grid	RP plan implementation effort		RP planning implications
Process	Strategic	Herculean	(6)	Any process is so hard to change that it takes great effort just to get the RP discussed. The importance of the RP is critical to the firm's activities.
	Turnaround	Herculean	(6)	
	Factory	Importunate	(5)	Even though an RP is not critical here, any movement or change toward an RP must be well documented with new policies and procedures being put into place throughout the process.
	Support	Difficult	(4)	The RP is a desirable that should be developed in the long run. Again, new policies and procedures must be clear and be put into place throughout the process.
Work Hard/ Play Hard	Strategic	Difficult	(4)	Impatience is the biggest obstacle. If benefits are clear, support for the RP is widespread, but people want it tomorrow. If past inefficiencies in the former process are clear, support for the RP is more consistent.
	Turnaround	Importunate	(5)	Again, impatience is the biggest obstacle. If benefits are clear, support for the RP is widespread, but people want it tomorrow. Not having been dependent on this process in the past, immediate support for RP is limited.
	Factory	Considerable	(3)	The need for an RP is evident based on today's activities. Since it is not expected to significantly affect sales in the next 24 hours, however, commitment wanes.
	Support	Considerable	(5)	Difficult to have much commitment to re-engineering of any kind. Management is often too short-term minded.
Bet-Your Company	Strategic	Facile	(1)	Planning and many meetings are important parts of day-to-day operations. With top management support, the RP will not be accomplished with facile effort (comparatively).
	Turnaround	Facile	(1)	Same as above. Time to plan and then make appropriate changs is not a problem in this situation. The RP will not be accomplished with facile effort (comparatively).
	Factory	Moderate	(2)	Very important to invest in the future. Even though direct link between the RP and future benefits is weak, previous importance of the process warrants attention to the RP.
	Support	Importunate	(5)	Senior Management makes the decisions. Need for an RP is not of strategic importance. Difficulty is getting senior management to be involved enough to take action and delegate responsibility.
Tough-Guy/ Macho	Strategic	Difficult	(4)	Even though the RP is seen as essential, the short-term perspective overshadows the persistence needed to implement the RP easily. Individual orientation and competition hinders cooperation.
	Turnaround	Difficult	(4)	Same as above. Benefits of the RP must be clear and specific and relate to a currrent specific decision even if that type of decision may not be relevant by the time the RP is in place
	Factory	Herculean	(6)	Without a clear benefit (over the old process) for future decisions, commitment to the RP is very low.
	Supprt	Herculean	(6)	

- *Process culture*: Benefits and projected results of the RP Plan must be clearly stated. Policies and procedures are critical to a successful re-engineering effort in a process culture. Everything must be put into a memo and/or documented. Job titles play an important role in process culture, so as new responsibilities are created or delegated, careful consideration should be given to job title and perceived status.

- *Work hard/play hard culture*: This is an action-oriented culture. Amount is more important than quality (eg sales). Listing the number of benefits of an RP will foster more commitment than giving details on a few benefits. Immediate benefits must be highlighted whenever possible. Success comes from persistence in this culture.

- *Bet-your-company culture*: The ritual of this culture *is* the business meeting. Important issues will get full discussion. Decision-making is top-down once all the inputs are in. Actions are measured and deliberate. Once the importance of the RP is evident, specific decisions are made by top management and the plan starts becoming a reality. The decision-makers have a great deal of character and self-confidence, which should enhance good follow-through on decisions. Also people in this culture become highly dependent on one another (they never 'burn any bridges'). This implies better-than-average cooperation and communication between departments during the implementation effort.

- *Tough-guy/macho culture*: The immediate feedback of this culture fosters a short-term perspective. The youth of many people typically in this type of culture does not support a strong planning orientation. These factors lead to difficulty in implementing a RP. Speed not endurance is often the focus. Not taking action, however, is as important as taking one. There is also extremely strong internal competition which breeds individualism and weak communication, another challenge for successful implementation of the RP.

Implementation considerations according to SRG position are then considered. The two independent variables in the culture re-engineering grid are reversed to obtain the re-engineered process implementation grid shown in Table 16.3. The re-engineered process implementation grid presents implementation patterns and concerns related to SRG position. The grid also serves to validate the RP plan implications presented in the culture re-engineering planning grid.

Similar to the process that was carried out with the culture re-engineering grid, the RP plan implications from the re-engineered process implementation grid (Table 16.3) are then analysed. General implications for each SRG position become apparent.

Table 16.3 Re-engineered process implementation grid

Strategic Relevance Grid	Culture	RP implementation effort		RP planning implications
Strategic	Process	Herculean	(6)	Any Process is so hard to change, that it takes great effort just to get RP discussed. The importance the RP is critical to the firm's activities.
	Work Hard/Play Hard	Difficult	(4)	Impatience is the biggest obstacle. If benefits are clear, support for the RP is widespread, but people want it tomorrow. If past inefficiencies in the process are clear, support for the RP is more consistent.
	Bet-Your-Company	Facile	(1)	Planning and many meetings are important parts of day-to-day operations. With top management support, the RP can be accomplished with facile effort (comparatively).
	Tough-Guy/Macho	Difficult	(4)	Even though the RP is seen as essential, the short-term perspective overshadows the persistence needed to implement the RP easily. Individual orientation and competition hinder cooperation.
Turnaround	Process	Herculean	(6)	The process is so hard to change, that it takes great effort just to get the RP discussed. The RP is critical to the firm's activities.
	Work Hard/Play Hard	Importunate	(5)	Impatience is the biggest obstacle. If benefits are clear, support for the RP is widespread, but people want it tomorrow.
	Bet-Your-Company	Facile	(1)	Planning and many meetings are important parts of day to day operations. With top management support, the RP can be accomplished with facile effort. Time to plan and then make appropriate changes is not a problem in this situation. The RP will not be accomplished quickly, however.
	Tough-Guy/Macho	Difficult	(4)	Even though the RP is seen as essential, the short-term perspective overshadows the persistence needed to implement it easily. Individual orientation and competition hinders cooperation. Benefits of the RP must be clear and specific and relate to a current specific decision even if that type of decision may not be relevent by the time the RP is in place.
Factory	Process	Importunate	(5)	Even though RP is not critical here, any movement or change toward it must be well documented with new policies and procedures being put into place throughout the process.
	Work Hard/Play Hard	Considerable	(3)	The need for the RP is evident based on today's activities. Since it is not expected to significantly affect sales in the next 24 hours, however, commitment wanes.
	Bet-Your-Company	Moderate	(2)	Very important to invest in the future. Even though direct link between the RP and future benefits is weak, previous importance of the process warrants attention to the RP.
	Tough-Guy/Macho	Herculean	(6)	Without a clear benefit (over the old process) for future decisions, commitment to the RP is very low.
Support	Process	Difficult	(4)	The RP is a desirable that should be developed in the long-run. Again, new policies and procedures must be clear and be put into place throughout the process.
	Work Hard/Play Hard	Importunate	(5)	Difficult to have much commitment to re-engineering of any kind. Management is often too short-term minded.
	Bet-Your-Company	Considerable	(3)	Senior Management makes decisions. Need for an RP is not of strategic importance. Difficulty is getting senior management to be involved enough to take action and delegate responsibility.
	Tough-Guy/Macho	Herculean	(6)	Without a clear benefit (over the old system) for future decisions, commitment to the RP is very low.

- *Strategic position*: The re-engineered process is critical to the current and future performance of the firm. The RP plan must be closely linked to corporate planning. Planning for RP implementation should have immediate attention from the firm's top management team. Implementation of the RP would tend to be slightly easier due to the strong perceived need for it.
- *Turnaround position*: Again, the RP is very important to the future performance of the firm. Without the RP, performance will suffer significantly in the long run. Planning for RP must be closely linked to corporate planning. The RP implementation effort varies greatly depending upon the organization's ability to adapt to new strategies.
- *Factory position*: The current process is needed for the organization's activities to be coordinated and to run smoothly. It is important to current company performance, but the RP is not expected to be a critical factor in the future. The RP implementation effort is significant since it is difficult to communicate the need for such radical change. Even though a smooth running RP is not critical to future strategies, current dependence on the old process lends some support to the RP implementation effort.
- *Support position*: The current process is still needed for the organization's activities to be co-ordinated and to run smoothly. It is not, however, viewed as critical to current company performance and the RP is very unlikely to be of strategic importance in the future. Without clear benefits (over the old process) for future decisions, commitment to the RP is very low and implementation especially difficult.

FRAMEWORK PLACEMENT

In order to add a practical element to the analysis presented, procedures for assessing one's position within the strategic relevance grid (SRG) and the corporate tribes culture model are included here.

Strategic Relevance Grid Placement

In order to assess the SRG position the questions described in Figure 16.5 should be answered. These questions are divided into two groups, one group for assessing the strategic relevance of the current processes and one group for assessing the strategic relevance for the proposed re-engineered process.

Strategic Relevance of <u>CURRENT PROCESSES</u> (Related to the Proposed Re-engineered Process)

CURRENT PROCESSES

Please indicate the significance of the following items in terms of their significance to current processes.

	V LOW	= Very Low Significance.
	LOW	= Low Significance.
	MODERATE	= Moderate Significance.
	HIGH	= High Significance.
	V HIGH	= Very High Significance.
	N/R	= Not Relevant or Don't Know.

SIGNIFICANCE

1. Impact of one-hour shut down of existing processes, on major operational activities (eg customer service, plant shutdown)   VLOW LOW MODERATE HIGH V HIGH N/R

2. Impact of total shut-down of existing processes (3 to 4 weeks) on major organizational activities   VLOW LOW MODERATE HIGH V HIGH N/R

3. Extent of reliance of existing processes on outside vendors and consultants   VLOW LOW MODERATE HIGH V HIGH N/R

4. Difficulty of coping manually with critical existing processes (or difficulty of doing it another way)   VLOW LOW MODERATE HIGH V HIGH N/R

5. Degree of dispersion in the locations of existing processes   VLOW LOW MODERATE HIGH V HIGH N/R

6. Amount of recovery time needed after a one day failure in existing processes   VLOW LOW MODERATE HIGH V HIGH N/R

Strategic Relevance of the <u>PROPOSED RE-ENGINEERED PROCESS</u>

SIGNIFICANCE

1. The RP (Re-engineered Process) will give cost displacement or cost reduction   V LOW LOW MODERATE HIGH V HIGH N/R

2. The RP will help the firm to develop and offer new products or services for sale (including significant new features to existing product lines)   V LOW LOW MODERATE HIGH V HIGH N/R

3. The RP enables development of new administrative control and planning processes   V LOW LOW MODERATE HIGH V HIGH N/R

4. The RP offers significant tangible benefits through improved operational efficiencies (eg, reducing inventory; improved credit collection)   V LOW LOW MODERATE HIGH V HIGH N/R

5. The RP offers new ways for the company to compete (eg fast delivery, higher quality, etc)   V LOW LOW MODERATE HIGH V HIGH N/R

Figure 16.5   Strategic relevance grid assessment instrument

After answering the SRG questions it is relatively simple to place a process in the SRG. Assign the following values to the answers given:

V. LOW	=	1
LOW	=	2
MODERATE	=	3
HIGH	=	4
V. HIGH	=	5
N/R	=	None; ignore

Average the answers for each of the two groups of questions. If the average is 3 or more for a group, placement should be in the High section of the grid for that dimension (see Figure 16.3). If the average is less than 3, placement should be in the Low section of the grid for that dimension.

Culture Classification Placement

In order to assess an organization's type of overall corporate culture, the questions presented in Figure 16.6 were developed from Deal and Kennedy's (1982) description of the corporate tribes model. After completing the questions, add up the total number of points given for each type of organization (A, B, C and D) for the three questions (see Figure 16.7). The organization type with the most points is then translated to the culture type using the scheme shown on the right side of Figure 16.7.

	A	B	C	D		Culture Types
Q 1					A	= Bet-Your-Company
Q 2					B	= Tough-Guy/Macho
Q 3	—	—	—	—	C	= Process
TOTAL					D	= Work Hard/Play Hard

Figure 16.7 Summing and conversion of culture types

CONCLUSION

The current popularity of BPR is a signal that many organizations believe they need to perform much better than they currently are. In addition, Hammer (1990, 1993) has consistently stated that BPR is an ongoing process rather than a one-time 'cure', As such, it is particularly important to be able to implement new re-engineered processes with a minimum amount of difficulty (or failure!). We have significant help through literature and consultants in determining how to go about the re-engineering effort. We have little assistance, however, in fully understanding implementation.

ORGANIZATIONAL CULTURE ASSESSMENT

These questions relate to the type of organization that your institution is most like. Each of these items contains four descriptions of institutions. Please distribute 100 points among the four descriptions on how similar the description is to your own organization. None of the descriptions is any better than the others; they are just different. *For each question, please use all 100 points*.

FOR EXAMPLE: In question 1, if organization A seems very similar to mine, B seems somewhat similar, and C and D do not seem similar at all, I might give 70 points to A and the remaining 30 points to B.

1. DECISION TYPE (Please distribute 100 points)

points for A	In institution A, decisions involve a **high degree of risk**. **Feedback is slow** and results from decisions are not known for a **long time**.	points for B	In institution B, decisions involve **high stakes** and one decision may be critical to its survival. Results from decisions are known almost **immediately**.
points for C	Decisions in institution C are characterized by a **low degree of risk**. There is virtually **no feedback**. Results from decisions may **never be known**.	points for D	In institution D, one decision will neither make you nor break you. **Feedback is quick** and often **intensive**.

2. MANAGEMENT STYLE (Please distribute 100 points)

points for A	The management style in institution A is characterized as **team work, consensus** and **participation**.	points for B	The management style in institution B is characterised as individual **individual initiative, freedom** and **uniqueness**.
points for C	The management style in institution C is characterized as **security of employment, longevity in position** and **predictability**.	points for D	The management style in institution D is characterized as **hard-driving competitiveness, production and achievement**.

3. CRITERIA OF SUCCESS (Please distribute 100 points)

points for A	Institution A defines success on the basis of its development of **human resources, teamwork** and **concern for people**.	points for B	Institution B defines success on the basis of its having **unique** or **newest** products. It is a product **leader** and **innovator**.
points for C	Institution C defines success on the basis of **efficiency. Dependable delivery, smooth scheduling** and **low-cost production** are critical.	points for D	Institution D defines success on the basis of market penetration, and **market share**. Being **number one** relative to the competition is a key objective.

Figure 16.6 Corporate culture assessment

The contribution of this chapter is its use of two well-established models, the strategic grid and the corporate tribes model, from other disciplines to provide some insight into the difficulty of implementing BPR successfully. Davenport (1993) advocates that early on in the BPR process it is important to assess the strategic relevance for a process and qualify its culture. It is the position of this chapter that what is vital to consider in the beginning is critical to understand at the end (implementation).

Research is clear that BPR has a high failure rate, corporate culture is a key variable in implementing any major business change, and the strategic relevance of a proposed change affects implementation difficulty and success. The individual and combined impact of culture and strategic relevance on BPR implementation was therefore analysed and presented in a thought-provoking framework. The need for research in successful implementation of BPR is great. Hopefully, this work is one step forward in solving the unavoidable challenge of implementation.

REFERENCES

Allen, R F (1985) 'Four Phases for Bringing About Cultural Change' in Kilmann, R, Saxton, M J and Serpa, R (eds), *Gaining Control of the Corporate Culture*, Jossey-Bass, San Francisco, 332–350.

Arogyaswamy, B and Byles, C M (1987) 'Organizational Culture: Internal and External Fits', *Journal of Management*, 13(4), 647–658.

Belmonte, R W and Murray, R J (1993) 'Getting Ready for Strategic Change: Surviving the Process of Business Process Redesign', *Information Systems Management*, 10(3), 23–29.

Brousell, D (1993) 'A Word with Michael Hammer', *Datamation*, 39(15), 24.

Cash, J I, McFarlan, F W, McKenney, J L and Vitale, M R (1988) *Corporate Information Systems Management: Text and Cases*, 2nd edn, Richard D. Irwin, Homewood, Ill.

Davenport, T (1993) *Process Innovation: Re-engineering Work through Information Technology*, Harvard Business School Press, Boston, Mass.

Davenport, T H, Eccles, R G and Prusak, L (1992) 'Information Politics', *Sloan Management Review*, 34(1), 53–65.

Deal, T E and Kennedy A (1982) *Corporate Cultures*, Addison-Wesley, Reading, Mass.

Deshpande, R and Parasuraman, A (1986) 'Linking Corporate Culture to Strategic Planning', *Business Horizons*, 29(3), 28–37.

Flaatten, P O, McCubbrey, D J, O'Riordan, P D and Burgess, K (1992) *Foundation of Business Systems*, 2nd edn, Dryden Press, Fort Worth, Tex.

Hammer, M (1990) 'Re-engineering Work: Don't Automate, Obliterate', *Harvard Business Review*, 68(4), 104–112.

Hammer, M (1993) 'Re-engineering', *Retail Business Review*, 61(3), 10–19.

Hammer, M and Champy, J A (1993) *Re-engineering the Corporation*, Harper Business, New York.

Kilmann, R H, Saxton, M J and Serpa, R (1986) 'Issues in Understanding and Changing Culture', *California Management Review*, 28(2), 87–94.

Meek, L V (1988) 'Organizational Culture: Origins and Weaknesses', *Organization Studies*, 9(4), 453–473.

Moad, J (1993) 'Does Re-engineering Really Work?' *Datamation*, 39(15), 22–28.

Peters, T J and Waterman, R H (1982) *In Search of Excellence*, Harper and Row, New York.

Raghunathan, B and Raghunathan, T S (1990) 'Planning Implications of the Information Systems Strategic Grid: An Empirical Investigation', *Decision Sciences*, 21, 287–300.

Reimann, B C and Wiener, Y (1988) 'Corporate Culture: Avoiding the Elitist Trap', *Business Horizons*, 31(2), 36–44.

Saffold, G S III (1988) 'Culture Traits, Strength, and Organizational Performance: Moving Beyond 'Strong' Culture', *Academy of Management Review*, 13(4), 546–558.

Stanton, S, Hammer, M and Power, B (1993) 'Getting Everyone on Board', *I.T. Magazine*, 25(4), 22–27.

Stewart, T A (1993) 'Re-engineering: The Hot New Managing Tool', *Fortune*, 128(4), 32–37.

'The Role of IT in Business Re-engineering' (1993) *I/S Analyzer*, 31(8), 1–16.

Thompson, A A and Strickland, A J (1987) *Strategic Management: Concepts and Cases*, 4th edn, Business Publications, Plano, Tex.

Part Five

FLAT ORGANIZATIONS – OPPORTUNITY OR THREAT?

Many proponents of BPR would claim that the structure of an organization will become more 'horizontal' as a result of the successful implementation of a BPR initiative. Functions and departments will cease to exist; the focus of the organization will be on the processes through which it delivers value to its customers; teamworking will be the norm. The outcome will be a flatter and less hierarchical structure that will be more responsive to market dynamics. While this may sound logical, is it realistic? In this part, we present two chapters which address the question of whether the move towards these new structures poses an opportunity or represents a threat.

In a thought-provoking essay, James Hoopes compares the flat organization with Western civilization. He argues that there is a significant parallel between developments in organizations and a new way of thinking in the humanities and social science domains. This new way of thinking might be described as a growing conviction that the universe is nothing but organizations and that they are all relatively flat. He elaborates on this idea by considering, of all the things in the universe, the one thing that on the face of it seems the least like a flat organization – the individual human being. He takes us on an excursion into the history of metaphysics and moral philosophy, drawing on the ideas of philosophers such as Aristotle, Peirce, Popper, psychoanalyst Freud and linguist de Saussure. He then weaves these ideas into an argument which lends support to the notion of the superiority of the flat organization. He contends that while we have modelled our organizations after minds, our culture's model of mind is profoundly individualistic and profoundly mistaken. He proposes that a semiotic model of mind could help in our understanding of organizations, and in particular the flat organization.

In Chapter 18, Hugh Willmott laments the lack of consideration given by BPR to the human aspects of organizing. He focuses on the re-engineeering of human resources, arguing that a successful transition from a specialist function-based organization structure to one orientated around business processes will necessarily depend upon the people who enact, and are also (re)constituted by, BPR. He sees in the BPR literature no discussion of why, or how, managers and other employees may directly or covertly oppose its demands for change. He raises the question of how human resource managers are to address BPR's neglect and trivialization of the human dimensions of organizing and managing change.

17

WESTERN CIVILIZATION VERSUS THE FLAT ORGANIZATION

*James Hoopes, Babson College, Massachusetts**

Abolish hierarchies, manage with teams, focus on process and satisfy the customer. The flat organization is the new orthodoxy of organizational science. Whether this new orthodoxy passes under the name of re-engineering, total quality management or some other fashionable rubric, it amounts, says *Business Week*, to 'much more than just another abstract theory making the B-school lecture rounds. Examples of horizontal management abound' (20 December 1993: 78).

That an idea is actually being used, however, is no reason to believe that it will work. Managers must decide, before all the evidence is in, whether they should structure their organizations horizontally. In the absence of proof, is there any reason to accept the assurance of gurus, pundits and publicists that the flat organization is not just another trendy fad that will soon be last year's buzzword?

There is a significant parallel between developments in organizations and a new way of thinking in university humanities and social science departments. This new way of thinking might be described as a growing conviction that the universe is nothing but organizations and that they are all relatively flat. This idea can be made clear by considering, of all the things in the universe, the one thing that on the face of it seems the least like a flat organization – the individual human being.

Understanding the present conventional notion of what constitutes a human being requires a quick survey of the history of Western philosophy. For thousands of years philosophers have been committed to the idea of essential substances, whether the substance be the indivisible atoms out of which the ancient Greeks believed matter was composed or the

*   The author wishes to thank Allan Cohen, Thomas H Johnson, and C J McNair for their helpful comments on earlier versions of this chapter.

invisible substance of mind out of which Descartes believed individual souls were formed. In this tradition a living being was created whenever a soul was added to a material body. A vegetable soul enabled a body to grow. An animal soul made a body grow and move. A human soul resulted in growth, motion and *thought*.

Thus a human soul or mind was a sort of chief executive officer, engaged in the top- down management of the rest of the human organism. From Aristotle's *Nichomachean Ethics* to the self-help literature or our day, people have tried to understand why this mental CEO or soul has difficulty managing its unruly subordinates whether these have been known in Aristotelian terms as the passions, in Freudian terms as the unconscious, or in behaviourist terms as drives. Aristotelianism was a pure top-down model in which the mind was supposed to direct the passions. Freudianism and other depth psychologies suggested a more complex relation in which the mind's difficulty was due to its being partly unconscious and more responsive to the passions than had been previously believed. Behaviourism essentially threw up its hands and abandoned any notion of mind altogether.

About a century ago, a different view got a foothold in philosophy and linguistics, has slowly gained ground there, and in recent years has begun to influence other academic disciplines, especially in the humanities but to an important degree in the social sciences as well. This new view holds that the essence of matter and mind do not lie in whatever substance composes the universe but in *relations* among bits of that substance, which is why this view amounts to a description of the universe as an organization. More often than not this new way of thinking passes under the name of 'semiotic', the science of signs.

So much foolishness is perpetrated in some humanities disciplines under the cover of 'semiotic' that some will find it difficult to believe that semiotics could offer anything useful to management science. The problem lies in the large influence in some of the humanistic disciplines of the Swiss linguist Ferdinand de Saussure (1857–1913) who emphasized the arbitrariness of verbal signs (de Saussure, 1959). That is, D-O-G might just as well signify a supreme being and G-O-D a four-legged animal if those were the arbitrarily chosen conventions. The obvious truth of this assertion masks the errors that follow when the doctrine of the arbitrariness of signs is applied to broader relations than those between words and their meanings. For example, there have been attempts to apply this doctrine of the arbitrariness of meaning to social relations, and de Saussure himself held that 'every means of expression used in society is based ... on convention.' (de Saussure, 1968). Such a view renders semiotic irrelevant to organizational reality. All managers, even or perhaps especially those who despair of truly understanding their organizations, are at least tacitly aware that organizations have a measure of logical, non-arbitrary meaning in the signifying relations by which their people work together with some commonality of purpose.

Another conflict between de Saussure's semiotic and the everyday experience of managers is that if his more extreme adherents were correct it would be impossible for human beings to communicate at all. For example, de Saussure's notion of the arbitrariness of signs has led to the notion that 'literary works' are free to violate 'the codes that define them, and this is what makes the semiological investigation of literature such a tantalizing enterprise' (Culler, 1977). The literary critic is thus licensed to find all sorts of new and arbitrary meaning in texts while ignoring the author's intentions. But managers are authors in the sense that they use words to attempt to convey intended meanings. If words are free to run away from intentions, managers should find language useless. Again, the experience of at least some managers in using words to get the results they intended must make them suspicious if not contemptuous of those extreme semioticians who hold that signs operate entirely apart from human intentions.

A far broader and more useful tradition in semiotic derives from the philosopher, Charles Sanders Peirce (1839–1914), whom the late Sir Karl Popper called 'one of the greatest philosophers of all time'. (Popper, 1972). Peirce is usually credited with founding the philosophical school called pragmatism. As is widely known, pragmatists believe that the meaning of an idea can only be learned by considering what would be the practical consequence of the idea if it were acted on in the external world. What is less well understood is that Peirce arrived at this conclusion as a result of his revision of the Western metaphysical tradition. Rejecting the two substances of matter and mind as they had been defined by Descartes, Peirce held that there was one substance and that the varying phenomena that we call mind and matter are two different kinds of relations within that one substance. What we call material phenomena are relations in which one object is affected physically by a second object. Peirce therefore gave the name 'secondness' to this category of experience. Mental phenomena or what Peirce called 'thirdness' are relations in which one object is represented to a second object by a third, a sign (Hoopes, 1990). Since mind or thirdness is a relation among bits of the same substance involved in material phenomena there is no boundary between thought and the external world as in Descartes' system. The test of truth is not whether a thought conforms to what Descartes called the 'interior light of reason' but whether the idea is a sign that accurately represents the external world.

Moreover, Peirce's study of signs led him to the conclusion that there are three broad classes of signs – *indices, icons* and *symbols* – only the last of which is arbitrary (Hoopes, 1990). An *index* possesses a real rather than arbitrary relationship with its object as does a weather vane with the wind whose direction it signifies. An *icon* is not an arbitrary sign but resembles the object it represents, as does, say, a portrait its subject. *Symbols* – for example, the octagonal shape of stop signs – are the only arbitrary signs; we would stop just as readily for a triangular sign if that were the arbitrarily chosen convention.

Peirce's semiotic, rather than unrealistically denying the possibility of communication, explains how both the success and failure in communication that we have all experienced is possible. Similarly, the fact that it is possible for some signs to be arbitrary while others are not is explainable in Peirce's triadic semiotic, where a first object is represented to a second by a third, a sign, which mediates between them. The thought that interprets the sign as a representation of the object is called the 'interpretant':

OBJECT   SIGN   INTERPRETANT

Whether communication is successful or not depends on whether the interpretant accurately interprets the sign as a representation of its object. Miscommunication occurs when the interpretant inaccurately interprets the relation between the sign and its object. Since the interpretant as well as the object determines the meaning of the sign, miscommunication may occur even when the sign is an index really related to its object. Such realistic understanding of the possibility of both success and failure in communication is impossible within the terms of a dyadic semiotic such as de Saussure's where the emphasis is on the relation between the object and the sign ('signified' and 'signifier' in his terminology) and no attention is given to interpretation.

From the point of view of managerial theory and practice, the most interesting and useful aspect of Peirce's semiotic is the new understanding it offers of what constitutes both an individual and an organization. Taking first the case of the individual, Peirce rejected the entire Cartesian tradition which had sanctioned the conventional Western idea of the atomistic individual. In Descartes' view, a mind or soul or self is an immaterial essence added to a material body, which owes its life to the presence of the soul and loses life when the soul departs. The enormous influence of this atomistic individualism in Western culture is too obvious to need documentation. It has exerted great influence on Western management, which in many cases is a heroically individualist style or, as it has been aptly called after the style glorified in the myth of the American frontier, the 'Lone Ranger' style of management (Bradford and Cohen, 1984: 26).

Peirce's view is more relevant to organizational science, for he sees the mind not as something tacked onto the human body but as an organization within the body, a series of semiotic relations among the body's parts including especially, of course, the brain cells. Yet while Peirce clearly recognizes the 'firstness' of the body and the necessity of 'secondness' or physiological relations among its parts before there can be thought, his system is anything but materialistic. Physiological relations or feelings in the brain are not thought; they are strictly material relations or 'secondness'. Thinking and knowing only occur when physiological relations in the brain are given meaning, and meaning is a matter of semiotic interpretation or 'thirdness'. The patient reader's 'knowledge' that he or she is gazing at this paper comes from a relation in which a 'second' object, a neurological state, interprets a 'third' object, a prior neurological state, as a sign of a 'first' object, a thin, white external sheet with black letters imprinted on it.

The important point for managers in this admittedly rather technical account of Peirce's philosophy is that a human being is not an atomistic soul but is an *organization* or series of semiotic relations. 'You never can narrow down to an individual,' said Peirce. Consider any historic person. We call him an individual in 'common parlance, but in logical strictness he is not. We think of certain images in our memory – a platform and a noble form uttering convincing and patriotic words – a statue – certain printed matter – and we say that which that speaker and the man whom that statue was taken for and the writer of this speech' are the man. 'Thus, even the proper name of a man is a general term or the name of a class, for it names a class of sensations and thoughts. The true individual term[,] the absolutely singular *this* and *that*[,] cannot be reached. Whatever has comprehension must be general' [Kloesel, I, 461]. The same is true of all our supposedly singular thoughts; they are a series of relations because thought itself is a relational process. Thought is the process most closely related to our identity as human beings, which means that we, like organizations, are a process.

Reality being 'that which is represented in a true representation', the process of thought being the essence of man, and representation or signification being the essence of thought, it follows that in reality 'the word or sign which man uses *is* the man himself'. This notion of Peirce's that 'man is a sign' (Hoopes, 1990) is not as ethereal as it seems at first glance. As emphasized above, Peirce never denied the reality of the body but, rather, recognized its necessity. Nevertheless, thought or semiotic interpretation creates human identity. A small child makes no distinction between its own body and the rest of the universe. But through experience the child learns that the rest of the universe refractorily resists desire while 'that peculiarly important body called Willy or Johnny' does not (Hoopes, 1990). The child thus learns, correctly, to interpret this Willy or Johnny, this body, as what constitutes itself. And since the self derives its identity

301

from thought, what the self is thinking is what the self *is*. And since thought is in signs, the self is in signs.

Abstruse as the concept of the self as a sign may seem, it has utterly revolutionary implications for organizational science, for it breaks down the barriers between individual human beings that, in the Western tradition, have always been supposed to be impassable. If the human soul is not an immaterial atom added to a body but a series of semiotic relations within the body, the use of external signs, such as words, may carry the soul beyond the body

> ... are we shut up in a box of flesh and blood? When I communicate my thoughts and my sentiments to a friend with whom I am in full sympathy, so that my feelings pass into him and I am conscious of what he feels, do I not live in his brain as well as in my own – most literally? True, my animal life is not there; but my soul, my feeling, thought, attention are ... There is a miserable material and barbarian notion according to which a man cannot be in two places at once; as though he were a *thing*! A word may be in several places at once ... because its essence is spiritual; and I believe that a man is no whit inferior to the word in this respect. (Kloesel, I, 498)

The result of this ability of people to live, so to speak, outside their bodies is of potentially profound importance to managers though, so far as I know, managerial literature contains not even a single reference to such a view. It means that the spiritual line between the person and the organization is blurred. Words enable people not merely to communicate but to unite with others, to become at least sometimes literally one: 'two minds in communication are ..."at one", that is are properly one mind in that part of them.' (Hoopes, 1990). Here is an explanation of the satisfaction that people sometimes find in communicating and working with other people – an expansion of one's selfhood beyond one's own body and brain to that of another person: 'Man is conscious of his interpretant, his own thought in another mind...is happy in it, feels himself in some degree to be there.' (Kloesel, I,499).

Just as a mind is an organization, an organization can be a mind. Just as the individual mind is not an atomistic soul but an organized system of relations within the body, larger organized systems of relations within the body, larger organized systems of relations may come to constitute a larger mind in which people happily participate. Organizations can be more than mere associations of atomistic individuals represented mechanistically on an organization chart:

> There should be something like personal consciousness in bodies of men who are in intimate and intensely sympathetic communion ... Esprit de corps, national sentiment, sympathy, are no mere metaphors. None of us can fully realize what the minds of corporations are, any more than one of my brain-cells can know what the whole brain is thinking. But the law of

mind clearly points to the existence of such personalities, and there are many ordinary observations which, if they were critically examined and supplemented by special experiments, might, as first appearances promise, give evidence of the influence of such greater persons upon individuals. (Hoopes, 1990)

It surely is of enormous importance to managers if their organizations are not merely individuals connected more or less mechanically by shared tasks and the need to communicate about them. If organizations are potentially minds themselves, getting the most out of them may depend on letting them function as minds.

It is difficult, however, for a manager to let an organization function as a mind if the manager's entire cultural tradition has taught him a mistaken notion of how the mind works. The top-down model of the mind, with the understanding or consciousness serving as CEO and striving to control its unruly subordinates, is precisely the model by which many Western organizations are structured. The problem is not that we have not modelled our organizations after minds, for we seem, at least implicitly, to have done just that. The problem, rather, is that our culture's model of mind is profoundly individualistic and profoundly mistaken. How might a semiotic model of mind help?

A semiotic model of mind makes it possible to get a new hold on the problem of psychological conflict that led to the Aristotelian, Freudian and behaviourist models. These models of the human organism assume that maximum self-control and minimal self-conflict are the most desirable human state. The newer view puts all this in question by suggesting that the soul or mind is not a CEO, or at least not a CEO with a top-down style. Conflict, therefore, is not due to resistance to an authoritarian CEO by the soul's unruly subordinates. The soul or mind is the relationship among the bodily parts hitherto thought of as the soul's subordinates, including especially, of course, its brain cells (though as stated above, to assume, as materialists and atheists might, that relations within the brain are strictly physical or mechanical is to miss the interpretive or spiritual element – thirdness – within those relations). In such an organization some conflict is to be expected and is probably necessary to its most creative achievements.

Of course it might be argued that if the human organism does not have a CEO with absolute top-down authority, it ought to, for human beings have often done very badly. Certainly much psychological conflict results in terrible suffering. Worse, the organization of individual human beings into larger social organizations, be they companies or countries, has often had lamentable results. Yet it might help mitigate some of this evil to abandon our top-down notion of how both human beings and organizations ought to manage themselves.

Taking first the individual human organism, consider the damage done by our traditional moralism in which the mental CEO or soul is supposed to subdue the passions. This naive faith in the CEO-mind leads to the powerful and mistaken tendency in our culture to reform ourselves by resolution, by simply deciding to adopt different values and act according to them. This method of reform usually fails. For a drug addict to 'just say no', as if his desire were not a powerful part of himself but only a low-ranking flunky who ought to be easily controlled by a simple order, is worse than useless; it is destructive. The addict's difficulty in *just* saying no can only add to his feeling of weakness and inadequacy. The moral strength the addict needs cannot come from futile attempts to subdue desire. The needed moral strength can only come from considering the drug in the largest possible series of relations so that present pleasure and future well-being can be compared. Even then, of course, victory is hardly assured, as is attested by the experience even non-addicts have with other moral struggles over such issues as sexual behaviour, weight control and living within one's income.

Analogous to this naive faith that the individual CEO-mind can reform itself by resolving to adopt new values and act according to them is the reliance of managerially intense organizations on culture change. Who has not met the zealous young manager out to 'change the culture'? As with the West's traditional Cartesian notion of the individual mind, the idea of culture is that it exists somehow apart from structure, apart from the body of the organization. Just as the drug addict is thought to need to do nothing more than to assert the supremacy of mind over matter and 'just say no', so, too, the organization needs nothing more than the wilful adoption of a new set of values. (This same manager would piously avow the need to accept and respect the existing culture if the question were how to operate in a foreign land rather than in one's own organization.)

This command and control model of mind poses a much greater threat to organizations than to individual human beings. People at least have the advantage of being, in reality, relatively flat organizations even if they are somewhat harmed by the myth of the mind as a CEO. But corporations turn the myth into reality; the CEO is a fact. The passions often say no to the mind, but employees much less frequently challenge the boss.

The failures of communication that result from the failure of employees to imitate the passions and speak up all the time are more damaging to a corporation than would be the quieting of the passions in an individual (if such a thing were possible). For the relations, both internal and external, that need to be considered to determine what course will lead to the future well-being of the business organization are almost infinitely more complex than in the case of the individual human organism.

In another important respect, however, the business organization has recently come much closer to resembling an individual human being – in the quantity and complexity of the information it must process and in the rapidity with which it must do it. The argument for the flat organization is that it allows for more rapid information processing and decision-making in our increasingly complex world. Keeping in mind that even by the standard of today's technology, the individual human being is still a marvel at information processing, it is of some significance that the individual is a flat organization rather than a top-down hierarchy.

Therefore this fairly esoteric excursion into the history of metaphysics and moral philosophy lends a bit of support to the notion of the superiority of the flat organization. The importance of this support could easily be overestimated since it is drawn from philosophy as well as from managerial experience. But neither is this philosophical support for the flat organization insignificant. Managers always have to act before experience has taught them all they would like to know. Managers therefore cannot afford to ignore the lessons of philosophy or at least of pragmatic philosophy, which is only one more way of saying that they live in a universe organized fairly flatly where the answers to their most important questions are not given from the top down.

REFERENCES

Bradford, D I and Cohen, A R (1984) *Managing for Excellence: The Guide to Developing High Performance in Contemporary Organizations,* Wiley, New York.

Culler, J (1977) *Ferdinand de Sausssure,* Penguin, New York

de Saussure, F (1959) *Course in General Linguistics,* trans. Baskin, W, The Philosophical Library, New York.

Giddens, A (1979) *Central Problems of Social Theory: Action, Structure and Contradiction in Social Analysis,* University of California Press, Berkeley, Calif.

Hoopes, J (ed.) (1990) *Peirce on Signs: Writings on Semiotic by Charles Sanders Peirce,* University of North Carolina Press, Chapel Hill, NC.

Kloesel, C J W *et al.* (eds) (1982) *Writings of Charles S. Peirce: A Chronological Edition,* Indiana University Press, Bloomington, Ind.

Popper, K (1972) *Objective Knowledge: An Evolutionary Approach,* Clarendon Press, Oxford.

18

WILL THE TURKEYS VOTE FOR CHRISTMAS? THE RE-ENGINEERING OF HUMAN RESOURCES

Hugh Willmott, Manchester School of Management, UMIST

INTRODUCTION

> There is a new-look menu over at the Consultants' Cafe. Good old soupe du TQM and change management pâté are off. Perhaps you would care to try some business process re-engineering instead? (Oliver, 1993)

During the 1980s, executives were invited to sample and digest a series of 'recipes' for enhancing corporate performance. Notably, they were urged by Peters and Waterman (1982) to emulate the successes of 'excellent' companies by strengthening their corporate cultures. (For a critique of this literature see Willmott (1993).) More recently, Total Quality Management (TQM) has been widely promoted and adopted as a means of achieving continuous improvement. (See, for example, Oakland (1989). For a critical examination of the theory and practice of quality initiatives, see Wilkinson and Willmott (1995).) However

> A recent study indicates that around 85% of the organizations using TQM are disappointed with the outcome ... experts are predicting that TQM will be replaced by corporate re-engineering as the technique most favoured by organizations anxious to maximize their people and material resources. (Oates, 1993)

Making the transition from specialist function-based to business process-oriented organizing practices necessarily depends upon the 'human resources' who enact, and are also (re)constituted by, BPR (Watson, 1994). Given BPR's focus upon *processes*, it is remarkable how little attention is given by BPR to the *human* aspects of organizing and the implementation of change programmes.

The chapter begins by reviewing the BPR vision of radical business process change* focusing upon its use of information technology to facilitate a move away from linear/sequential work organization towards parallel processing and multidisciplinary teamworking. The neglect of the human dimension within BPR is then identified. Finally, the chapter reflects upon how human resource management (HRM) specialists, in particular, may respond to BPR's trivialization of the human and organizational complexities and dilemmas associated with its recipe for radical organizational change. The chapter concludes by suggesting that the human aspects and implications of BPR have been woefully neglected, and that these should provide a strong focus for future management research.

IT'S A VISION THING

Business consultants have a vested interest in emphasizing the novelty and potency of whatever variety of 'snake oil' they dispense to managers. But their prior investment in more established recipes for business success means that they are inclined to interpret the new in terms of the old. In turn, this may promote an excessive scepticism about the novelty of new recipes, such as BPR, which are then dismissed by academics as well as practitioners as 'old wine in new bottles'. This reaction is very understandable given the hype that accompanies every fashion and fad (Eccles and Nohria, 1992). But it is unhelpful when it blinds us to the possibility that BPR may be distinctive in its approach to the restructuring of business practices.

Though it may represent a new nadir in the inelegance of its terminology, BPR has proved to be at once sufficiently striking, flexible and ambiguous to encompass many programmes and techniques, such as teamworking, networking and even EPOS (electronic point of sale), that have contributed to the reorganization of work during the 1980s. In common with previous recipes for improving business performance – from Taylorism to TQM – BPR draws together, synthesizes and provides an articulation for ideas and practices that have been floating around in

---

*   Since the term was coined by Hammer (1990), articles and books on business process re-engineering have mushroomed. See, for example, Morris and Brandon (1993). Since these books are frequently derivative as well as repetitive, I focus upon Hammer's (1990) original article, his subsequent book with Champy (1993) and Johansson *et al.* (1993).

the business world without a catchy label or a champion.

What Hammer, BPR's principal advocate, has done is not so much concoct a novel recipe but has put a name to an emergent trend in business organization towards the use of information and communication technologies (ICTs) to redesign work processes – a trend that has been prompted by, and has subsequently contributed to, an intensification of (global) competition. Hammer's contribution, like that of earlier guru figures, resides in a flair for packaging and promoting an appealing product in a market where status-conscious consumers are, like the proverbial Emperor, anxious to espouse and sport the latest in management fashions. Not undeservedly, BPR has been likened to the curry house special: no one knows exactly what it is (Oliver, 1993: 18). Nonetheless, what Knights and Morgan (1991) have observed of top managers' espousal of the discourse of corporate strategy also seems applicable to current enthusiasm amongst top management for BPR, namely that through its discourse

> ...managers are constituted as subjects either in support of, or in resistance to, its plausibility. Insofar as [BPR] discourse would seem to facilitate general concerns with personal as well as organizational well-being and control, individuals readily participate in its practices and internalize its discipline. In this respect they are transformed into subjects who secure their sense of meaning, identity and reality through participation in the discourses and practices of [BPR]. (Knights and Morgan, 1991: 269)

Hammer's formulation of BPR promises radical (not just incremental) improvements in such areas as product development, product quality and speed of delivery through the innovative use of ICTs. How is this to be accomplished? Instead of using ICTs to 'automate' existing, functionally organized methods of production, its leading advocates urge that ICTs be mobilized to redesign processes in ways that 'obliterate' established practices. The most basic and common feature of re-engineered processes, Hammer and Champy (1993) contend is 'the absence of an assembly line; that is, many formerly distinct jobs or tasks are integrated and compressed into one'. More generally, Hammer has argued that

> It is time to stop paving the cow paths. Instead of embedding outdated processes in silicon and software, we should obliterate them and start over. We should 'reengineer' our businesses: *use the power of modern information technology to radically redesign our business processes in order to achieve dramatic improvements in their performance.* (Hammer, 1990: 104, emphasis added)

The embeddedness of outmoded mechanisms both within organization structures and their IT systems is diagnosed as a principal source of competitive decline. Their symptoms are legion: lengthy product development cycles, poor customer responsiveness and service, capital locked up in operations that add little or no value. Even in companies that have embraced the principles of TQM and JIT, it is claimed that their bureaucratic structures have been left largely intact, or have even been reinforced by such programmes, making possible room for dramatic improvements in performance.

> Despite [the application of TQM and JIT principles], most Western companies remain *highly bureaucratic*, with departments acting individually and 'throwing over the wall' to the next department designs, information, product, and most of all problems ...barriers to overall business effectiveness are raised and turf is jealously guarded ...This kind of organizational linking *needs to be broken apart and rebuilt as a process-oriented business ... where everyone regards working in cross-functional teams as the norm ...and where everyone knows that the key goal is to produce a service or product that the marketplace perceives to be best.* (Johansson *et al.*, 1993: 7, emphases added)

To achieve this goal, the champions of BPR demand that old assumptions, values and rules are challenged and superseded. For example, BPR encourages a fundamental questioning of received wisdoms – such as the assumption that merchandising decisions are best made at headquarters; or the assumption that customers don't (and perhaps won't) make even straightforward repairs to their own electrical equipment. By exposing and replacing assumptions that lock companies into existing paradigms of production and distribution, BPR promises to make quantum leaps in processes of service delivery, product development cycles, etc. Whilst acknowledging that major disruptions and job losses accompany BPR, its leading exponents are confident that strong leadership from top management can persuade sufficient turkeys to vote for Christmas.

PEOPLE: ACHILLES' HEEL, OR PARSON'S NOSE, OF BPR?

When it comes to identifying the new organizing practices that are to replace old, outmoded mechanisms, the advocates of BPR are more vague. Its methodology of change is also quite opaque. However, certain contours are comparatively well defined. BPR's special weapon is the power of ICTs and its principal targets are functionally based structures and sequentially organized processes. Both are criticized for their tendency to differentiate rather than integrate elements of product design, manufacture and delivery.

BPR presents a novel challenge to organizational structures, processes and cultures. Its promise of greater productivity and shorter time to market is predicated on making major shifts in managerial practice and culture. Yet the question of how such shifts are to be smoothly achieved remains unanswered. Whilst BPR espouses multidisciplinary integration of business processes, it is dominated by the logic and language of computer science and production engineering. Within this logic, people are deemed to be malleable, predictable and willing to be programmed in accordance with the requirements of a rationally designed system. However, in practice, people are unpredictable, wilful and recalcitrant. Perhaps for this reason, if no other, David Nadler, president of Delta Consulting Group, is reported to have said that

> 'We have watched a number of re-engineering projects fail. They have involved huge promises of savings, but have either stopped because they don't seem to be leading anywhere, or they have been completed but with none of the promised gains to show for it. Moreover, such projects generate payments to consultants of upward of $5 to $20 million. It's a nasty little secret.' (Quoted in Thackray, 1993)

By promising to provide the means of leaping ahead of the global competition, the BPR vision of the future of work presents a beguiling answer to the problems of declining competitiveness. However, it also promotes the continuing casualization and contraction of full-time employment as organizations (continuously) re-engineer their processes. Those who remain are obliged to work at an ever-quickening intensity and pace. For this group, there is the prospect of eventual 'burnout' and disposal. For those whose jobs have been re-engineered out of these companies, there is the increasingly restricted prospect of occupying the low paid, temporary jobs that service tomorrow's 'networkers' 'information brokers' and 'symbolic analysts' (Reich, 1991).

This – the human element – is the Achilles' heel, or perhaps the parson's nose, of BPR. HRM specialists, in particular, may question whether the ambitions of BPR are consistent with the effective stewardship of 'human resources'. More specifically, it might be asked whether 'enlightened' and 'progressive' ideas about the creativity, empowerment and fulfilment of employees are compatible with the engineering-led theory and practice of BPR. The posing of such questions implies that it is not so much BPR's inflated sense of its own novelty as its shallow, technicist appreciation of the human dimension of organizational change that renders it vulnerable to hostile evaluation, not least by HRM specialists.

(AD)DRESSING THE TURKEYS

BPR's sketchy, or perhaps cynical, comprehension of the human aspects of organizing and the management of change is remarkable, even by the standards of leading proponents of TQM and Excellence. It is simply assumed that strong and sustained leadership from top management, supported by an adequate level of resourcing, will ensure the conversion of employees to the brave new world of BPR. Little consideration is given to the very practical issue of *how BPR's (universal) remedies are to be reconciled with the (particular, contingent) conditions in which its pre-scriptions are to be applied.* When examples are given, these are presented as unequivocal success stories.

In what is one of the most celebrated examples of BPR, Hammer describes how Ford (North America) reduced its accounts payable staff from over 500 to 125 by redesigning the payment process and using ICTs in a way that dispensed with invoices altogether. Perhaps those who lost their jobs (or were redeployed) were entirely supportive and cooperative in this change...? In this respect at least, the parallels between BPR and Taylorism are quite striking (Hosseini, 1993). Like Taylor, who rose to become chief engineer at the Midvale Steel Company, Hammer, the computer scientist, is quick to transfer the language of computing and recent developments in parallel processing to the complex and frequently perverse world of human relations.

In any event, Hammer unreservedly represents the re-engineered process as a means of 'empowering' employees. When commenting upon the re-engineering of insurance applications at US Insurer Mutual Benefit Life (MBL),* he observes that 'empowering individuals to process entire applications ...has eliminated 100 field office positions, and case manag-ers can handle more than twice the volume of new applications the company previously could process' (Hammer, 1990: 17). Here empow-erment is equated with the integration of tasks made possible by the development of expert systems and relational databases rather than with the expansion of discretion, or even an increase in task variety. No consideration is given to the loss of employment opportunities associated with such change. Nor does Hammer consider the probability that the VDU operators ('case managers') are stuck in a dead-end job that in all likelihood has become more intensive, routine and isolating as a conse-quence of the re-engineering .

To be sure, champions of BPR (again in common with Frederick Taylor) acknowledge that the radical changes envisioned by BPR may encounter some opposition. But any employee hostility to BPR is inter-preted not as warrantable resistance but as irrationality or inertia which can be overcome by effective leadership and commitment from top management. Hammer notes that the disruption and confusion generated by re-engineering can make it unpopular. But he is equally confident that

---

*   MBL was the eighteenth largest life insurer in the US.

any opposition can be effectively surmounted by top-level managers. The commitment of top-level managers to BPR is deemed to be sufficient 'to enlist those who would prefer the status quo' (Hammer , 1990: 112; a similar emphasis upon leadership occurs in Johansson *et al.*, 1993: Chapter 8). So, despite an admission that 'the strain of implementing a re-engineering plan can hardly be overestimated' (Hammer, 1990: 112), Hammer is sure that employees can be convinced of its virtues.

However, employees are not infinitely malleable, passive commodities. They are not indifferent to how they are managed. Accomplishing the full and effective implementation of BPR is likely to prove more difficult than is contemplated by its advocates' faith in the persuasive powers of senior management. Which does not mean that *some* features of the changes envisaged by process re-engineering will not be welcomed. For example, despite the increased routinization and depersonalization of their work, 'case managers' at MBL (see above) may have favoured the removal of supervisors or preferred the reduced fragmentation of tasks. But even those who, on balance, are inclined to endorse such changes are also likely to have reservations about their implications for future job security. They may also recognize, and resent, the extent to which the pace and accuracy of their work can now be continuously monitored, albeit indirectly, by information systems. For example, the implementation of these systems makes it possible to monitor the speed and accuracy of the case managers' work. Where cooperation with BPR programmes is achieved under duress, it is likely that their impact will be sustained only by the same old coercive methods condemned by the new prophets of business management (Oliver, 1993).

When addressing new programmes intended to achieve organizational objectives, Legge (1977) identifies two possible responses: those of 'conformist' and 'deviant innovation' , respectively. In broad outline, the difference between them is that the former, 'conformist' innovator accepts as given whatever programmes are embraced by management, and then 'tries to demonstrate the worth of his [sic] activities within this framework (Legge, 1977: 79). In contrast, the 'deviant' innovator adopts a more questioning orientation that does not necessarily accept the favoured framework. Accordingly, the HRM specialist who is a 'deviant innovator' may strive to 'gain acceptance for a different set of criteria for the evaluation of organizational success and his [sic] contribution to it (Legge, 1977: 85). Indeed, when reflecting upon the role of HRM specialists in relation to TQM, Wilkinson and Marchington (forthcoming) have argued that a preparedness to take a questioning stance towards its assumptions and prescriptions is essential if they are 'to maintain [their] professional integrity and claim to expertise'.

As a *conformist innovator*, the HRM specialist may suggest ways in which the implementation of BPR can be expedited through the use of organizational communication media, training programmes and forms of internal marketing. Whether or not he or she is conscious of the inconsistencies of its hard-nosed, engineering mentality with 'progressive', humanistic human resource thinking, he or she disregards such knowledge by indicating how HRM expertise may facilitate BPR without directly questioning its assumptions or consequences – in terms of staff morale, commitment, turnover, etc, and its compatibility with other programmes, codes of practice or mission statements. In effect, conformist innovators keep their heads down, perhaps because they do not recognize any wider responsibilities attaching to the HRM profession. Or it may be that they willingly disregard such responsibilities in order to safeguard the credibility of the specialism within the organization and/or for more self-interested career motives.

Deviant innovators, in contrast, are more inclined to apply their professional expertise in ways that raise questions about the advisability of pursuing particular programmes which may have unintended consequences for current or future organizational effectiveness. Indeed, such 'deviants' may deem their professional responsibilities to extend beyond a managerial orientation towards organizational effectiveness by acting as the interpreters, or even the advocates, of broader social values when these are perceived to be in conflict with the values inscribed in organizational programmes such as BPR. Even though the HRM specialist may be unable to change dominant organizational values, he or she may, in this way, provide an alternative perspective on organizational development – for example, by reminding fellow managers that the legitimacy of their actions, and the uncoerced cooperation of employees, is dependent upon wider social norms and standards.

CONCLUSIONS

Neglect of the human dimension in BPR may reflect a growing sense of confidence and/or desperation amongst corporate executives and their consultants: *confidence* inasmuch that the 1980s have seen a successful employer offensive, supported by New Right industrial policy, that has weakened the power of employees to promote as well as resist change, but *desperation* too because this weakening of employee power has not been sufficient to reverse the loss of competitiveness and market share to Japanese businesses and Pacific Rim companies. Commercially speaking, it may be true that many companies struggling to survive in national and world markets are 'burdened' with 'layers of unproductive overhead and armies of unproductive workers' (Hammer, 1990: 112) in comparison to their competitors. It may also be true that other 'softer' and more incremental recipes for (re)gaining competitive advantage have not done enough to reduce this burden. But it remains questionable whether those who comprise the 'overhead' – corporate managers no less than other employees – will willingly recognize themselves, or even be persuaded to understand themselves, either as a 'burden' or as 'unproductive'.

The architects of BPR assume either that employees will unequivocally welcome the changes brought by BPR or will be persuaded by top management to support them. As a consequence, there is no discussion of why, or how, managers and other employees may directly or covertly oppose its demands for change. This then raises the question of how HRM specialists are to address BPR's neglect and trivialization of the human dimensions of organizing and managing change. Are HRM specialists content simply to provide the relevant HR techniques that are claimed to smooth the implementation of programmes that have been designed by others? Or does their distinctive concern for the human dimension of work enable and spur them to question the rationality of remedies that contribute to the dis-ease for which they profess to dispense a cure? The introduction of BPR in organizations will be as much a test of the meaning of professionalism for HRM specialists as it will be a trial for those who are subjected to, or displaced by, its zeal to obliterate jobs as well as established practices. Examining and assessing the relevance and role of HRM theory and practice in relation to the interpretation and implementation of BPR presents an important item on the agenda of contemporary management research.

ACKNOWLEDGEMENT

The preparation of this chapter has been supported by an Economic and Social Research Council (ESRC) award under the Programme on Information and Communication Technology (PICT) and an ESRC award for a project on Quality Initiatives in the Financial Services.

I would like to thank Fergus Murray for his assistance and comments in preparing an earlier version of this chapter. I am also grateful to Adrian Wilkinson for suggesting that I revisit Karen Legge's study of innovation and problem-solving in personnel management.

REFERENCES

Eccles, R G and Nohria, N (1992) *Beyond the Hype: Rediscovering the Essence of Management*, Harvard Business School Press, Boston, Mass.
Hammer, M (1990) 'Re-engineering Work: Don't Automate, Obliterate', *Harvard Business Review*, 67(4), July–August.

Hammer, M and Champy, B (1993) *Re-engineering the Corporation: A Manifesto for Business Revolution*, Nicholas Brealey Publishing, London.

Hosseini, J (1993) 'Revisiting and Expanding Taylorism: Business Process Re-Design and Information Technology', *Computers and Industrial Engineering*, 25(1), 533–535.

Johansson, H J, McHugh, P, Pendlebury, A J and Wheeler, W A (1993) *Business Process Re-engineering*, John Wiley, London.

Knights, D and Morgan, G (1991) 'Corporate Strategy, Organizations, and Subjectivity: A Critique', *Organization Studies*, 12(2), 251–277.

Legge, K (1977) *Power, Innovation and Problem-Solving in Personnel Management*, McGraw-Hill, London.

Morris, D and Brandon, J (1993) *Re-engineering Your Business*, McGraw-Hill, New York.

Oakland, J (1989) *Total Quality Management*, Heinemann, London.

Oates, D (1993) 'Buzz Words: Learning the Language of Business', *Accountancy*, August.

Oliver, J (1993) 'Shocking to the Core', *Management Today*, August, 18–23.

Peters, T J and Waterman, R H (1982) *In Search of Excellence: Lessons from America's Best Run Companies*, Harper & Row, New York.

Reich, R B (1991) *The Work of Nations: Preparing Ourselves for 21st Century Capitalism*, Simon & Schuster, London.

Thackray, J (1993) 'Fads, Fixes and Fictions', *Management Today*, June, p 41.

Watson, T J (1944) *In Search of Management*, Routledge, London.

Wilkinson, A and Marchington, M (forthcoming) *TQM – Instant Pudding for the Personnel Function?* Mimeo, Manchester School of Management for the *Human Resource Management Journal*.

Wilkinson, A and Willmott, H C (1995) *Making Quality Control*, Routledge, London.

Willmott, H C (1993) 'Strength is Ignorance; Slavery is Freedom: Managing Culture in Modern Organizations, *Journal of Management Studies*, 30(4), 515–553.

INDEX